CW00348864

British Asian fiction

Manchester University Press

For Philip

British Asian fiction

Twenty-first-century voices

Sara Upstone

Manchester University Press
Manchester and New York
*distributed in the United States exclusively
by Palgrave Macmillan*

Copyright © Sara Upstone 2010

The right of Sara Upstone to be identified as the author of this work has been asserted by her in accordance with the Copyright, Designs and Patents Act 1988.

Published by Manchester University Press
Oxford Road, Manchester M13 9NR, UK
and Room 400, 175 Fifth Avenue, New York, NY 10010, USA
www.manchesteruniversitypress.co.uk

Distributed in the United States exclusively by
Palgrave Macmillan, 175 Fifth Avenue, New York,
NY 10010, USA

Distributed in Canada exclusively by
UBC Press, University of British Columbia, 2029 West Mall,
Vancouver, BC, Canada V6T 1Z2

British Library Cataloguing-in-Publication Data
A catalogue record for this book is available from the British Library

Library of Congress Cataloging-in-Publication Data applied for

ISBN 978 0 7190 7832 3 hardback
ISBN 978 0 7190 7833 0 paperback

First published 2010

The publisher has no responsibility for the persistence or accuracy of URLs for any external or third-party internet websites referred to in this book, and does not guarantee that any content on such websites is, or will remain, accurate or appropriate.

Edited and typeset
by Frances Hackeson Freelance Publishing Services, Brinscall, Lancs
Printed in Great Britain
by MPG Books Group in the UK

Contents

Acknowledgements

The final stages of this project were facilitated by a sabbatical from the Field of English Literature, Kingston University. I would like to those at the university who assisted in this project, in particular Erica Longfellow, Shehrazade Emmambokus, and students on the modules 'Dwelling and Diaspora' and 'City and Suburb'. I am also grateful to those attending the 2008 Kingston Readers' Festival; the Millennial Fictions Conference, Brunel University, 6–7 July 2007; the Colonial and Postcolonial Spaces Conference, Kingston University, 6–7 September 2007; and the Unsettling Women Conference, University of Leicester, 11–13 July 2008. Ravinder Randhawa, Gautam Malkani, and Suhayl Saadi were all incredibly gracious in answering my questions, and I am grateful for their generosity.

Additional thanks go to Christine Dailey, Sheila Ling and all those at Victoria Drive, whose prayers and friendship have been such a blessing. Finally, I would like to thank all at Manchester University Press for their enthusiasm and professionalism.

Introduction

'Your American accent is charming.'
'Oh, don't say that. I've been trying to get rid of it and seem more Indian again, particularly since Indians have become so hip.'
'Yes, there can't be one of them who hasn't written a novel.'[1]

labels can be useful. Things need to be categorized to identify trends and developments, which does not mean that everything under that category is the same.[2]

Growing up in the West London borough of Hounslow in the 1980s and 1990s, British Asian culture was something taken for granted. At my Church of England secondary school, 50% of the students came from South Asian backgrounds. Morning prayers were juxtaposed by bhangra dancing in the classrooms at lunchtime; Diwali, Eid and Ramadan were familiar yearly observances; and a fusion of English, Urdu and Punjabi echoed in the hallways. In history, we studied the Mughal Empire alongside the history of its British counterpart. Yet while the curriculum was filled with Asian voices, the study of literature was not: we never studied an Asian writer, let alone one born or raised in Britain.

This absence exists despite the fact that there have been Asian writers in Britain for almost as long as there have been Asians in Britain: since the seventeenth century.[3] In the wake of mass migration from the 1950s, however, for the first time there exist in large numbers Asians born in Britain or settled since childhood and, now as a result, British-born or British-raised Asian authors. This book focuses on the works of fiction produced by this new generation. Its central contention is that such authors, who have emerged only in notable numbers in the late twentieth and early twenty-first centuries, mark the establishment of a definitive genre of British Asian writing deserving recognition in its own right.

In isolating such authors as 'British Asian' this book

1

distinguishes between this writing and a now well-estab-
lished wider field of black British literature, outlined in studies
such as James Procter's *Dwelling Places* (2003), Victoria Arana
and Lauri Ramey's *Black British Writing* (2004), C. L. Innes' *A
History of Black and Asian Writing in Britain 1700–2000* (2002), and
in anthologies such as *Charting the Journey* (1988).[4] Such texts
recognise the connections between black and Asian authors as
a result of a shared minority experience, particularly important
in the 1980s when it was felt that resistance to racism would be
best achieved through broad coalition politics.

At the same time, however, that anthologies were being produced which emphasised a universal blackness, others such as
Right of Way (1988) and later, *Flaming Spirit* (1994), emphasised,
particularly from a feminist perspective, a more specifically
Asian identity.[5] From the 1990s universal 'black' identity has
increasingly been called into question as a construct that,
while politically useful, does not by itself effectively allow
for full consideration of individual ethnic identities.[6] There
is, undoubtedly, a common context of racism in Britain that
means black and Asian cultures share important perspectives
on living in Britain. This is supplemented by a complex history of colonial settlement and migration, for example the use
of Indian indentured labour in the Caribbean and East Africa
which has complicated notions of belonging and led to dynamic
fusions of black and Asian influence. These fusions, however,
have also produced tensions between black and Asian populations. Moreover, analyses of black culture often centre on the
experience of slavery which, while essential to understanding
British African and Afro-Caribbean identities, is often – though
as the Caribbean context illustrates not always – less relevant
to the British Asian experience.[7] That a large amount of the
theory surrounding both black British literature and identity
more generally comes from an African or Afro-Caribbean perspective, exacerbated perhaps by the dominance of American
critical perspectives (where 'black' has a very different meaning), has perhaps led to the differing experiences of British
Asians – especially from India, Pakistani, and Bangladesh –
being underestimated.[8] For Rupa Huq, for example, writing in
1996, British Asians are 'the "invisible community" in British
academic and popular discourse'.[9] At the same time, a more specific British Asian identity has been productive in providing a
counterpoint to negative representations through an explosion
of what has been referred to as 'Asian cool'.[10] For Hari Kunzru,

one of the authors featured in this book, 2003 was the 'year of the Trendy Asian in London'.[11] The mainstream popularity of Asian film, music and comedy – Gurinder Chadha's *Bend it Like Beckham* (2002) and *Bride and Prejudice* (2004), the film adaptation of Ayub Khan-Din's *East is East* (1999), television shows *The Kumars at Number 42* and *Goodness Gracious Me*, the musical *Bombay Dreams*, music artists Jay Sean, Asian Dub Foundation, Punjabi MC, and the rise of Desi Beats – have all contributed to the sense of a distinctly British, distinctly Asian, thriving cultural scene.[12]

Recognising this does not underestimate that the term 'Asian' carries its own problems. As British Muslims face challenges in relation to issues such as the Rushdie Affair, the Gulf War, and 9/11 and its aftermath – including the London Tube bombings of 7 July 2005 – so even more specific frameworks are perhaps increasingly vital. This position is most usefully summed up by Ziauddin Sardar:

> Calling Muslims 'Asians' is ridiculous because Muslims consciously reject all racial and geographical categories – as a Universalist worldview, Islam seeks global, Universalist notions of identity. Furthermore, Asia is not a race or identity, it's a continent. Even in Asia, where more than half of the world's population lives, no one calls him or herself 'Asian' ... Moreover, the meaning of the term changes from place to place. In the US, the Asian label is attached to Koreans, Filipinos and Chinese. In Britain, we do not use the term Asian to describe our substantial communities of Turks, Iranians or Indonesians, even though these countries are in Asia. So, at best the label 'Asian' is meaningless.[13]

Moreover, Britishness itself is an increasingly contested term. The Labour government which came to power in 1997 has emphasised the need to reclaim Britishness from nationalist discourse, and to rework it in the terms of Britain's diverse population.[14] Yet this reworking leads to debates as to how precisely an inclusive definition of Britishness might be forged to avoid the mistakes of previous definitions privileging white English values, while at the same time honouring Britain's long history. Tension between inclusive national identities – the idea of 'community cohesion' – and a multicultural, cultural pluralist politics that advocates instead a 'community of communities'[15] recognising ethnic and cultural differences have polarised political debates.[16] The call for a 'new Britain' – while well-intentioned and important for multiethnic politics – marks an anxiety about the term's relevance.[17] Despite its title, therefore,

British Asian Fiction at times calls into question the 'British Asian' label, as texts not only assert its value, but also point to its inappropriateness in specific cultural contexts.

This book also is written with conscious awareness of the complexities of its own definition of British-born/raised writers. Such distinction is made in recognition of the fact that authors with such shared backgrounds are part of a complex chronology of settlement refusing easy grouping by either time or birth. British-born Asian writers are not new: they exist as far back as Aubrey Menen, whose first novel was written in 1947. Equally, contemporary British Asian authors do not necessarily meet the criteria of having been born/raised in Britain: a number settled in adulthood. Some of these, such as Rukhsana Ahmad – who describes herself as a 'British-based South Asian writer or a writer of Pakistani origin living in London' – maintain an expatriate attitude, while others would not distinguish themselves from those born in Britain.[18] The length of what is not even an exhaustive list – Tariq Ali, Tahmima Anam, Anita Desai, G. V. Desani, Leena Dhingra, Farrukh Dhondy, Romesh Gunesekera, Sunetra Gupta, Attia Hosain, Aamer Hussein, Abdullah Hussein, Syed Manzurul Islam, Kamala Markandaya, Suniti Namjoshi, Kamila Shamsie, Farhana Sheikh, A. Sivanandan, Sanjay Suri – points to a much broader dynamic Asian presence.

To focus on birth and early experience in the contemporary context, however, reflects how citizenship legislation has increasingly made birth central to definitions of Britishness. Both the 1914 and 1948 British Nationality Acts gave commonwealth citizens the right of British citizenship. Under the premises of this later act the first large wave of Asian migrants came to Britain. The subsequent 1968 Act, however, made Britishness contingent on the birthplace or citizenship of one's parents or grandparents. This was further sedimented by both the 1971 and the 1981 Acts, the latter restricting right of settlement to those whose parents or grandparents were British citizens. As being born to a British citizen became what made one British, so the birthplace of a British citizen frequently became Britain itself, against an earlier generation of migrants whose British citizenship preceded entry into Britain, and was dependant not on ancestral connection, but on membership of the British Empire. In being born in Britain, British Asian authors have a particular relationship to citizenship which marks them out as distinct, often representing those defined as British within the confines of increasingly restrictive legislation. Although the

British-raised individual does not have this claim, nevertheless they too are distinct by way of a cultural familiarity shared
with the British-born. As Roger Ballard argues, not youth generally but 'more specifically *those who have spent the greater part of
their childhood in Britain*, usually participate much more actively
... they are constantly on the move between a variety of social
arenas, which are often organised around differing, and sometimes radically contradictory, moral and cultural conventions'.[19]
Kadija Sesay's emphasis on the newness of black British writing, and its assertion of an explicit and confident British – rather
than migrant – identity, is equally relevant in a British Asian
context:

> In essence, the new generation of black writers in Britain cannot
> write about some faraway home from a position of remembrance;
> they write about Britain from their own British viewpoints and put
> their own British spins on the world as seen from their very own
> perspectives. What characterized an earlier black British literature,
> the migrant's otherness, emanated from their coming to Britain and
> searching for a particular kind of perceived Britishness that did not
> necessarily exist. Black writers born in England have none of these
> illusions. They are developing within the British landscapes and
> social groups that they have been born into, writing about their own
> impressions of Britain from a new British perspective.[20]

As Kunzru himself notes, first-generation writing was 'the story
of immigrants, of outsiders gaining or failing to gain acceptance
into a world whose terms are set by a white population. Only
recently has a body of second-generation fiction arisen, dealing
with the experience of those of us who have always already
found ourselves "here", and whose Britishness eclipses our
relations with the other countries in which our parents grew
up.'[21]
Defining the significance of a British-born/raised generation is therefore a distinction from an earlier generation who
arrived as adults. It is for this reason that, throughout the book,
the term 'British-born/raised' is employed in preference to the
terms 'second generation' (for those born in Britain) or '1.5 generation' (for those raised in Britain). Frequent suffixing of these
'generation' terms with the word 'migrant' means they have
a tendency to blur the distinctions between these two experiences.[22] It is also in this sense that this book most notably
differs from existing critical discussions. A number of studies
do reflect specifically on British Asian experience.[23] Yet only
one of these, Yasmin Hussain's *Writing Diaspora* (2005), focuses

explicitly on the British-born/raised generation. Even when the term 'British Asian' is employed, it may signify something quite different: Neil Murphy and Wai-Chew Sim, for example, use this term to refer not only to British-born/raised authors, but also those who have migrated to Britain in adulthood and, further than this, also to those authors who come from West and East Asia.[24] For these critics there is a strong element of continuity, directed by a cultural theory which replicates this position, centred around a category of 'diaspora' which is seen to unite both migrants and their descendents, as '"diaspora space" is a conceptual category … "inhabited" not only by those who have migrated and their descendants but equally by those who are constructed and represented as indigenous'.[25] They reflect a dominant tendency in the study of black British-born literature in general which, as Sesay argues, has frequently been seen as an extension of earlier black writing.[26]

What matters here, given the complexities of birth, is less about specifics of place and time, and more about a particular subject positioning. It reflects the awareness that identifying an author via ethnic categorisation is less about ethnicity per se than about an attitude which may come with this: a term 'ideological rather than geographical'.[27] For Hanif Kureishi and Kunzru, for example, this positioning in relation to issues of identity is apparent in their books, even when the subject matter is not British Asianness. What is inferred by these writers, instead, is a particular sensibility. This is not to suggest that ethnicity in itself determines outlook; indeed, throughout the chapters that follow a recurring theme is the 'burden of representation': the pressure placed on ethnic authors not only to write about certain themes, but also to present them in a particular light.[28] Rather this book suggests that what we find in such authors is that unique social and cultural circumstances encourage, as for migrant writers, or even women writers, particular perspectives. Such perspectives are not singular, but they are given additional depth and resonance through the experience of being British Asian.

Such distinction should not be taken to mean that these authors necessarily differ from their migrant forebears in all respects; as Avtar Brah argues, inter-generational difference should not necessarily be assumed to be inter-generational conflict.[29] The definition of diaspora as 'collective trauma, a banishment, where one dreamed of home but lived in exile'[30] is inappropriate for a generation who have not relocated, justifying perhaps the assignation 'post-diaspora'.[31] Nevertheless diaspora raises the importance of connections between migrant and British-born populations. Brah's formulation of 'diaspora space', that it may be 'possible to feel at home in a place and, yet, the experience of social exclusions may inhibit public proclamations of the place at home' illuminates how British-born Asians might experience similar alienation to the preceding migrant generation. [32] Such alienation, however, springs from very different circumstances in the British-born subject: not from physical dislocation, but from the very lack of this alternative space of belonging because of an often-distanced relationship to an ancestral physical geography. [33] Moreover, this generation must negotiate feelings of racial or religious rejection against their own inherent sense of British citizenship as a birthright.

While alienation indicates the need to negotiate identities in the wake of difficult relationships to both a distant ancestral homeland and a very present yet contested Britain, yet the confidence of many British-born protagonists suggests they are not as confused as their classic representation as 'caught between two cultures' implies.[34] Whereas, for Homi Bhabha, minorities 'have no option but to occupy … interstitial spaces', the British-born/raised generation announces its agency so that, against alienation, there is also a more defiant British-born sensibility.[35] Negotiation of complex cultural positionings means a fusion of different influences celebrated as a powerful new identity, rather than as detrimental to a stable sense of self. Taken a step further, fusion itself becomes a defining identity, as both traditional Britishness and diasporic identities are rejected. Such fusion may be established in opposition to British citizenship but may also, in Kureishi's words, reflect 'a new way of being British after all this time',[36] as the British Asian subject refuses assignation either as eternal minority in relation to a mythical whiteness or as perpetual immigrant, 'ethnicity or blackness … experienced less as an oppositional identity than as a way of being British'.[37] Like the black British writer more generally, these authors affirm Arana and Ramey's conclusion that 'they do not write about their staying power because they are not the ones who migrated. Britain, they affirm, is their country'.[38] Part of a 'home-grown British political discourse', for these Asian writers 'Britain really is home'.[39] As Ravi, one of the young men in Gautam Malkani's Londonstani (2006) so eloquently puts it, 'We didn't fuckin come here, innit … we was fuckin born here'.[40]

British Asian confidence has consequences for the politics of British Asian texts. Monica Ali's *Brick Lane* (2003) and Kureishi's *The Black Album* (1995) capture the anti-establishment protests of British Asian youths in the name of their own specific religious and cultural identities which reflect Ash Amin's characterisation of a new generation who 'have begun to make demands as full citizens that cannot be sidelined as minority claims for minor spaces of recognition'.[41] They draw into stark relief the chasm between citizenship legislation and the realities of social inclusion, 'the informal notion of who really did or could belong': that one may hold a British passport, and yet by the colour of one's skin or religion be denied full access to advantages which should come with such citizenship.[42] It is these informal notions, as much as institutional or state-sanctioned racism, which these texts engage with: suggesting legislation matters less than everyday encounters which define national belonging. Yet, at the same time, confidence also produces, as in the fiction of Atima Srivastava, less overtly political novels: characters reflective of a new generation of British Asian youth for whom issues of cultural identity have faded in comparison to other social concerns. This reflects a world in which issues of ethnic tolerance are less concerns to be fought for, and rather elements of urban British life now taken for granted. As David Lammy suggests, there is a version of British society in which multiculturalism and internationalism are 'lived through our everyday experiences' instead of being 'abstract concepts that need to be artificially "celebrated"'.[43] These authors also take politics in new directions. Part of their confidence is a concern not simply with racism, but with internal politics, a representation Ruvani Ranasinha recognises as a movement away from culture clash to 'discord between generations and within communities'.[44] From the earliest British Asian feminist texts of authors such as Ravinder Randhawa, for example, a desire is evident to complicate racial politics with concern for patriarchy and thus to announce 'we are no longer prepared to wholeheartedly and uncritically accept all and sundry from our "cultures" as good'.[45]

These changes mean that in some instances frameworks commonly used to define migrant literature become problematic. British-born ethnic authors have often been included in postcolonial frameworks, reflecting the universalising of postcoloniality as the contemporary condition.[46] Yet as one of the complaints against postcolonial theory is its devaluation

of specificity, so the blurring of black British (and by implication British Asian) literature with postcolonial texts does
little to alleviate such concerns. While postcolonial terminology therefore continues to be useful when considering points
of continuity between migrant and British-born perspectives,
nevertheless the uniqueness of British-born/raised writing
demands revisions to key critical concepts. In this sense, British
Asian writing engages directly with Peter Childs and Patrick
Williams's question: 'When is postcoloniality going to end?
How long does the postcolonial continue?'[47]

This need to revise postcolonial frameworks is particularly
urgent in relation to perhaps the central concern of postcolonial theory: hybridity.[48] Poststructuralist theories of fluidity
well suited to postcolonial literature are often tempered in the
British Asian text by representation more suited to analysis via
more culturally and geographically located social theory. While
Kureishi and Nadeem Aslam may re-affirm the 'multi-location-
ality' that is associated with the diasporic experience, other
authors establish more rooted and stable identities.[49] They
reflect the recognition in postcolonial theory itself that terms
like hybridity may become as exclusionary as the more ostensibly 'stable' identities they were identified as subverting.[50]

Finally, these changes in emphasis have consequences in
terms of form and structure. The majority of the texts here,
while sophisticated and often lyrical, lack the magical-realist
elements of the novels of Salman Rushdie, or the modernist
flourishes of Sam Selvon which, for Elleke Boehmer, defines the
postcolonial genre and offers a powerful subversion of colonial
style.[51] More rooted, realist prose reflects a desire to actively
represent, rather than posit alternative possibilities, but also
confidence that traditional forms need no longer be subverted
as acts of political rebellion. Strategies of postmodernism are
inappropriate to thematic concerns less about disorder and
fluidity, and more about tempering that fluidity within the context of stability and rootedness. This difference filters into the
language used: as Sesay notes, the new voices born in Britain
are less concerned with the reconstruction of the language of
their parents, preferring a 'London English' which defines their
cultural complexity.[52] Moreover, their imagery comes not from
the landscapes of the migrant's 'home country', but rather from
influences 'directly connected to England'.[53] This may be to the
detriment of the progressive potential of these texts as utopian
fictions, but does increase their power as social commentaries.

The dream-like visions of lost spaces pervading migrant novels are replaced with hard-hitting reflections on a directly and immediately experienced Britain.

The writers looked at here have been chosen because their fiction embodies the complexities of the new British Asian perspective. They exist within a wider context: the large number of writers working in poetry, in the short story, and in drama, whose work falls outside the scope of this book, but is nevertheless central to its vision, and also works, such as Zadie Smith's *White Teeth* (2000) or Marion Molteno's 'In Her Mother's House' (1987), which are not written by authors of British-Asian ethnicity, but nevertheless address issues related to this cultural background.[54] The book is structured to trace a chronology, though not necessarily a linear development. Chapter 1 explores the transition between migrant and British-born/ raised positioning through the figures of V. S. Naipaul and Salman Rushdie, arguing that the common reading of their liminal positioning can be reconsidered to emphasise the transition from migrant to British-Asian consciousness. Each subsequent chapter explores a single British Asian writer. Finally, in conclusion, I explore the work of the newest writers yet to establish a significant corpus of work, examining the writings of Niven Govinden, Malkani, and Nirpal Singh Dhaliwal. Each chapter concludes with a set of questions for further study. These are designed to encourage further thought about the author, texts, and issues discussed. In addition, a short selection of recommended further reading identifies the most comprehensive sources specifically in relation to each author.

Bearers 'of complex cultural practices that disrupt easy definitions of Britishness', the fiction of British Asian authors marks a crucial intervention in how British identities are imagined and enacted in the twenty-first century.[55] The newness of their voices is not simply a dynamic presence in the framework of ethnic fictions, but also in the broader context of contemporary British literature.

Notes

1   Kureishi, *Something to Tell You*, p. 200.
2   Lima, 'Interview with Kadija Sesay', p. 22.
3   For history of Asian writing in Britain see Innes, *History of Black and Asian Writing*; for general history of Asians in Britain see Fisher *et al.*, *South-Asian History of Britain*.
4   Grewal *et al.*, *Charting the Journey*.

5 Asian Women Writers' Workshop, *Right of Way*; Ahmad and Gupta (eds), *Flaming Spirit*.
6 See, for example, Brah, *Cartographies*, pp. 96–7; Modood, 'Political Blackness and British Asians'; Alexander, 'Beyond Black'.
7 See Alibhai-Brown, *Who Do We Think We Are?*, p. 10.
8 See, for example, Boyce Davies' summary of black gender theorists, *Black Women, Writing and Identity*, p. 49.
9 Huq, 'Asian Kool?', p. 71.
10 *Ibid.*, pp. 61–80.
11 'Interview with Hari Kunzru', www.book-club.co.nz/features/harikunzru.htm.
12 For discussion of these cultural forms see Fisher *et al.*, *South-Asian History of Britain*, pp. 198–204.
13 Sardar, 'The Excluded Minority', p. 52. For recent discussion of British Muslim youth see Lewis, *Young, British and Muslim*.
14 See Dodd, 'Challenges for New Labour'.
15 Parekh, *Future of Multi-Ethnic Britain*, p. 3.
16 For these debates see Alexander, 'Imagining the Asian Gang', p. 539; Kundnani, 'The Death of Multiculturalism'.
17 For contemporary debates surrounding Britishness see Cook, 'Relocating Britishness'. For projects to construct a 'new Britain' see Leonard, *Britain™*.
18 Schlote, '"I'm British But …"', p. 87.
19 My emphasis, Ballard, 'Introduction', *Desh Pardesh*, p. 30.
20 Sesay, 'Transformations Within the Black British Novel', p. 107. See also Lee, 'Changing the Script', pp. 69–76.
21 Kunzru, *'Art, Writing: White Teeth'* (2000). This notion of generational difference is also reflected in King, *The Oxford English Literary History*.
22 I follow here Skinner, 'Black British Interventions', p. 136, who employs 'British-born' in discussion of black British literature. For 1.5 generation see Modood *et al.*, *Changing Ethnic Identities*, p. 13.
23 Most notable are Nasta, *Home Truths*; Ranasinha, *South Asian Writers*; Murphy and Sim (eds), *British Asian Fiction*.
24 Murphy and Sim (eds), *British Asian Fiction*.
25 Brah, *Cartographies*, p. 181; Nasta herself quotes this, *Home Truths*, p. 8.
26 See, for example, Lawson Welsh, 'Critical Myopia', p. 132.
27 Skinner, 'Black British Interventions', p. 128.
28 For this debate see Julien and Mercer, 'De Margin and de Centre'.
29 Brah, *Cartographies*, p. 42.
30 Cohen, *Global Diasporas*, ix.
31 Mishra, *Literature of the Indian Diaspora*, p. 229.
32 Brah, *Cartographies*, p. 193.
33 The best documentation on this experience is the first-hand accounts in Phillips and Phillips, *Windrush*.
34 For the origin of this phrase see Anwar, 'Young Asians Between Two Cultures'. For discussion see Burdsey, 'One of the Lads', p. 760, Ballard, 'Introduction', pp. 7–9, Brah, *Cartographies*, pp. 40–45.
35 Bhabha, 'Vernacular Cosmopolitan', p. 139.
36 Kureishi, 'Rainbow Sign', pp. 9–38, p. 38.

37   Modood, *Multicultural Politics*, p. 199.
38   Arana and Ramey (eds), 'Introduction', *Black British Writing*, p. 3.
39   Brah, *Cartographies*, p. 47; Hussain, *Writing Diaspora*, p. 132.
40   Malkani, *Londonstani*, p. 127.
41   Amin, 'Unruly Strangers', p. 460.
42   Paul, *Whitewashing*, p. xii.
43   Lammy, Rediscovering Internationalism', p. 36.
44   Ranasinha, *South Asian Writers*, p. 225.
45   Grewal *et al.*, 'Preface', p. 3.
46   See, for example, comments in Gikandi, *Maps of Englishness*, p. 213, and Walder, *Post-Colonial Literatures*, p. 199.
47   Childs and Williams, *Introduction to Post-Colonial Theory*, p. 7.
48   For Boehmer, *Colonial and Postcolonial Literature*, p. 227, the migrant text is 'hybridity writ large and in colour'.
49   Brah, *Cartographies*, p. 197.
50   See, for example, Mitchell, 'Different Diasporas and the Hype of Hybridity'; San Juan Jnr., *Beyond Postcolonial Theory*; Chrisman, *Postcolonial Contraventions;* Shohat, 'Notes on the "Post-Colonial"'.
51   Boehmer, *Colonial and Postcolonial Literature*, p. 236.
52   Sesay, 'Transformations', p. 105.
53   *Ibid.*, p. 105.
54   Smith, *White Teeth*; Molteno, 'In Her Mother's House'. There are too many writers to note here: including poets Sindamani Bridglal, Chila Kumari Burman, Varun Chandra, Jeanne Ellin, Shahidah Janjua, Shamshad Khan, Tariq Latif, Srabani Maitra, Irfan Merchant, Prachi Momin, Maya Naidoo, Selina Rodrigues, Saiaah Salim, Seni Seneviratne, Taslima Shahjahan, Gerry Singh, Shazia Sohail and dramatists Ayub Khan-Din, Meera Syal, Sudha Bhuchar, Tanika Gupta, Maya Chowdhry, and Gurpreet Kaur Bhatti.
55   Amin, 'Unruly Strangers', p. 460.

1

Salman Rushdie and V. S. Naipaul

> Diaspora that we were, we became static and in this stasis relapsed
> into mythology, initially through epic remembrance of the Indian
> past and subsequently through Bombay cinema. Nor did our lives in
> the end find an alternative vitality through the postcolonial celebra-
> tion of the hybrid; rather we remained half and half. [1]

Visit the University of London Library located at Senate House,
Bloomsbury, and the problem of classifying authors by ethnicity becomes immediately apparent. A researcher wanting
to consult work on Salman Rushdie finds this material – and
indeed Rushdie's fiction – in the English Literature section. Yet
you are directed within this section not to the British authors,
but rather to a separate section on World Literature including
postcolonial authors such as Chinua Achebe, Wole Soyinka and
Arundhati Roy. Look for the work of V. S. Naipaul, and related
critical writings, and you encounter an even more perplexing
scenario. These works are not located on the fifth floor of the
library with the English Literature books at all. Instead, you
must take the winding stairs up to the seventh floor – the final
public floor, and one not served by lift – to the 'Latin American
Studies' section: an interdisciplinary collection where you find
(undoubtedly because of the location) the largely untouched
works of writers including not just Naipaul, but also his brother
Shiva, Wilson Harris and Derek Walcott, in a special section
devoted to 'West Indian Literature'.

Classification of Rushdie's and Naipaul's works in this way
is not a failing of the library. Rather, it points to these writers'
problematic status. Are they postcolonial authors, important
principally for their relationship to ideas of empire? Are they
national authors, whose relevance lies most in their relationship
to their countries of birth? Or, indeed, are they British authors,
needing to be read within the context of an increasingly multicultural British literature?

The latter possibility is the one denied by both library classifications. Rushdie and Naipaul, it seems, are 'expatriates': they
'belong' elsewhere.[2] Their accolades seemingly acknowledge
not British success, but the success of those 'English-language
authors living in Britain whose origins were not British'.[3]
Having been born in Bombay, India, in 1947 (the year of Indian
independence and the creation of Pakistan), Rushdie first
came to Britain in 1961 as a 13-year-old to attend Rugby public school, going on to read History at Cambridge University.
Similarly, Naipaul – who was born to parents of Indian origin in the Caribbean colony of Trinidad in 1932 – arrived in
England on a scholarship to Oxford University to read English
Literature as an 18-year-old in 1950. Yet despite spending all of
their adult lives in Britain, Rushdie and Naipaul are rarely read
as British authors. As Graham Huggan notes:

> It is rare for either to be designated as a *British* writer. Even some of
> the most culturally sensitive of critics have been known to persist
> in the view that Naipaul and Rushdie originally come from 'other'
> places – to suggest that in some deep-rooted, atavistic sense, they are
> immigrant writers who 'really' belong somewhere else. Are these
> two obviously well-known writers still marginal on account of their
> ethnicity? Or because they choose in their work to fictionalise their
> own experiences of displacement? Or because they are seen, in spite
> of themselves, as First World informants for their native Third World
> cultures?[4]

Naipaul, for example, is largely related primarily to 'Third-
World subjects', seen to be of relevance in Caribbean and
postcolonial contexts.[5] Fawzia Mustafa places Naipaul's first
'English' novel, *Mr Stone and the Knights Companion* (1963), in a
section entitled 'abroad', and chooses to discuss him in terms
of 'contemporary writing in English' rather than as a British
author.[6] Elsewhere, it is declared that 'Naipaul is a Caribbean
writer and will never be a British/English writer'.[7] The circumstances of his birth in Trinidad as a consequence of the colonial
practice of indentured labour that took Indian migrants to the
Caribbean in the nineteenth century illuminates in these terms
the complexity of designations such as 'black' or 'Asian', and
the potential for shared points of reference, but also the possible tensions resulting from the complex racial politics of the
Caribbean. Rushdie, equally, is seen because of his focus on
the migrant as a postcolonial writer: he inspired the title of
the 'founding' work of postcolonial criticism, *The Empire Writes
Back* (1989), and *The Satanic Verses* (1988) has been interpreted

as indicative of his feelings of being a 'foreigner in England'.[8] Both *Midnight's Children* (1981) and *Satanic Verses* have been read as being directed at Indian audiences, rather than British readers, leading to reviews describing Rushdie's work as 'very Indian'.[9] For Ruvani Ranasinha, Rushdie's work differs 'from the British-born generation that came after ... in significant ways'.[10] He is not British, but 'South Asian Anglophone'.[11]

Yet, despite this, a converse movement reads both authors as British and even – more narrowly – as English. In Naipaul's case this begins as early as the 1960s, as V. S. Pritchett refers to him as one of 'the younger English novelists',[12] while in the 1970s William Walsh credits Naipaul's *Mr Stone* on the grounds that 'the Englishry ... is solid and accurate', and the 'English' stories in *A Flag on the Island* (1967) because 'the British reader cannot but be struck by the clear authenticity'.[13] Later authors, such as Aijaz Ahmad and Gamini Salgado have identified him as an 'English novelist';[14] British broadcaster Melvyn Bragg refers to him as 'one of *our* most distinguished novelists'.[15] Rushdie, equally, is seen by some critics as 'un-Indian'.[16] His early work has been criticised as representing the 'exotic fantasia' of British fiction.[17] Conversely, it is celebrated for its connection to the English literary tradition, and Rushdie has been called 'the best known contemporary English writer'.[18] Critical work frequently associates him not with migrant authors, but with later writers such as Hanif Kureishi.[19] More recently, both authors have been featured in a host of anthologies dealing with 'British Literature'.

For themselves, Naipaul has at times refused all national identification in favour of simply 'Writer'.[20] In doing so, he foreshadows debates surrounding the burden of representation that have consumed black British literature: the question as to what extent writers from ethnic backgrounds should be held responsible for how their communities are perceived. At other points he has identified himself with India and Britain, and as someone who 'can't think of myself as being displaced'.[21] He has until recently explicitly disassociated himself from Trinidad, stressing the 'accident' of his birth.[22] In contrast, despite his valorisation of the migrant, and his narrator's declaration in *Satanic Verses* of the 'hollowness' of concepts of land, belonging, and home,[23] Rushdie has far more often associated himself with his place of birth, identifying himself on a number of occasions as Indian, or as an 'Indian writer',[24] and discussing 'the British' as a term from which he is excluded as a 'foreigner'.[25]

Naipaul and Rushdie are not alone in being based for the

majority of their lives in Britain but being born elsewhere: one could equally focus on Sam Selvon, who shares the complexity of Naipaul's Caribbean background, or Farrukh Dhondy who, like Rushdie, came to Britain from India for his university education. Settling when they were slightly older, however, these authors do not in quite the same way straddle definitions of postcolonial and British literature. Moreover, they have not achieved the same notoriety that has made Naipaul and Rushdie the two most significant voices in the establishment of a tradition of Asian writing in Britain. Naipaul has won probably every major literary prize, including the 2001 Nobel Prize for Literature, and, in 1993, the first David Cohen British Literature Prize: he was also knighted in 1990. Rushdie, likewise, has won numerous prizes, including the 'Booker of Bookers' in 1993 and he, too, was knighted in 2007. Both have been immured in controversy: Rushdie most notably for the *fatwa* – a death sentence passed by the Iranian Ayatollah Khomeini in 1989 for supposed blasphemy against Islam in *Satanic Verses* – and Naipaul for his alleged 'racism' in his negative portrayal of the developing world in both his novels and travel writing.[26]

What is neglected in a large amount of the vast literature on Naipaul and Rushdie is how their writings are concerned with the construction of a specifically British Asian identity. As Mustafa points out, writers such as Naipaul are part of the first generation to feel the absence of an 'imperial theme'; they cannot posit themselves as 'anti-colonial' in the same way as their predecessors writing under the oppressive cultural influence of colonialism.[27] Naipaul 'is part of, yet not part of the English world';[28] he 'moves between the stance of insider and outsider' in a 'transitional space'.[29] Even those texts identified as locating him as English are more complicated than they first appear. For example, in his critique of Naipaul, Selwyn R. Cudjoe cites Patrick Swinden as indicating Naipaul's acceptance as an English writer. Return to the original source, however, and what is evident instead is a more complex positioning:

> One of the final living novelists writing in English is not by birth an Englishman ... Yet an English writer is what Naipaul is. All his writing life has been based in London. His publishers are London publishers selling books directly to English readers. The rhythms of his prose are English rhythms, and the speech his characters speak ... is English speech ... Naipaul values this culture, and feels himself to be very much a part of it. *Nevertheless he is a Trinidadian and he is an Indian.*[30]

Thus while Anthony Powell would identify Naipaul as a new English talent in the early 1970s, Dennis Potter would reply with the riposte: 'Our? Well, yes, no'.[31]

Rushdie, equally, occupies a position of 'third world cosmopolitan' simultaneously positioned both inside and outside any national identity;[32] Homi Bhabha's reading of him as occupying a disruptive space of ambivalence speaks to this potential, as do readings that extend Bhabha's criticism.[33] Rushdie has placed himself in this in-between position, declaring 'There are ways in which I am no longer Indian. There are ways in which I've never been English'.[34] Discussing his collection of short stories *East, West* (1994), he has said 'I am that comma'.[35] In this positioning, the transition from the concept of postcolonial literature to British Asian writing – from immigrant to citizen – is writ large. Naipaul and Rushdie exemplify some of the central concerns of British Asian writings as they are presented by a generation raised or born in Britain and, in doing so, illustrate continuity between these concerns and those of the earlier generation of postcolonial authors. Yet, at the same time, they are not quite the same as the later writers considered in the following chapters of this study.

Intepreting Rushdie and Naipaul in such terms is to position them distinctly as transitional figures in the development of British Asian literature, as the connecting forces between migrant postcolonial narratives and the new British Asian literature. They are, in this sense, liminal figures; liminal not simply in the negative or clichéd sense of being caught between cultures, but in the positive sense of marking a space of potential and transformation. Their liminality is not about being caught between competing South Asian and British identities, but of occupying the space between migrant and British Asian perspectives. Such positioning is not a site of stagnation for Rushdie and Naipaul, but one of movement: it is a site of positive ambivalence which recognises the refusal of the status as eternal immigrant in favour of the powerful and forceful claims of British Asian communities for public recognition.

'Double perception'[36]

To read Rushdie and Naipaul in this way as occupying a similar positioning is to question the common tendency – evident in the work of critics including Ian Baucom, Michael Gorra, Bharati Mukerjee, Revathi Krishnaswamy and Jaina C. Sanga

– to juxtapose their work.[37] Rushdie is identified as the master of experimental form, while Naipaul is seen as the colonial inheritor of a nineteenth-century English literary tradition, a writer who 'has long positioned himself closer to the heart of the "borrowed culture" than at the brink of any "new" identity formation'.[38] While Rushdie is celebrated for his supposed evocation of a hybrid, optimistic and positively chaotic vision of an anti-colonial diasporic identity, 'splendidly inauthentic',[39] Naipaul is criticised for what are identified as his pessimistic, assimilationist discourses, which supposedly privilege ideas of cultural purity, order and Western privilege.[40]

What these oppositions neglect, however, is that, in reality, there is considerable overlap, as Graham Huggan, Susheila Nasta, and Michael Wood emphasise.[41] Stylistic differences, in particular, are less pronounced than often suggested. Although Naipaul's supposed realism is often contrasted to Rushdie's hyper-real magical-realism, Naipaul in fact has enacted his own more subtle subversion of form through fusions of autobiography and novel, autobiography and reportage, and fiction and memoir. Richard Allen, for example, declares that Naipaul's style is 'every bit as complex as the magical realist style developed by Salman Rushdie'.[42] In Farrukh Dhondy's comments on Naipaul one sees the hidden spectre of Rushdie through those he has been frequently compared to; it is the former, Dhondy declares, who is the more skilled writer:

> They are not imitations of Laurence Sterne or Gunter Grass. Their prose is nowhere an egregious attempt to imitate the childish and finally meaningless linguistic experiments of Joyce, and nowhere calls attention to its own self regard. Transparency, the attention to the object beyond the prose, is all.[43]

At the same time, popular readings of Rushdie's subversive use of language[44] are complicated by recent readings by Vijay Mishra, who argues that Rushdie's neologisms may be connected to the earlier colonial project of Hobson Jobson,[45] and therefore to colonial desire, as much as being a subversion of colonial language use:[46] a specific example of what Peter Morey defines as Rushdie's 'ambivalence ... to those cultural values the fiction ostensibly sets out to interrogate'.[47] The simplistic opposition constructed between Rushdie's positive hybridity and Naipaul's negative decay neglects how, in reality, Rushdie's texts are often depressing in their conclusions about the possibilities of a British identity that could incorporate its Asian citizens, while Naipaul is far more optimistic in these same terms than he is often is presented as being. Instead, both writers are located in a space of transition between migrant identity and the reality of a confident, British Asian identity as it is confronted by later authors.

Both Naipaul and Rushdie reflect their status as postcolonial, rather than British Asian, authors, in their principal concern for the trauma of migration. Preoccupied with those who have come to Britain as adults, they offer a similar vision of migrant struggle to that presented in other black British fictions.[48] Naipaul's *The Mimic Men* (1967) – the story of Ralph Singh, an exiled Caribbean politician – is a classic text in such terms, presenting London as a 'marvel of light' which fails to live up to its promise as Ralph declares 'so quickly had London gone sour on me'.[49] *The Enigma of Arrival* (1987) can be read similarly as a document of migrant alienation. Again the story of a migrant, it draws heavily for inspiration from Naipaul's own life, documenting the gradual acculturation of its unnamed narrator to rural England. Although, as I suggest below, to read the novel as a simplistic vision of alienation is to underestimate its irony and performative qualities, nevertheless the same familiar imagery is rehearsed in this later work. The narrator's early experiences in London are classic of migrant disillusionment: 'I had come to London as a place I knew very well. I found a city that was strange and unknown'.[50] His history in Britain – living almost all of his adult life there – foregrounds the disabling long-term effects of diasporic consciousness. When, only two pages into the narrative, the narrator declares that 'After all my time in England I still had that nervousness in a new place, that rawness of response, still felt myself to be in the other man's country, felt my strangeness, my solitude' (5–6) the repetition of 'still' emphasises a weariness accompanying many failed attempts to feel 'at home'.

Reading Rushdie in similar terms challenges those who interpret his texts as interrogations of migrant alienation in favour of confident and celebratory hybridity. From his third novel, *Shame* (1983), Rushdie has been associated with a discourse of celebratory migration. Yet, in fact, from this novel onwards it is more accurate to identify in Rushdie's work a discourse of liminality. *Shame*'s narrator's belief that 'something can *also* be gained' by migration points to a concomitant loss; the 'hopefulness' of migration is juxtaposed by 'the emptiness of one's luggage'.[51] Although *Shame* is a novel about Pakistan, such discussions are filtered through a British Asian perspective, the 'ghosts' of an honour killing and an Asian girl attacked by white men on an underground train.[52] Juxtaposing these two contexts, Rushdie positions his narrative not between migrant and British identity, but between a migrant perspective and a specifically British Asian alternative. *Verses* – Rushdie's most explicit engagement with Britishness – can in these terms be read as an extension of such earlier concerns. In Rushdie's own words, it is a narrative of both 'stresses and transformations'.[53] The story of the fortunes of two immigrants, Gibreel Farishta and Saladin Chamcha – who fantastically fall into Britain as a result of an aeroplane terrorist bombing – it has been read through Gibreel's final transformation of London as indicating the reverse colonisation of Britain by its former colonial subjects.[54] Such readings neglect, however, that this interrogation is largely a failure. Gibreel emerges as much a mimic as Ralph Singh; from his first encounter in a smoking jacket with the police at Rosa Diamond's house it is clear that part of what has been transplanted in the fusion of the two migrants' personalities during their magical fall is Chamcha's colonial sensibility. The method Gibreel uses to position himself as 'England's cultural redeemer' is a colonial one and those who overlook its failure, such as Baucom, also overlook this reality.[55] It is a desire for order, for a 'Geographer's London' (322), as strong as that felt by any of Naipaul's protagonists, as Gibreel 'depends on his adversary's maps'.[56] This act of colonial mapping – to 'redeem the city square by square' (326) and instil 'clarity' (353) – mimics the linear project of colonial settlers.[57] It is, as the novel's direct references point to (353), an act of Fanonian self-hatred, which traps Gibreel permanently in the colonial relationship.

Likewise, Chamcha can only survive by returning to his ancestral home of India, reinforcing the traditional connection – little different from that evoked in the 1981 Nationality Act – between ancestry and national belonging, but also Rushdie's own pronouncements of attachment to India, often neglected in discussion in favour of his more postmodern statements.[58] Despite his British passport, Chamcha's migrant status means his liminality is permanent. He has an 'essence' that cannot be obscured; 'long suppressed locutions' refuse to be denied, 'betraying him' (49) by revealing an alternate ethnic self.[59] This affirms what Simon Gikandi refers to as the fact that the novel 'is condemned ... to reinscribe the very normativities – nation and empire – that it seeks to negate',[60] a 'capitulation of form' in Marc Delrez's terms, which means the novel abandons its radical potential for conventional realist closure.[61] Ultimately, Rushdie cannot imagine a positive Britain, in the same way that he cannot in *Shame* positively re-imagine Pakistan outside of its authoritarian politics, and in *Midnight's Children* can only lament the fading of a heterogeneous India in the wake of the rise of Hindu nationalism. As an author writing from the location of simultaneously British citizen and migrant, in the context of a Conservative national government openly hostile to such individuals, the vision of a contented British Asian population remains at least partially unrealised. Returning to London eleven years later in *The Ground Beneath Her Feet* (1999) the situation is little different: Britain remains a space of disillusionment; again associated with both madness and death it is a place where 'everything shifts'.[62]

Rushdie's hybridity therefore is profoundly limited, and emphasis on his celebration of the nomadic, itinerant subject neglects the concomitant discourse of stability in Rushdie's work. Rushdie's own criticism points towards this; in 'In Good Faith' (1990) his discussion of Chamcha's triumph at the end of the novel as one of 'wholeness' points to the continued significance of belonging.[63] One critic to notice this is Andrew Teverson. Discussing the alternative perspectives on migration developed in *Verses* through the philosophies of Lucretius and Ovid, Teverson notes that Chamcha's success is not, as other critics have argued, because he adopts the hybrid perspective of Ovid.[64] Rather his survival is because he fuses both tradional Lucretian and Ovidian ways of thinking.[65] This awareness, combined with Gibreel's failure, means the realisation of hybrid Britain is incomplete; it is a space of illegal immigrants not delighting in the possibilities of exile, but desperately yearning to be 'made permanent' (264). Britain is represented as a nation of violence and objectification, where police racism is institutional, deportation frequent, and the objectification of the 'other' is made explicit by Chamcha's fantastic transformation into both animal and devil.[66] Indeed, the furore surrounding *Verses* was itself a declaration of this desire for permanency, rather than a rejection of citizenship: the anger of British Muslims focused on the fact that British blasphemy laws only protected the nation's Christian population and thus served to make Muslims second-class citizens unrecognised by British law.[67]

How newness enters the world

Such migrant sensibility affirms Huggan's suggestion that both Rushdie and Naipaul are on one level 'deeply pessimistic writers'.[68] Yet, at the same time, existence in a liminal space between this pessimism and the dynamism of British Asian identities means both writers coterminously hint towards what succeeds the trauma of migration: the 'newness' of British Asian consciousness that will regenerate Britishness and reconfigure it for the twenty-first century. It is in this context that liminality becomes the marker of possibility. Although Chamcha and Naipaul's unnamed narrator both fail to entirely realise a British Asian identity, they nevertheless exist within the context of the broader potential of achieving this positioning.

In *Verses*, Rushdie traces this possibility through opposition between his immigrant characters and a British-born Asian generation, foreshadowing the voices presented by the writers focused on in the later chapters of this book. Indeed, his book is an early example of a specific engagement with the term 'British Asian' (415). In interview, it is clear that Rushdie sees a definite difference between this new generation and an earlier one, of which he himself is a part:

> Forty percent of what are called immigrants are born in England. They are all young, they've grown up in England, and they all have exactly the same expectations from that society as the white kids ... It's not uncommon for the first generation of the immigrants to come for a quiet life ... The second generation doesn't do that.[69]

Against the celebration in *Verses* of borderless existence through its migrant figures – 'when you throw everything up in the air anything becomes possible' (5) – stands an equally powerful declaration of permanence by this next generation. A quotidian expression of Britishness on the level of the street based on location of abode and birthplace reclaims nationality from narrow, parochial values.

In this way, Rushdie's novel stands as the statement behind Hanif Kureishi's claim in 'The Rainbow Sign' from his British-born standpoint that 'there must be ... a new way of being British after all this time'.[70] In a strategy that all of the authors included in this book take up in greater detail, this new generation does not adapt itself to Britishness; rather it demands that Britishness itself adapts to include them. Hanif Johnson (his name drawing attention to the figures of Hanif Kureishi and black British dub poet Linton Kwesi Johnson) does not reject

Enoch Powell's 'Rivers of Blood' speech, but rather demands its revision to include him, to 'reclaim the metaphor ... make it something we can use' (*Satanic Verses* 186). The 'minor hero'[71] of Jumpy Joshi refuses 'to accept the position of victim' (253), exemplifying the next generation of Black Britons' refusal of passivity; he exists within a context of 'self-defence patrols ... determined not to take it lying down' (451). The 'brashly punky second-generation Sufuyans' with their tank-tops, rainbow hair, and 501 jeans, equally, offer a challenge to Chamcha's old-school Englishness with a model of assertive youth identity.[72] Mishal stands at her window as 'the recording angel and the exterminator' (283), secure in her 'turf' (284). That the Sufyans are accepted, whereas Chamcha – as his transformation into a devil suggests – is objectified as 'other', identifies their newness as the route to social inclusion. Chamcha's colonial Britishness must die to make way for the confident assertions of a very different, impure, contemporary Britishness that these young people represent. The novel's leitmotif, that 'to be born again ... first you have to die' (31), thus stands as a direction for the remaking of Britishness. The old Britain must die for a new Britain to be born but, equally, the migrant must give way to a British Asian consciousness that will take its rightful place at the centre of the reform of national ideology. Whereas Gibreel fails, and Chamcha must return 'home' to find something 'solid and real' (534), it is these individuals who confidently proclaim their home within Britain, declaring '*We have to live in it; we have to live here, to live on*' (469).[73] And while their parents die, they survive, the migrant again giving way so that newness can be born. Ironically, the Rushdie Affair is itself implicated in this 'newness': it was the solidarity driven by reaction to Rushdie's novel that led British Muslims to define themselves as a distinct community.[74]

If Rushdie announces the possibility of a different British-born experience that foreshadows a British Asian literature written from such a perspective, then Naipaul does something even more radical, announcing not just, as Rushdie does, the development of a British Asian sensibility but, even more powerfully, the possibility of that sensibility for all Asians in Britain, *regardless of birthplace*. The narrator of *Enigma*, like Naipaul himself, comes to Britain as a student: he is not born or raised there. Nevertheless, the novel documents his eventual establishment not only as British, but also as English. Here Naipaul enacts his own statement against the 1981 Nationality Act; what makes one connected to a place is not ancestry, as Thatcher's legislation would argue, but personal attachment. This possibility – for not simply being British Asian, but *becoming British Asian* – makes Naipaul, perhaps ironically, better placed than Rushdie to point towards the realisation of a British Asian identity.[75]

As *Enigma*'s narrator reconfigures his relationship to an English tradition he feels excluded from, he obliterates his colonial ideas but also, in doing so, re-imagines a landscape he can finally make claim to, becoming a Wiltshire 'local'. The narrator 'heals', finding that the place where he 'was truly an alien' offers him finally 'a new life' (111); he becomes attuned to the place 'in a way that I had never been in Trinidad or India' (189). There is, as for Rushdie, a rebirth here: a 'second life ... second, happier childhood ... second arrival' (95). So Naipaul finally offers in his fiction a sense of self-assurance that Rushdie, born later, came to earlier in the trajectory of his career. But in his emergence he can travel further than Rushdie himself: to a place where it is the migrant, and not just the British-born Asian, who can achieve such positioning.

Answering the critics

The potential problem in making such a claim is that criticisms of Naipaul suggest his writings do not promote newness at all; rather, they mimic colonial identities, and promote both assimilation and a reassertion of a narrow, mono-cultural Britishness. To read Naipaul in such terms, however, neglects the subtle subversions enacted within his representations of English cultural traditions. Newness here may be less obviously pronounced than in Rushdie's explosive fictions, but it is equally present.

Take, for example, the argument that Naipaul elevates a nostalgic and prejudiced historical definition of Englishness which yearns for a 'lost' rather than never-existing ideal.[76] Look closely and it is clear this is only a partial reading of Naipaul's texts, neglecting Naipaul's own dislike of imperialism.[77] *In a Free State* (1971), for example, is a scathing critique of the British expatriate community. Both *Mr Stone* and *Mimic Men* illuminate England as a bleak space, associating it with 'fragmentation and isolation, a sense of futility, and the absence of belonging to a meaning-giving community',[78] reflecting Naipaul's early critique of London in his non-fiction writings, and also his harsh personal reflections on Britain as revealed by his letter writing.[79] Such early texts, written decades before Rushdie's work, play a crucial role, alongside others such as Selvon's *The Lonely Londoners* (1956), in beginning the disruption of Englishness, on English soil, a critique further extended in later works such as 'The Perfect Tenants' (1967), 'Tell Me Who to Kill' (1971), and *Magic Seeds* (2004).

Enigma itself is not to be read as a manifesto for colonial Englishness. Much criticism focuses, for example, on 'decay' in *Enigma* as evidence of Naipaul's nostalgia. Yet the narrative explicitly indicates that deterioration is something to be valued. It is Naipaul's own symbol of the 'death' necessary for newness, as the narrator tells us that 'I liked the decay' (55) because 'in that perfection, occurring at a time of empire, there would have been no room for me' (56). There must be a death of colonial Britain the narrator – like Chamcha – is aware, for a new, inclusive Britishness to emerge. The narrator's mapping of this shift means, as Helen Tiffin argues, that Naipaul's novel is transformed from simply marking the erosion of empire to in fact being 'an active agent of that decline'.[80] Decay becomes 'change' (228): if any alienation remains it is not a result of the experience of migration, but of the unique conjunction of a more complex personal history and a more specific colonial relationship of being born an Indian minority in Trinidad.[81]

There is, moreover, no 'true' Englishness here, either. This is why *Enigma* must begin with the story of 'Jack's Garden': it is the narrator's relationship with Jack that radically alters his sense of there being an 'authentic' Englishness from which he is excluded. When he first sees Jack, the narrator reads him as 'genuine, rooted, fitting: man fitting the landscape' (14). Only later does he come to learn that Jack is equally a symbol of newness:

> It did not occur to me that Jack was living in the middle of junk, among the ruins of nearly a century; that the past around his cottage might not have been his past; that he might at some stage have been a newcomer to the valley; that his style of life might have been a matter of choice, a conscious act. (14)

What is initially assumed to be 'traditional' is merely 'Jack's way' (49). And it is not just Jack: the Phillipses too are revealed to be 'rootless people' (241). Yet both have found belonging: 'Jack ... anchored by the seasons and the corresponding labours of his gardens', the Phillipses by 'festivities outside, that gave rhythm and pattern and savour' (242). Equally, Pitton, who is unsuited to his role as gardener, finds belonging after his employment is terminated, to become a 'new man' who finds 'community and a little strength' (310). This awakens the narrator's understanding that there are no barriers to his own assumption of Englishness, his own much-desired need to belong. The universality of newness or difference expressed here –'recourse to humanism'[82] – is something Naipaul shares with Rushdie's universe where 'none of us are ourselves' that has been equally defined as a 'postcolonial humanism'.[83] It marks him not as a purveyor of the authentic, as Baucom suggests, but, like Rushdie, as a believer in perpetual mimicry as an important part of establishing meaningful connection to place.[84] It is also, as explored in the later chapters of this book, something both authors share with the next generation: the awareness that 'the old authenticities were always inauthentic'.[85] Yet while Naipaul's characters are performers in all scenarios, Chamcha's return to India suggests his notion of performance is less universalised. It is therefore, in fact, more in Naipaul's fiction than Rushdie's that stability is to be replaced with continuous newness.

Naipaul's much discussed relationship to English literary tradition, classical English language, and the realist form associated with the English novel in its imperial heyday also must be considered within the context of this 'newness'; as Caryl Phillips asserts, 'That he has never allowed himself to be absorbed fully into the English tradition is something many critics have misunderstood.'[86] While Naipaul is often read as a mimic of this form, he is a subtle interrogator of its associations. In an early essay, 'Jasmine' (1964), he declares that 'the English language was mine; the tradition was not'.[87] Aware of the need to renew English in a postcolonial context he reworks it: 'all Dickens's descriptions of London I rejected ... Dickens's rain and drizzle I turned into tropical downpours' (186). This subversion comes into *Enigma*, as the narrator declares that 'my Dickens cast, the cast in my head, was multi-racial'.[88] Such ironical employment of the English language and its literary forms is akin perhaps to what a writer such as Derek Walcott does in terms of poetry: a subtle subversion that lacks Rushdie's explicitness, perhaps, but is equally powerful. In his poem 'A Far Cry from Africa' (1956), Walcott asks 'how choose/Between this Africa and the English tongue I love?'[89] His answer to this question is the poem itself: not a turn to dialect or an extravagant corruption of standard English, but rather a subtle reworking of language through application against its own original purposes: a language against empire, used to describe a land-scape and experience dramatically removed from an English context. Naipaul's own work offers a similarly 'quietly ironic allusive gestures to the tradition of domestic nineteenth- and twentieth-century British literature'.[90] As Walcott finds Africa through English, so through the English landscape the narrator of *Enigma* finds Africa too: 'the Wiltshire I walked in – began to return Africa to me' (187). Naipaul's extensive reference to the English literary canon – his nods to Wordsworth, to Dickens – in these terms is not simple mimicry, but subversive repeti-tion. Naipaul is reclaiming these sources as rightfully his but also transforming their meaning as they speak for a very differ-ent voice.[91] They are potentially opened up to critique as their voicing in this manner draws attention to the narrow cultural values they once stood for, so that it is for the migrant 'the very heart of the English literary tradition ... reconverted and rede-signed to tell and celebrate their story'.[92]

There is further irony here, in that Walcott is one of Naipaul's most virulent critics, calling *Enigma* 'predictable' as it resurrects the prejudices of Naipaul's earlier writing and allows Naipaul to re-imagine himself as 'English squire'.[93] While the basis of Walcott's criticism in Naipaul's travel writing – which is at times problematic – is not to be into called into question, nev-ertheless, as Robert M. Greenberg has argued, it is important not to uncritically transfer these problems to Naipaul's fiction.[94] Emerging in *Enigma* is not mimicry in negative Fanonian form, but rather self-conscious employment in Bhabha's more subver-sive rendering of the term, a copying 'almost the same, but not quite' and, as such, a profoundly destabilising intervention into imperial identity.[95] That Naipaul sets up such subversion inten-tionally, against Bhabha's suggestion it is an unintended effect, not only again unites Naipaul with Rushdie, but also points to Naipaul's position not as colonial subject, but as self-aware British Asian critic of this positioning.[96] As discussed further in Chapters 2, 6 and the Conclusion of this book, his employ-ment of mimicry is the same strategy taken up subsequently by Kureishi, and problematised further in the self-conscious fictions of Meera Syal and Gautam Malkani.

In claiming Britishness in *Enigma*, Naipaul announces a new-ness in British identity centred upon the right to use its language and traditions, and a subtle transformation of these traditions through their employment by voices whose ancestry is not British, although their national identity is. One needs to ask, in these terms, why Naipaul is judged more harshly than Rushdie for the identifications his characters display. If Chamcha claims his Indian heritage, why is this less problematic than the claim of Naipaul's narrator to an English national identity? In such criticisms, particularly as they are expressed by Mustafa and Cudjoe, there seems to be a hint of what can only be defined as racism, an exclusionary rhetoric which states that Naipaul *cannot* be British. So for Cudjoe the fact that England is accepted as home is 'saddening', evidence of Naipaul's neurosis-driven 'wish-fulfilment'.[97] In this analysis, there is a national identification that Naipaul is *supposed to have*. Critics who make such assumptions go against the notion of belonging as something that is transferable and open to all. They consign Naipaul – and with him all with a similar history – to the status of eternal immigrant, to be ceaselessly traumatised, endless wanderers, without acknowledging the intensely painful reality of such existence. As Rushdie's migrants in *Verses* declare their desire to be made 'permanent' (264), so Naipaul's narrator has achieved this. Such achievement enacts its subversion without recourse to postmodern excess, but is evident nevertheless, and more so for the contribution it makes to a changing notion of British identity. For while Rushdie's migrants leave, Naipaul's stay: it is they who forge the conditions under which the next generation will make their claims.[98]

Staging marginality

To re-vision liminality as a transiently occupied location gesturing towards the possibility of British Asianness is to recognise in part the positioning of Rushdie and Naipaul themselves, and their implied authors, within a space of confidence that points towards the transformation of the migrant voice into a British Asian consciousness. While each authors' characters straddle alienation and confident belonging, the authorial voice in both cases is testament to the latter. In this respect, marginality is only employed strategically: what Huggan refers to as both authors' 'staged marginality', a double-voiced discourse equally apparent in both authors' work.[99] In Rushdie's short story, 'The Courtier' (1994), for example, the narrator declares his lack of cultural knowledge despite long-term settlement in Britain: he is no more comfortable than his more recently arrived father.[100] Yet Rushdie's own knowledge seeps through, as he tracks the stores of Oxford Street and Kensington.[101]

Equally, in *Verses* one can see the difference between Rushdie's own confident mapping, and the experience of his migrants. Gibreel's inexperience of the Underground leads him to flee 'in every direction' as 'he did not have any idea of the true shape' (201). Yet the description of this confusion is replete with Tube stations and landmarks – the Bank of England, Tufnell Park, the Metropolitan Line, Oxford Circus – to reveal an author whose own experience is profoundly different, with a legibility that – as I discuss in relation to Atima Srivastava – is a significant feature of British Asian narratives. Equally, in Naipaul's 'Tell Me Who to Kill' the narrator has no insider knowledge, proclaiming 'I can't see where I am going'.[102] Yet Naipaul's knowledge cannot help but infuse the text, tracking Dayo's brother's movement from Oxford Circus, down Oxford Street, into a Lyons' tea shop, down Great Russell Street, and to the British Museum.[103] In later texts, such as *Half a Life* (2001) and its sequel *Magic Seeds*, this strategy is repeated. The central character of Willie, whose life as a migrant student in London mimics Naipaul's own, expresses his confusion on his arrival in the city:

> He didn't know what he was looking at. The little booklets and folders he picked up or bought at Underground stations didn't help; they assumed that the local sights they were writing about were famous and well understood; and really Willie knew little more of London than the name.[104]

Yet Naipaul recounts Willie's movements in great detail, from the streets to the bus numbers and their destinations, from 'the city' to the suburbs of Cricklewood and Turnham Green.[105] For Naipaul – despite his status as a migrant – such geography is indeed 'well understood'.

Enigma is unique in these terms, as the novel's self-referential structure allows not just author but also migrant protagonist (being the same person) this experience. Liminality is impermanent: for the migrant as much as the British-born the visible signs of alienation betray a more deep-rooted process of both embedding oneself with Britain and redefining simultaneously what that 'Britain' represents. As *Enigma*'s migrant protagonist *is* its confident author, insider knowledge is more openly available: the irony of Rushdie's and Naipaul's unknowing migrants versus their own ease is finally exposed. Use of past tense in *Enigma* is profoundly significant: akin to the classical *bildungsroman* it reminds us that the experience of the protagonist is very different from that of the storyteller. The former, for much of the novel, lacks knowledge. But reporting of this in the past tense – 'it *was* hard for me to distinguish one section or season from the other; I *didn't* associate flowers or the foliage of trees with any particular month' (my emphasis, 4) – indicates how far the protagonist has moved from this earlier relationship. The storyteller has an understanding that exceeds many of the 'insiders'; 'what had come out at the top of the hill was not the hawthorn, but the blackthorn' (41), he is able to tell us. This is not just further marking of the potential for *becoming* British Asian; it also means, as Allen suggests, the novel is simultaneously a transparent English narrative *and* a statement of postcolonial identity, each symbol having a dual register of meaning so the reader is 'reading two novels at the same time; one in which the language appears transparently to record the everyday life of rural England, the other in which every detail can be read as carefully symbolic of post-colonial identity and culture'.[106] Naipaul himself points towards this duality, a metaphor for two different ways of reading, but also two different ways of Britishness, as his narrator announces 'Two ways to the cottage. Different ways: one was very old, and one was new.'(6) Such duality moreover reveals, as I discussed in the introduction, the positionality as a British Asian author which is always present. As Naipaul's writer narrator declares that 'in my writing those days, I was hiding my experience[s] from myself ... yet at the same time revealing them to anyone who looked beyond the conventional words and forms and attitudes I was aiming at' (314) so the conscious double-voicing of his later narrative is merely the next step in a textual creation that *always* occupies a unique position informed by ethnic experience.

That Huggan continues his discussion of staged marginality in terms of Kureishi points again to continuity, evidence of strategic ambivalence that has filtered into the work of Naipaul's and Rushdie's successors.[107] This becomes, for example, the ideology of Kureishi: his identification of the British Asian subject as 'English born and bred, almost' points, similarly, not to an alienated 'in-between' so much as to the British Asian's entry into British culture as the destabilising of its imagined homogeneity.[108] Formally, too, both Naipaul and Rushdie are profoundly influential: be this the magical-realist lyricism of Nadeem Aslam or the hyper-active prose of Hari Kunzru – both owing much to Rushdie – or the subtle reworkings of realism and understated postmodernism employed by Syal and Monica Ali, both drawing more obviously from Naipaul's strategies.

The influence of Rushdie and Naipaul also translates, at least in some of these authors, to similar positioning in more problematic terms. Rushdie and Naipaul offer similarly secular viewpoints which, although having more explosive consequences in the case of Rushdie, have led to both authors being accused of furthering anti-Islamic sentiment.[109] In Chapters 2 and 5 on Kureishi and Aslam I respectively emphasise the continuance of these problematic liberal positionings although, as explored in Chapter 8 on Ali, it is evident that British Asian texts may also interrogate as well as support such earlier standpoints.

What these continuities indicate is a gradual transition, rather than a radical departure. As postcolonial authors become British Asian, so those who are British-born/raised develop their concerns. If there is a tangible difference, it is perhaps in the level of confidence. Sanga argues that for Rushdie there is a doubt surrounding identity that makes his texts thematically modernist, even if formally postmodernist.[110] For British Asian authors, formal qualities are less defined, but they are on the whole thematically postmodernist: the doubt which lingers in Rushdie's texts is replaced by buoyancy and self-assurance, and the universality of experiences of alienation are more accepted as a manifestation of contemporary society, on which the British Asian author is only the most insightful of commentators.

Conclusion

Both Rushdie and Naipaul capture a Britishness being changed to accommodate its ethnic citizens, the sense in which, as Michael Gorra argues, the task isn't 'to assimilate them to England but rather to suggest how England, and English, might assimilate itself to them'.[111] Their texts are liminal not in the often-used sense of sitting uncomfortably between two alternative sites of absolute belonging, but rather in the sense of sitting between a conventional migrant positioning, and a newly emerging, as yet unrealised, British Asian sensibility. Jumpy Joshi is a 'failed' hero; Mishal and Anahita's assimilation, 'growing up refusing to speak their mother tongue' (250), has yet to give way to Shahana's acculturation in *Brick Lane* with sandwiches of cream cheese and mango pickle. Naipaul's sense of decay surrounding his rejection of birth as indicative of roots has yet to give way to the assertive rendering of becoming as offered by Suhayl Saadi. Yet, in Rushdie and Naipaul, we find the beginnings of this later confidence: the self-assurance, in part, of narrative voices which stand in opposition to the more obvious themes of alienation in their novels. It is to the next generation that we must turn, however, for the completion of such experiences.

Discussion

- How do the narrative voices employed by Rushdie and/or Naipaul lay claim to the British landscape?
- How, and with what level of success, do Rushdie's and/or Naipaul's central protagonists 'change' Britishness?
- Both Naipaul and Rushdie have been criticised for their representation of the developing world. How do the potentially problematic aspects of their fiction reflect on them as 'British authors'?

Notes

1 Mishra, 'The Familiar Temporariness', p. 200.
2 Harrison, *Salman Rushdie*, p. 125.
3 Ishiguro on Rushdie's Booker Prize win for *Midnight's Children*, quoted in Teverson, *Salman Rushdie*, p. 4.
4 Huggan, *Postcolonial Exotic*, p. 85.
5 Mustafa, *V. S. Naipaul*, p. 1, p. 2.
6 *Ibid.*, p. 90, p. 219.
7 Inder Singh, *V. S. Naipaul*, p. 49.
8 Hennard Duthell de la Rochère, *Origin and Originality*, p. xiii.
9 Smale (ed.), *Salman Rushdie*, p. 9, p. 15. See also Afzal-Khan, *Cultural Imperialism*, p. 143.
10 Ranasinha, *South Asian Writers,* p. 186.
11 *Ibid.*, p. 209.
12 Pritchett, *New York Review of Books*, 11 April 1968, as cited in French, *The World Is What It Is*, p. 257.
13 Walsh, *V. S. Naipaul*, p. 44, p. 47.
14 Ahmad, *In Theory*, p. 111; Salgado, 'V. S. Naipaul and the Politics of Fiction', p. 314.
15 As cited in Cudjoe, *V. S. Naipaul*, p. 225.
16 Krishnan, '*Midnight's Children*: An Un-Indian Book About All Things Indian', p. 51, p. 53.
17 Mahanta, 'Allegories of the Indian Experience', p. 244.
18 Webb, 'Salman Rushdie: Satanic Verses', p. 87. Morey, 'Salman Rushdie and the English Tradition'.
19 See, for example, Brennan, *Salman Rushdie*, p. 150; Gorra, *After Empire*, p. 8, and Holmes, 'The Postcolonial Subject Divided Between East and West'.
20 Mustafa, *V. S. Naipaul*, p. 8.

21 See Kundu, 'Naipaul: "An Indian who is not an Indian"', p. 122, p. 124.
22 Naipaul maintained this position for the majority of his career. He does, however, mellow in *A Way in the World*, where Trinidad is referred to as 'home' in both opening and concluding pieces, p. 1, and pp. 343–68.
23 Rushdie, *The Satanic Verses*, p. 4. Hereafter *Verses*. Subsequent references cited parenthetically.
24 See, for example, Tripathi, 'Salman Rushdie Interview', p. 25; Rushdie, 'Imaginary Homelands', p. 16.
25 Tripathi, 'Salman Rushdie Interview', p. 24; Haffenden, 'Salman Rushdie', p. 56. See also Webb, 'Salman Rushdie', p. 93.
26 For a survey of the criticism of Naipaul see Nixon, *London Calling*, pp. 4–6. There is a large literature on 'The Rushdie Affair'. However, the best objective summary is offered by Mishra, *Literature of the Indian Diaspora*, pp. 233–41.
27 Mustafa, V. S. *Naipaul*, p. 13.
28 Weiss, *On the Margins*, p. 3.
29 Hayward, *The Enigma of V. S. Naipaul*, p. 4. Nasta, *Home Truths*, p. 94.
30 My emphasis, Swinden, *The English Novel of History and Society*, p. 210.
31 Potter, *The Times*, October 1971, as cited in French, *The World Is What It Is*, p. 284.
32 Brennan, *Salman Rushdie*, p. viii.
33 Bhabha, *Location*, p. 168, See also Sanga, *Salman Rushdie's Postcolonial Metaphors*, p. 17, Nasta, *Home Truths*, p. 136.
34 Ross, *'Contemporary Authors* Interview', p. 5.
35 Anonymous, 'Homeless is Where the Art Is', p. 162.
36 Wood, 'Enigmas and Homelands', p. 84.
37 Baucom, *Out of Place*, pp. 187–91; Sanga, *Salman Rushdie's Postcolonial Metaphors*, p. 43; Gorra, *After Empire*, p. 170; Krishnaswamy, 'Mythologies of Migrancy', pp. 138–9; Mukerjee, 'Prophet and Loss'. For a more subtle account of the authors' differences see Gurnah, 'Displacement and Transformation'.
38 Mustafa, *V. S. Naipaul*, p. 4.
39 Baucom, *Out of Place*, p. 187. Similar readings are offered by Bhabha (*Location*, pp. 166–9 and 225–9), Gandhi, '"Ellowen, Deeowen"' and Sachdeva Mann, '"Being Borne across"'.
40 See, for example, Mustafa, *V. S. Naipaul*, p. 7; Baucom, *Out of Place*, p. 182; Mishra, *Literature of the Indian Diaspora*, p. 129.
41 Huggan, *Postcolonial Exotic*, p. 86. Nasta, *Home Truths*, p. 96. Wood, 'Enigmas and Homelands', p. 77.
42 Allen, 'A Post-Colonial World', p. 149. See also Niven's comment that Naipaul has 'created a new form': 'V. S. Naipaul Talks to Alastair Niven', p. 5.
43 Dhondy, 'The Gutter Inspector's Report?', p. 55.
44 See, for example, Hennard Duthell de la Rochère, *Origin and Originality*, p. xxiv, Sanga, *Salman Rushdie's Postcolonial Metaphors*, p. 31, Dawson, *Mongrel Nation*, p. 135.
45 Rushdie's interest in this project is expressed in 'Hobson Jobson'.

46 Mishra, 'Rushdie-Wushdie: Salman Rushdie's Hobson-Jobson', Kingston University Literary Series, Kingston University, England, 28 October 2008.
47 Morey, 'Salman Rushdie', p. 32.
48 See, for example, Selvon, *Lonely Londoners* or Lamming, *Emigrants.*
49 Naipaul, *Mimic Men*, p. 17.
50 Naipaul, *The Enigma of Arrival*, p. 146. Hereafter *Enigma*. Subsequent references cited parenthetically.
51 My emphasis, Rushdie, *Shame,* p. 29, pp. 86–7.
52 *Ibid.*, p. 116.
53 Rushdie, 'Choice Between Light and Dark'.
54 See, for example, Baucom, *Out of Place*, and Bhabha, *Location*.
55 Baucom, *Out of Place*, p. 209, p. 211. Critics to note this problem are Huggan, *Postcolonial Exotic*, p. 92; Clement Ball, *Imagining London*, pp. 207–8; Gikandi, *Maps of Englishness*, p. 220; Delrez, 'Political Aesthetics', p. 14, and Mcleod, *Postcolonial London,* pp. 151–6.
56 Gikandi, *Maps of Englishness*, p. 222.
57 For this act of colonial mapping in *Verses* see Upstone, *Spatial Politics*, pp. 85–114.
58 'Imaginary Homelands' is suffused with such sentiment, the desire for 'a city and a history to reclaim' (p. 10). For Spivak, this return is autobiographical, 'Reading The Satanic Verses', p. 226.
59 Rare critical acknowledgment of this shift comes in Clement Ball, *Imagining London*, pp. 210–11.
60 Gikandi, *Maps of Englishness*, p. 208.
61 Delrez, 'Political Aesthetics', p. 14.
62 Rushdie, *Ground Beneath Her Feet*, p. 278.
63 Rushdie, 'In Good Faith', p. 397.
64 For the former position see Sawhney, 'Satanic Choices', p. 260.
65 Teverson, *Salman Rushdie*, p. 151. See also Bhabha, *Location*, p. 224.
66 Rushdie explores institutional racism in 'The New Empire in Britain'.
67 See Mishra, 'Postcolonial Differend', p. 14.
68 Huggan, *Postcolonial Exotic*, p. 104.
69 Tripathi, 'Salman Rushdie Interview', p. 27.
70 Kureishi, 'Rainbow Sign', p. 38. This connection is further established by Rushdie's nonfiction. See 'The New Empire in Britain': 'British racism, of course, is not our problem. It's yours', p. 138.
71 Baucom, *Out of Place*, p. 206.
72 Ross, *Race Riots*, p. 212.
73 For a positive reading of *Verses'* British-born figures see Hennard Duthell de la Rochère, *Origin and Originality*, p. 110.
74 Gorra, *After Empire*, p. 166.
75 '[B]ecoming British Asian' is used in the very different context of Syal's fiction by Bromley, *Narratives for a New Belonging*, p. 147.
76 Baucom, *Out of Place*, p. 178.
77 In his authorised autobiography, French reveals how critical of empire Naipaul has been, comparing it negatively to Nazism. See French, *The World Is What It Is*, p. 137.

78 Weiss, *On the Margins*, p. 88.
79 See Hayward, *Enigma of V. S. Naipaul*, pp. 42–3: the most obvious example of this early feeling is 'London'. In a letter to his mother in 1954 Naipaul writes 'Do not imagine that I am enjoying staying in this country. This country is hot with racial prejudices, and I certainly don't wish to stay here'. See Naipaul, *Letters Between a Father and Son*, pp. 313–14. For a good summary of this alienation in Naipaul's early fiction see Gurr, *Writers in Exile*, pp. 65–91.
80 Tiffin, 'Rites of Resistance', p. 43.
81 See, for example, 'Reading and Writing', p. 12. Both facets of this experience are explored in *Enigma*, pp. 120–6.
82 Mustafa, *V. S. Naipaul*, p. 19.
83 Rushdie, *Satanic Verses*, p. 65; Weiss, 'V. S. Naipaul's "Fin de Siècle"', p. 116.
84 Baucom, *Out of Place*, p. 188.
85 Corner, 'Beyond Revisions', p. 167.
86 Phillips, 'V. S. Naipaul', p. 198.
87 Naipaul, 'Jasmine', p. 26.
88 Naipaul, *Enigma*, p. 186.
89 Derek Walcott, 'A Far Cry from Africa', p. 2588.
90 Mustafa, *V. S. Naipaul*, p. 160.
91 Suleri, *Rhetoric of English India*, p. 155.
92 King, *V. S. Naipaul*, p. 148.
93 Walcott, 'The Garden Path', p. 27, p. 31.
94 Greenberg, 'Anger and the Alchemy', p. 220.
95 Bhabha, *Location*, p. 86.
96 Here I concur with Nasta's positive reading of Naipaul, in *Home Truths*, p. 105.
97 Cudjoe, *V. S. Naipaul*, p. 212, p. 213, p. 214.
98 At the end of *Enigma*, the narrator does return to his place of birth. However, the self-referential nature of the narrative makes it clear that this is only a stage in the narrator's assumption of Britishness.
99 Huggan, *Postcolonial Exotic*, p. 87.
100 Rushdie, 'The Courtier', p. 185.
101 *Ibid.*, pp. 187–8.
102 Naipaul, 'Tell Me', p. 60.
103 *Ibid.*, pp. 93–4.
104 Naipaul, *Half a Life*, p. 52.
105 Naipaul, *Magic Seeds*, p. 194, p. 200, pp. 222–3, p. 279.
106 Allen, 'A Postcolonial World', p. 149.
107 Huggan, *Postcolonial Exotic*, pp. 94–104.
108 Kureishi, *Buddha*, p. 3.
109 Mustafa, *V. S. Naipaul*, p. 27. For an overview of Naipaul's anti-Islamic sentiment see Kapur, 'A Million Neuroses', and Wheatcroft, 'A Terrifying Honesty'. Although the *Satanic Verses* affair was driven by accusations of Orientalism, recent Rushdie criticism renews this claim: see Sawhney and Sawhney, 'Reading Rushdie after September 11, 2001'.
110 Sanga, *Salman Rushdie's Postcolonial Metaphors* p. 20.

111   Gorra, *After Empire*, p. 174.

Further reading

Michael Gorra, *After Empire: Scott, Naipaul, Rushdie* (Chicago: University of Chicago Press, 1997).

Damian Grant, *Salman Rushdie* (Plymouth: Northcote House, 1999).

Abdulrazak Gurnah (ed.), *The Cambridge Companion to Salman Rushdie* (Cambridge: Cambridge University Press, 2008).

James Harrison, *Salman Rushdie* (New York: Twayne, 1992).

Helen Hayward, *The Enigma of V. S. Naipaul: Sources and Contexts* (Basingstoke: Palgrave Macmillan, 2002).

Fawzia Mustafa, *V. S. Naipaul* (Cambridge: Cambridge University Press, 1995).

David Smale (ed.), *Salman Rushdie: Midnight's Children/The Satanic Verses: A Reader's Guide to Essential Criticism* (Basingstoke: Palgrave Macmillan, 2001).

Andrew Teverson, *Salman Rushdie* (Manchester: Manchester University Press, 2007).

Timothy F. Weiss, *On the Margins: The Art of Exile in V. S. Naipaul* (Amherst: University of Massachusetts Press, 1992).

2

Hanif Kureishi

They pretend they're democrats but they're little Lenins.[1]

In 1967, my grandparents moved to a council flat in West Kensington. Their excitement at this, I have been told since, was so strong it was palpable. Having waited years to escape poor living conditions and exploitation by Hammersmith's private landlords, the possibility of secure tenancy and guaranteed standards was as close as this working-class generation would get to the home ownership their children and grandchildren later enjoyed.

Forty-one years later, my grandmother still lives in that same council flat. Now a widow, she finds the estate is not what it was, though it is still better than many. There is little communication amongst the international inhabitants of my grandmother's block, and the right-to-buy scheme introduced by the Thatcher Government in the 1980s has meant she is one of the few council tenants left, the majority of properties rented to students or local workers on short-term leases.

As a child, I would travel every week with my mother on the bus from our house in the suburbs to visit my grandparents. For me, like Karim in *The Buddha of Suburbia* (1990), this journey into the city was filled with anticipation. I repeat this journey to the present day: from a different suburb, and – admittedly – with less of the sense of exhilaration it produced during my childhood. A result of this, however, is that I know the terrain of most of Kureishi's novels and short stories (and also some of his films), intimately: the West London in which he situates a large proportion of his writings I consider to be my 'second home'.[2] I can see *Buddha's* 'rows of five-storey peeling stucco houses' (126); I can identify Kureishi's Nashville public house with its Wurlitzer jukebox facade (127) as The Three Kings, a public house on the corner of North End Road near West Kensington

Tube station so well known to its local population that it is now renamed 'The Famous Three Kings'.

Yet while for Kureishi these stucco houses are the spaces of 'itinerants and poor people' (*Buddha* 126) I also know the real poor people in the spaces Kureishi does not recount in his seemingly realist narrative, filled as it is – like all his texts – with street names and landmarks. The world we inhabited had a different sort of poverty from Kureishi's world. Broaden out the geography, and change time frames, and my perspective shifts little. I can place exactly the circus and sex shops in contemporary-set *Something to Tell You* (2008) but my picture also includes the tramps who sit opposite, drinking each day from early morning until evening.[3] While Philip Dodd, interviewing Kureishi, cites him as saying that there are *'enough stories in west London to keep you in work forever'* it is difficult not to think that, in Kureishi's late fiction at least, this West London setting has largely facilitated the *same* story.[4]

Such an anecdote draws attention to what good literary critics already take for granted, particularly in terms of ethnic authors for whom the burden of representation is great: a literary work, however 'realist', is not the real world. Yet how Kureishi imagines his world is central to his identity as a British Asian author. His vision of London, and of the communities that inhabit it, has become the scaffolding for an ideological perspective that infuses his fiction.

Being British Asian: Kureishi's posed/post-ethnicity

For Mark Stein, Kureishi's novels fall into two groups, identified respectively as 'posed-ethnic' and 'post-ethnic'. Posed-ethnic works are *'self-consciously* postcolonial', applying ethnic reference points ironically and manipulating reader expectations.[5] Post-ethnic work sees 'ethnicity ... displaced but not evaded, without entirely ceasing to be of concern'.[6] The former term Stein applies to Kureishi's early work; the latter identifies later writing. Further examination of Kureishi's work, however, calls into question this distinction: the early plays *The King and Me* and *Tomorrow Today!* (1980) are undoubtedly post-ethnic works.

Nevertheless, Stein's categories do broadly apply. Most of Kureishi's early work is posed-ethnic: the plays *The Mother Country* (1980), *Outskirts* (1981), *Borderline* (1981), *Birds of Passage* (1983), the novels *The Buddha of Suburbia* and *The Black Album*

(1995), the films *My Beautiful Laundrette* (1985) and *Sammy and Rosie Get Laid* (1992) all illustrate the ironic assumption of ethnic identities. *Buddha* is perhaps the high point in these terms: Karim's father plays at being 'the Buddha', Charlie forges a career 'selling Englishness' (247), Karim himself is a wonderful version of Homi Bhabha's subversive mimic. He portrays an 'authentic' Indian in his acting career for popularity and prosperity: 'I sent up the accent and made the audience laugh by suddenly relapsing into cockney at odd times' (158).

In between these two novels, Kureishi's first self-directed feature, *London Kills Me* (1993), is his first consciously post-ethnic work. Its multicultural cast of young people, with racial backgrounds taken for granted, foreshadows films such as *Kidulthood* (2006) and *Adulthood* (2008) in which urban landscapes provide the backdrop for hard-hitting drama with a diverse cast of characters.[7] This is developed in Kureishi's later fiction, the novels *Intimacy* (1998) and *Gabriel's Gift* (2001), and the majority of the short stories in the collections *Love in a Blue Time* (1997), *Midnight All Day* (1999), and *The Body and Seven Stories* (2002), where the central characters are often white, or their race is not indicated.[8] This is also the case for Kureishi's later screen and theatre work: *Sleep with Me* (1999), *The Mother* (2003), *When Night Begins* (2004), *Venus* (2006). Yet, at the same time, broader questions of identity are always being posited, be this the debate surrounding authenticity raised by Gabriel's painting in *Gabriel's Gift,* or the preoccupation with the body in Kureishi's later short stories and *Intimacy.*[9]

Born in Bromley, Kent, on 5 December 1954, Kureishi is the first author of note *born* in Britain, although, as I shall discuss in Chapter 3, he is not the first author to focus on the issues of this generation. His posed-ethnicity may be connected to this, ironic reference to ethnicity marking the confidence of the British Asian subject to manipulate racial codes and binaries. Kureishi is not interested in the migrant relationships that preoccupy Salman Rushdie and V. S. Naipaul; 'he is not a displaced postcolonial wiring *back* to the centre, he writes *from* the centre'.[10] He has, on a number of occasions, refused any description of him as caught between cultures, alienated, or confused.[11] The most often cited statement by Kureishi, that there must be 'a new way of being British after all this time', is an assertion of such positioning: Britain's racist past should not mean a rejection of Britishness by its ethnic populations, but rather a call to redefinition.[12]

At the same time, post-ethnicity, refusing to present race as the defining feature of an individual life, is a powerful way of portraying this confidence: being Asian and British is, Kureishi stresses, nothing to make a fuss about. He refuses definition as an Asian author[13] and, moreover, challenges the definition of any fiction in such terms: there is, he says, 'no such thing as a gay or black sensibility'.[14] He is more likely to cite influences from classic British or contemporary American fiction than postcolonial writing.[15] The post-ethnic is crucial to the refusal of the burden of representation, reflecting Kureishi's belief that 'If contemporary writing which emerges from oppressed groups ignores the central concerns and major conflicts of the larger society, it will automatically designate itself as minor, as a sub-genre.'[16] It is also essential to understanding the concept developed through this book, that British Asian writers offer a particular sensibility. Despite his resistance to such readings, Kureisi's work is undoubtedly informed by his personal experiences of racial politics in Britain. His texts offer perspectives on identity which, even when not explicitly about ethnicity, are framed nevertheless by a unique positioning.

Kureishi's posed-ethnicity is also undoubtedly foregrounded by his own mixed-race background – born to an English mother and a Pakistani father – a physical symbol of the problematic nature of accepting simplistic ethnic identifications. This mixed-race identity is reflected in, and also informs the relationships of *My Beautiful Laundrette*, *Sammy and Rosie Get Laid*, *Buddha*, and *Black Album*. Blurred ethnic identities are contextualised within a broader rejection of categories: fluid sexuality sees the performance of ethnic identities mirrored in equal performances of gender, frequently manifested in bisexuality. This reinforces, however, the argument made for post-ethnicity too: even when not discussing ethnicity, Kureishi is making relevant comments. An assertion such as Karim's that, in terms of his sexuality, 'I felt it would be heartbreaking to have to choose one or the other' (*Buddha* 55) might equally be applied to the novel's position on ethnicity.

In essence, Stein has not identified modes of representation specific to Kureishi, but rather the preoccupations of the majority of British Asian writers. In one way or another, all of the authors in this book follow one of these two models or, like Kureishi, engage in both of them. What is more interesting in terms of Kureishi therefore are not these terms, but rather the nuances of his engagement with them. The term 'post-ethnicity' is not Stein's own, but is borrowed from David Hollinger.

Yet Hollinger's original definition has notable features inappropriate to Kureishi's work. These features, which Stein perhaps sensibly overlooks, are in fact the aspects of Kureishi's work which *are different* to a number of the other authors in this collection.

Taking for granted, therefore, the idea that Kureishi's writings are both posed-ethnic and post-ethnic, it is more useful to ask what are the reasons for, and the consequences of, post-ethnicity less broad than Hollinger's original definition? Moreover, how has such representation changed across Kureishi's prolific career? What is evident is that Kureishi's specific engagement with post-ethnicity brings with it a unique relationship to the founding concepts of postcolonial literary theory, and – ultimately – an engagement that leads to its own unravelling.

Kureishi's postmodern didacticism

In his application, Stein takes up Hollinger's idea that 'ethnicity, "race," or history are only some of the possible determinants delineating the symbolic boundaries of cultures'.[17] He neglects the fact that a central alternative identification is what Hollinger refers to as 'moral communities'.[18] Rather than inherited allegiances, Hollinger envisages religious affiliations with 'the right of exit, and also the dynamics of entry', considering how the model of provision provided in the United States to separatist groups such as the Amish might be modified to allow for the recognition of religious values within a multicultural society.[19] Yet there is little advocating of religious community in Kureishi's works, which favour instead a life of, in Kureishi's own words, 'class, race, fucking and farce' (*Buddha* 189). Exclusions such as these offer an image of Kureishi as a far more didactic writer than critics often suggest. Once these exclusions are established, it is possible to identify in Kureishi's work a notable ideological positioning.

Exclusion of religious commitment from Kureishi's post-ethnic world makes the application of Hollinger's framework problematic. This exclusion is most notable in Kureishi's treatment of Islam, the focus of both *Black Album* and *My Son the Fanatic* (2000).[20] As I have argued elsewhere, these texts critique fundamentalist Islamism without recourse to alternative manifestations which would provide more positive representations of the relationship between religion and politics.[21] Kureishi's objection is not to Islam *per se*, however, but to religion itself.

The narrator of *Intimacy*, for example, proclaims: 'We have reached such a state that after two thousand years of Christian civilization, if I meet anyone religious – and, thankfully, I do only rarely these days – I consider them to be mentally defective and probably in need of therapy.'[22] In his non-fiction and interviews Kureishi's critique of Islam is interwoven with critiques of Christianity, and religion in general:

> There are all kinds of things in Islam which are clearly not compatible with liberalism ... There's a lot of stuff in there that you wouldn't want around now. And that, clearly, one can't make compatible with what goes on now ... It is a very, very unpleasant religion in all sorts of ways.
> *And so is Christianity.* You have to jettison those bits, you know, in order to live in this country. It seems to me the basis of our living in England, of our living in England together, is liberalism. And liberalism and certain parts of Islam don't go together at all ...
> I mean, *a religion* isn't only something that you just swallow whole. It is a pick and choose thing too.[23]

Religion, *in general*, cannot be integrated into Kureishi's post-ethnicity: his assertion that it is a 'pick and choose thing' is the statement of a proclaimed atheist.[24] Religion, *in any form*, has no relevance.

This irrelevance is woven into Kureishi's texts. In *Intimacy* Victor has a Bible, but 'no one read it, not even the Song of Solomon' (58); in 'The Body' (2002) religion is already extinct: the narrator tells us 'There *was* religion, once'.[25] In *Buddha*, religion of any form is associated with a lack of creativity; in the suburbs 'it was a lovely day but their routine never changed ... People in hats and suits were coming back from church and they carried Bibles' (39). The association is not just with stifling conformity, but with mental weakness: in *Something to Tell You* Kureishi's choice of similes indicates this: 'like a madman always with the Bible' (267) suggests, in reverse reading, that a man always with a Bible is a madman. The comment in 'Lately' (1997), 'to everyone their own religion, these days. Who was not deranged, from a certain point of view?', can be similarly read. [26]

Kureishi's rhetoric here forcefully stresses the danger of systems of fundamentalist thought. That religion represents such a system for Kureishi is evident, but it is not his only target. Family, too, is fundamentalist:

> There is a profound relation between the sort of families that exist in a particular society – the family ideal, as it were – and the kind of

political system that's possible. You couldn't have a liberal, democratic political system in a society in which families were Muslim,
strictly organised around the symbolic position of the absolute
father.[27]

The notion of the 'perfect family' is destabilised in the majority
of Kureishi's earlier texts, particularly *My Beautiful Laundrette*,
London Kills Me, and *Buddha*. Family values are fundamentalist because they are associated not with religion, but with
Kureishi's other target for critique: right-wing politics, especially
as they are manifested in the Thatcherite ideals of the 1980s.[28]
For Kureishi the politics of Margaret Thatcher's Conservative
administration were middle-class, conservative and intolerant,
and were embodied in a discourse of 'family values'.[29]

The movement from posed-ethnicity to post-ethnicity only
heightens this connection. In his comments on his screenplay
for *The Mother*, a post-ethnic tale questioning conventional ideas
of gender and ageing, Kureishi opposes the family with the
rights of the individual. The film ends with 'the mother' strid-
ing out alone, abandoning the judgements of her family and
their reliance on convention. An ideal family for Kureishi is not
about connection, but about the right to be disconnected:

> It seems to me that this is a pretty good family and the fact that there
> is a good deal of indifference in the family to the welfare of the other
> people probably seems to me to be quite a good thing as well. I
> mean one of the ways in which you might survive in a family is by
> ignoring the craziness of the other members of the family, otherwise
> you may be swept into the maelstrom of claustrophobia.[30]

This context allows us to reappraise perhaps Kureishi's most
famous post-ethnic work, *Intimacy*, which was attacked after
publication because Kureishi used his own life as subject matter.[31] The novel's position on adultery does not simply reflect
Kureishi's personal life, or even his conscious manipulation of
such reader assumptions, but rather a logical continuation of
earlier critique. Jay's belief that 'every day should contain at
least one essential infidelity or necessary betrayal. It would be
an optimistic, hopeful act' (6) is a rejection not of marriage *per
se*, but of everything it stands for: 'habit convention, morality
... doing what you are told' (36). While critics of *Intimacy* have
suggested the novel is misogynistic this neglects the fact that,
rather than a criticism of women, it is a criticism of marriage
more generally, representative of the conventional relationships which Kureishi has *always* represented as stifling and

unproductive while – in contrast – his representation of women is often applauded for its challenging of stereotypes.[32]

This critique is reinforced in *Love in the Blue Time* through the surrealist fable 'The Flies'.[33] The flies in question only infest the homes of long-married couples, who desperately but covertly attempt everything they can think of to destroy them; they are metaphorical of the boredom and stasis of family life: 'the only secret that everyone keeps'.[34] They mark the hegemony of marriage as a repressive institution, a suffering that potions or therapy cannot cure. There is therefore a trajectory to be traced between Kureishi's scathing attacks on the suburbs in *Buddha* as the place where 'divorce wasn't something that would occur to them. In the suburbs people rarely dreamed of striking out for happiness' (8) and the dramatic rejection of marital conventions in *Intimacy* and *Love in a Blue Time*. The suburbs are just a pertinent site of what Kureishi dislikes most: 'the sanctification of home'.[35]

The identities and behaviours Kureishi critiques are deeply interconnected. Kureishi refers to *Intimacy's* questioning of the sacred nature of marriage as challenging 'the Koran of the middle classes'.[36] Jay experiences marriage in terms of religion: it is 'the only kind of religious faith I've had' (64). In interview, Kureishi brings his critique of religion, the family, and Thatcherite politics together explicitly, with his own liberal individualist positioning as the posited alternative:

> We're moving away from the liberal notion that individuals can make up their minds. Throughout the Eighties we've seen a return to sacred books – as though the freedom of the Sixties and Seventies so unsettled people that they want to go back to older ways. Thatcher wants England to be like the Fifties, with the family of the Fifties.[37]

At the centre of Kureishi's critique of different 'fundamentalisms', therefore, is the explicit positing of an alternative world-view: one which can be defined as 'postmodern didacticism'. By this, I mean the privileging of a world-view that favours multiplicity and liberal individualism, but only to the extent that one cannot reject this way of thinking, so that ideas of community, conventional family life, and religious affiliation become impossible. Embodied in Kureishi's celebration of extra-marital sexuality, individualism and secularism, such privileging is not limited to Kureishi's treatment of ethnicity, but infuses his work in various forms of which the critique of religious fundamentalism is only one.[38]

A reading of postmodern didacticism in these terms relies upon seeing Kureishi's irony as being overestimated. Identifying an 'ironic distance', Ranasinha suggests readings of Kureishi as didactic result from lack of appreciation of his distance from the firm positions his characters occupy.[39] Yet Kureishi's own comments in interviews (unless we read these too as ironic) make such readings more difficult. For example, on faith, Kureishi has commented that 'we're moving back almost to a medieval state'.[40] His comments on his association of the suburbs with a limited existence, and of the association in his youth of marriage with unexciting routine, ideologically enforced by post-war politics, equally call into question readings aiming to complicate or render ironic his treatment of 'conventional' family life.[41] Any irony, too, is part of the ideological positioning his novels take. Ambivalence indicates a problematic lack of commitment which is itself indicative of an ideological perspective. When Kureishi proclaims 'I didn't want to write a book that took sides', this itself establishes a liberal, postmodern framework for his writings.[42] When Kureishi speaks of doubt as 'the most crucial human faculty of all' it is as an alternative to the definition of prejudice as 'the pursuit of certainty'.[43]

Ranasinha effectively reads *Buddha* as an example of this liberal positioning, but examination of *Black Album* provides even stronger evidence.[44] Noted as the most didactic of Kureishi's novels,[45] *Black Album* can be read as a story that implies that the worlds of religious belief and postmodern fluidity 'are so incommensurate that they cannot converge'.[46] In particular, *Black Album* illustrates how it is not enough in Kureishi's terms for culture to be diverse: the self, also, must embody this difference internally. The most vital symbol for this way of thinking is the artist who gives the book its title: Prince. Prince's own identity, and indeed his music, is a mixture of hybrid influences – black and white, male and female – which makes him an encapsulation of Deedee and Shahid's relationship. This is a world defined by cultural diversity rather than cultural conformity, not just between individuals, but within them:

> How could anyone confine themselves to one system or creed? Why should they feel they had to? There was no fixed self; surely our several selves melted and mutated daily? There had to be innumerable ways of being in the world. He would spread himself out, in his work and in love, following his curiosity. (274)

What results is, in Berthold Schoene's terminology, a

'polycultural remoulding of the notion of Britishness' or what Sukhdev Sandhu calls *aggregation*: 'the constant mutation and updating of the self'.[47]

It is not enough that the world is made up of different cultures, even if they live together and share experiences. Rather, cultural uniqueness must be abandoned for an endless process of dislocation. Consider the following appraisal of Kureishi's work by Anthony Ilona:

> It is the existential condition of migrancy that proves a significant trope in the reconfiguration of identity as an *wholly* interactive and mutable rather than fixed and timeless idea in *The Buddha of Suburbia*. Here, it is the concept of *continual* relocation, the *ongoing* encounter and interaction with the extrinsic world, the transformative negotiation between the idea of home and *changing* location abroad, that becomes a *constant* over and above the *oscillatory* return to a reified vision of Self.[48]

To read Kureishi as an upholder of multiculturalism, as do Kenneth Kaleta and Ranasinha, therefore, does not offer the most accurate rendering of his position.[49] For Kureishi does not subscribe to the concept of multiculturalism as a toleration of individual communities and ethnic differences. For example, in *Outskirts*, this multicultural politics is satirised while, in *Buddha*, the multicultural world produces only ethnic tensions: spatial demarcation that breeds racism as Ted tells Karim '"That's where the niggers live"' (43). Elsewhere, Kureishi's opinions on faith schooling go against the idea of the accommodation of communal provision.[50]

As a later text, it is *Intimacy* that offers the most refined version of Kureishi's ideological positing. When Asif asks Jay if he believes in anything, his reply might stand for the majority of Kureishi's male protagonists to this point: 'I believe in individualism, in sensualism, and in creative idleness' (132). The novella's title refers to Jean Paul Sartre's 1949 story of the same name, a connection cemented when Kureishi reprinted it in 2001 under the title 'Intimacy and Other Stories', the very title of Sartre's original publication. Reference to Sartre points to the existence of an isolated individual, celebrated at the expense of communal identity. Sartre's story, like Kureishi's, is one of adultery and abandonment, although in Sartre's case it is the wife, Lulu, who is responsible. While Kureishi's story ends with Jay leaving, Sartre's begins with Lulu leaving, ending with her reluctant return to her grieving husband. However, the conclusions are the same: marriage is a restrictive covenant that destroys the individual. Ranasinha's argument that Kureishi 'invokes post-sixties freedoms to give a socio-political framework and philosophy for self-indulgence' illustrates starkly the continuance between this and Kureishi's earlier posed-ethnic work: her critique of Kureishi's privileging here of individual desire could equally be a comment about *Buddha* or *Black Album*.[51]

It is perhaps sex and drugs that are the most dramatic symbols of this liberal indulgence.[52] In *My Beautiful Laundrette*, the capitalist Pakistanis complain that 'the country is being sodomized by religion'; not only does this draw together Kureishi's critique of religion with experimental sexual practice, it also identifies a dialogical relationship between liberal sexual practice, religious ideologies represented as illiberal and intolerant, and also a Thatcherite politics associated with homophobia.[53] *Sammy and Rosie Get Laid*, *My Beautiful Laundrette*, *Buddha* and *Black Album* all offer sexual experimentation as a better solution to social problems than political action, satirised and rendered ineffective. More widely, against monogamy, denial of sexual desire is represented as a rejection of all that is vital where, for Rosie, 'jealousy is wickeder than adultery',[54] and Jay, rejecting the conventional hierarchy, asks 'Why can't they be blamed for being bad at promiscuity?' (*Intimacy* 42). To see how this functions as a sustained ideology, one can consider these comments alongside *Buddha*. When Karim first becomes aware of his father's adultery his reaction is not moral disgust, but rather an appreciation of being removed from the dreariness of his everyday existence: 'I began to think the whole affair was over, and I rather regretted this, as our life returned to dull normalcy' (45). *Buddha* points, too, to how drugs, as much as sex, embody this reality. Karim's relationship with Eleanor is sexually adventurous, orgiastic, and drug-fuelled. Even when Kureishi does move from this position in his early work he finds his digression regrettable. In relation to *London Kills Me*, Kureishi has stated: 'I regret not having some scenes showing what a good time you can have on drugs'.[55]

Such themes are also evident in *Love in a Blue Time*: the drug-fuelled lives of the central characters of the title story; the memorable opening of 'D'accord, Baby' ('All week Bill had been looking forward to this moment. He was about to fuck the daughter of the man who had fucked his wife');[56] the pornographic pictures of 'Blue, Blue Pictures of You'; the multiple sexual encounters of 'Lately'.[57] The attitude to relationships, and to morality, is perhaps best summed up by the conclusion to 'Nightlight':

> All his life, it seems, he's been seeking sex. He isn't certain why, but he must have gathered that it is an important thing to want. And now he has it, it doesn't seem sufficient. But what does that matter? As long as there is desire there is a pulse; you are alive, to want is to reach beyond yourself, into the world, finger by finger. [58]

It is not that there is no recognition of the suffering encountered by following one's desires, but rather than this experience is essential. So as early as *Buddha*:

> I thought about the difference between the interesting people and the nice people. And how they can't always be identical. The interesting people you wanted to be with – their minds were unusual, you saw things freshly with them and all was not deadness and repetition ... Then there were the nice people who weren't interesting, and you didn't know what they thought of anything. Like Mum, they were good and meek and deserved more love. But it was the interesting ones, like Eva with her hard, taking edge, who ended up with everything, and in bed with my father. (93)

In *Intimacy*, likewise, Jay is aware of the limits of casual sex, of the bravery of commitment (20) and, through his friend Victor, knows the devastating effect leaving will have on his sons (115). In the wake of this, Jay's final decision, his rejection of convention, is startling. His assertion that 'I could only think there are some fucks for which a person would have their partner and children drown in a freezing sea' (120) potentially freezes the heart of the reader against Jay and – by association – his individualist ideology.[59] Read Kureishi's comment in *Ear* that 'the unwanted will always feel irrelevant wherever they are and whatever they do' (228) and one wonders why Jay cannot apply this to his own treatment of his children. He knows he 'will feel worse tomorrow, and the day after, and the day after that. All this, in the name of some kind of liberation.' Yet Jay chooses to go anyway: 'rather a fool than a fascist' (44).[60]

One final aspect of this liberal positioning is a skewing of class perspective. Kureishi's claims to be *lower* middle class are dubious given his father's Catholic public school education in Bombay,[61] and the comments of Kureishi's sister that 'My grandfather was not a '"cloth cap working class" person' in her corrections of Kureishi's 'false impression of our family life'.[62] As suggested in the opening to this chapter, this distance from *real* poverty is reflected in the texts: not just *Buddha*, but also later. In

Gabriel's Gift, Gabriel's statement to 'almost, but not quite' (10)
belong to the middle classes is problematised as his father is an
artist, and his family employs an au pair. If Kureishi's attachment to working-class culture is dubious, then his celebration
of London for its supposed grittiness is equally so. This is not a
case, as James Procter argues, simply of Kureishi inhabiting the
more prosperous West London, but that even when he inhabits
this space he does not really encounter its poverty, facilitating a
romanticisation of squalor.[63] In *Something to Tell You,* the narrator
captures this experience:

> However much you dislike the country, you drive back into the city
> on a Sunday night after a weekend away and your heart sinks: the
> dirt, the roughness, the closeness of everyone and everything, so
> much so that you can almost believe you like leaving London. (210)

Kureishi's prose here is at its most beautiful: complex meaning transmitted in deceptively simple sentences. And yet it is
also at its most troubling, with more than a hint of detached
modernist *flânerie.* In his film diary for *Sammy and Rosie Get Laid,*
Kureishi himself acknowledges this distance: the film is set
around 'estates that I walk past every day but haven't been
in since the last election'.[64] While for Kureishi this distance is
bridgeable by the imagination – 'outside the world I live but
not outside my mental world' – it can equally be argued that
it simply reinforces an unrealistic position on poverty located
firmly within liberal middle-class discourse.[65] Kureishi's position on the suburbs has been read as a conscious disruption: an
imaginative intervention which hybridises what is in reality a
closed space. One needs, however, to be equally aware of the
imaginative strategies at work in Kureishi's supposedly 'working-class' London: the space that 'is and is not Britain; it is and
is not the world'.[66]

One other way of considering this positioning is in terms of
hybridity, a notion central in postcolonial studies:

> Hybrid identities are never total and complete in themselves, like
> orderly pathways built from crazy-paving. Instead, they remain *per-*
> *petually* in motion, pursuing errant and unpredictable routes, open to
> change and reinscription.[67]

The focus here not just on change, but on *perpetual* change is
profoundly relevant to Kureishi's concerns. Jay's problem with
marriage is its lack of 'movement' (*Intimacy* 132); the purchase
of a house, of a mortgage, means 'you would never be able to
"move" again' (47), illustrative of how the postcolonial discourse

of nomadism can be transferred to the micro scale. Transferral to the notion of the family illuminates how potentially destructive such a discourse is; while one might not appreciate the possible consequences of dissolving national borders in the name of greater freedom and movement, the idea of dissolving familial bonds for the same reasoning draws into stark relief the destruction involved in such seemingly creative processes.

Such micro-politics draws attention to the contradictions now recognised as inherent in key postcolonial terms. The didactic way in which hybridity is presented by Kureishi as the *only* successful belief system renders it incompatible with the values of fluidity and individual subjectivity conventionally of equal importance to postcolonial theory. How different is this, we need to ask, from an assimilationist position; does it make any difference if the one identity that becomes acceptable is, paradoxically, mutable? The notion of post-ethnicity as facilitating choice is undermined by the idea that Kureishi privileges certain choices over others, even if that privileged choice is the liberal choice to *not choose*. Chad in *Black Album*, for example, *chooses* Islam: yet this 'fixed' choice is presented as a tragic failure; while Shahid may be the archetypal metamorphic subject, there is little sense that this translates to a wider hybrid society, which would find space for those whose identities are less fluid, and more rooted in a particular belief system. Such a critique of hybridity is offered by Tariq Modood:

> Both hybrid individuals and ethnoreligious communities have legitimate claims to be accommodated in political multiculturalism. The latter are no less hybrid in that their development, too, is a product of British opportunity structures and Asians and Muslims are continuously adapting to British influences. Hybridity and religious communities should not be pitted against each other in an either-or fashion as is done all too frequently by the celebrators of British Asian hybridity.[68]

Modood's example of such a 'celebrator'? None other than Kureishi.

'like questioning a religion while wanting to believe in God': the moral turn[69]

If *Intimacy* is the most nuanced example of Kureishi's ideology, it is also the point where it begins to unravel. In the novel's final paragraph, Jay's contentment offers a vision of rootedness. This may be definitively anti-establishment rootedness, yet it is the beginnings of a greater shift: one which suggests that, perhaps, concepts of community, and of post-ethnicity in its original form, are now less impossible for Kureishi than they might once have been.

The texts of 1999 are significant here. In the first of these, *Sleep with Me* – Kureishi's return to the theatre after sixteen years – indulgence gives way to doubt. Staple characters of adulterers and individualists, Stephen and Sophie, are paired with those who would interrogate such positions. Against Sophie's promiscuity, Julie declares 'the family is a point you can live from. I like ordinary, everyday life'.[70] When Stephen declares his desire to break up his marriage, Charles responds, 'It's so violent, leaving – Our fathers didn't leave. I'd notice men, after I left ... with their children, just on the street, going to the pictures ... holding hands ... Stephen ... it broke me.'[71] The conclusion of the play, with Julie comforting her crying child, contrasts with the celebratory individualism of earlier works.

In the second text of 1999, the short story collection *Midnight All Day*, the same progression is evident. Some of the stories – 'Strangers When We Meet', 'A Meeting, At Last', and 'The Umbrella' – are little different from Kureishi's earlier work.[72] In the latter the protagonist 'had not missed his wife for a moment'; the punishment she inflicts upon him (the denial of an umbrella in the pouring rain) is cancelled out by his lack of remorse: 'wet through, but moving forward'.[73]

It is interesting to note, however, that the initial publication of 'Umbrella' in *Granta* has a different conclusion: the final celebratory lines are absent.[74] This suggests, perhaps, that Kureishi cultivates an image as a shocking liberal, even as his ideas have begun to diverge from this position, an attempt which perhaps begins even earlier with the exclusion of a story such as 'Esther' (1989) from *Love in a Blue Time*.[75] The other stories in *Midnight All Day* are, like *Intimacy*, subtly different. 'Four Blue Chairs', for example, ends 'the four blue chairs will be there, around the table of their love'.[76] This love cannot yet be marriage, a pattern repeated in 'Girl' where a similarly romantic ending, 'knowing they would wake up with each other', is again possible within the confines of an extra-marital affair, and 'That Was Then', a story that continues to romanticise adultery but ultimately sees the protagonist return to his wife.[77] 'Midnight All Day' is a third rendering of the same circumstances: the central character is unhappy with his wife, engaging in an affair. Yet his motives are not the defiance of convention, but the securing of conventional happiness:

> Ian thought that he wanted to be at home, in a house he liked, with a
> woman and children he liked. He wanted to lose himself in the mun-
> dane, in unimportant things. Perhaps those things were graspable
> now. Once he had them, he could think of others, and be useful.[78]

The hedonistic life that accompanies individualism is no longer
unconditionally celebrated. In 'Morning in the Bowl of Night'
Alan has left his wife, and privileges his new girlfriend over
the needs of his children. Alan is aware, however, that 'no
amount of drink, drugs or meditation could make things better
for good'.[79]

Here Kureishi moves to a tentatively 'moral' perspective. An
earlier hint at this movement is offered in 'My Son the Fanatic'.
Although part of *Love in a Blue Time*, the story stands out from
the rest of the collection in its more critical approach to liberal
attitudes. For the first time liberalism is consciously presented
as an ideological position, which can be equally violent and
aggressive. This is best summed up by Susie Thomas:

> The paradox is that sceptical liberalism can be fanatical in its denun-
> ciation of fundamentalism. When Parvez tries to beat the fanaticism
> out of his son, it is clear that liberalism needs not only to ques-
> tion itself but also to rethink its relation to deeply held religious
> beliefs.[80]

The later screenplay does not retain this politics, where the
appeal of Islam is seen more sympathetically but liberalism,
too, is presented as less ideological,[81] and where the new ending sees Parvez freed from the constraints of his stereotypically
unadventurous Asian wife to pursue his relationship with
Bettina, in a return to celebratory liberal individualism.

In its discussion of the appeal of Islam, Bart Moore-Gilbert
does recognise in the film a new perspective, however; he refers
to this as 'the politics of recognition': the desire of communities to be acknowledged as such, and not simply to be given
individual rights.[82] In his next novel, *Gabriel's Gift*, description
of the local community is significantly different from earlier
accounts:

> The city was no longer home to immigrants only from the former col-
> onies, plus a few others; every race was present, living side by side
> without, most of the time, killing one another. It held together, this
> new international city called London – just about – without being
> unnecessarily anarchic or corrupt. [83]

To live 'side by side' is far from the vision of contamination offered by Kureishi's earlier fiction. It indicates an acceptance of a more conventional multiculturalism, in which distinct communal identities are given value, even as they tolerate the beliefs of others. With increasing sensitivity to the positive value of community Kureishi's individualism fades.

Such awareness is mirrored in *Gabriel's Gift*'s relationship to family, acknowledging not only the stresses of marriage but also the devastating effects of break-up, most noticeably for the 15-year-old Gabriel. The journey of Gabriel's father is distinctly a journey *away from* liberal individualism. He begins the novel idealising the musician Lester Jones: 'a free man. He can buy a house in any city in the world. He can look at glaciers and deserts whenever he wants.' (44) Yet by the end of the novel Dad has rejected this perspective and the novel celebrates his return home to Gabriel's mother. Their initial view that marriage is 'bourgeois ... they weren't of a generation that got married' (70) is reversed with a conventional – if secular – marriage ceremony. Dad's reflection on his relationship with Gabriel's mother could not be further from the attitudes of Jay:

> 'Excuse the details, but I'm telling you, Angel, that's what a man wants at the end of the day – and at my time of life – when he lays his tired head down. To know that a woman has chosen you, that she wants to be with you – it's an achievement' ... 'People are rarely a perfect fit. These days they walk away from one another too quickly. Why does everyone have to break up? If you can sit still through the bad bits you can find new things.' (160)

These interests are picked up in *The Body* (2002), a collection of stories where, 'in each case, a little bit of love and redemption are allowed to creep in'.[84] The title story indicates Kureishi's post-ethnicity: a focus on the relationship between body and self that resonates with concerns for racial and cultural identity. Exchanging his body for a younger model as part of a new secret technology, the protagonist, Adam, is offered both a female and a black body, but eventually selects the 'ideal': a young, white male. Yet he ultimately finds this new body, despite the experimentation it offers, unfulfilling. Adam's love for his wife is the one constant in his life, and his relationship with her is of greater power than any of the sexual encounters his new body facilitates. He longs to return to her, and – against previous liberal positions – espouses a belief in fidelity: 'What we used to call "promiscuity" had always bothered me. Impersonal love seemed a devaluation of social intercourse.'[85] This is, again, a subtle shift: in keeping with Kureishi's obsessive ambivalence both perspectives are still offered and, in this sense, postmodern didacticism continues; vacillation is still preferred to clear commitment. Yet the balance of power has changed: the conviction has become the afterthought. Now it is the protagonist who assumes the view conventionally interrogated. When Adam's original body is destroyed, the resulting conclusion makes 'The Body' a powerful morality tale. Adam gains a more exciting life, and realises the value of what he had. His new-found individualism, courtesy of the body of a dead man with no roots and no loyalties, is not a blessing, but a punishment: 'I was a stranger on the earth, a nobody with nothing, belonging nowhere, a body alone, condemned to begin again, in the nightmare of eternal life.'[86] This critique might also be read as a challenge to postcolonial motifs of hybridity: rootlessness not as a blessing, but as a curse.

Elsewhere in the collection, earlier judgements are equally modified: 'Straight' is a rejection of drug use;[87] 'The Real Father', with its question 'How could any love survive so many interruptions?' represents a powerful statement of the destructive impact of family break-up.[88] 'Remember this Moment, Remember Us', in which a couple record a birthday message for their young son for his fortieth birthday, is a powerful statement of family connection.[89] Kureishi followed *The Body* with a play, *When Night Begins*, similar in tone. An encounter between an adult step-daughter and her step-father it embodies Kureishi's ambivalence in their alternative remembrances of events. It is also, however, a sombre reflection on what it means to be 'decent', and the possibility of redemption.[90] In 2006, this attitude finally emerges in the area which previously has changed least: Kureishi's screenplays. Whereas *The Mother* simply transfers individualism and sexuality to the arena of old age, *Venus* is different. Kureishi characterises a relationship between a young woman and an old man across both age and class boundaries. This poignant relationship is, however, *not consummated*. Its quality, instead, comes from an abiding sense of the pressure of personal responsibilities, and the power of mental – rather than physical – connection.

Such change is surprising, given popular cinema's reliance on the power to shock. Perhaps more surprisingly, however, is how this shift has even begun to change Kureishi's perspective on religion. In *Something to Tell You*, Kureishi returns to the 'posed-ethnic' perspectives of his earlier work, with his first major novel with a British Asian protagonist since *Black Album*. The novel's central character, Jamal Khan, is almost the adult Karim: a mixed-race man who grew up in the London suburbs in the 1970s but now lives in the area of West London between Hammersmith and Shepherd's Bush. On one level, Jamal is still the liberal individual. He allows his son Rafi to 'watch TV, eat what he wanted and use bad words, the more creatively the better' (16). Yet Jamal also is willing to mediate his beliefs. His desire to become a psychoanalyst, for example, is not just an individual ambition, but deference to collective identities, 'something to do with "family honour", an idea which formerly I'd have found absurd' (68). Jamal tells his son, from whose mother he is separated, that 'No one gets married at twenty-five and stays with their partner until they're seventy unless they are deficient in imagination.' (240) Yet, by the end of the novel, he has come to recognise in relation to his wife that 'I knew I preferred her to anyone else.' (277) Jamal's encounter with his son over a meal Rafi has prepared, complete with a home-made menu that Jamal 'would never throw away' (243), is one of the most moving moments in Kureishi's fiction.

While religious belief is still not celebrated, here its appeal *is* characterised more positively. Faith makes one appear 'infantile', but 'God stories really keep everything together' (93). In post-9/11 and 7/7 contexts, Kureishi is more sympathetic about the abuse Muslims face: the novel documents the rise in rightwing politics and racist attacks (14, 320), and contrasts the fear felt in London after the terrorist attacks of 7/7 with the fear felt by the Iraqi people after Western invasion (319). Ajita's abusive father is not to be taken as an example of Islamic morality: 'he wasn't religious and never prayed' (190). At the same time Ajita herself becomes the voice for an interrogation of Jamal's middle-class liberalism: declaring that she never thought of him as a Muslim she suggests that Islam offers powerful cultural possibilities. Declaring 'war' (322) on the West, Ajita is Kureishi's most sympathetic portrayal of such a figure, in contrast to the intentionally confrontational images of Jamila in *Buddha*, the lesbian strippers of 'Wild Women, Wild Men' (1992) or, in this novel, Jamal's sister Miriam. Jamal understands that a critique of Islam can also be an equally exclusive right-wing discourse, as he sees 'how much Dad needed his liberal companions who approved of Reagan and Thatcher. This was anathema to me, but represented "freedom" in this increasingly Islamised land' (129). As Omar Ali of *My Beautiful Laundrette* makes an appearance as a gay Asian billionaire, his liberalism – a product of Thatcherite discourse – is no longer celebrated, but satirised. Hollinger's original definition of post-ethnicity is now almost, if not quite, possible.

Conclusion

In 'The Rainbow Sign', Kureishi explains his experience of visiting Pakistan as a young man:

> The family scrutiny and criticism was difficult to take, as was all the bitching and gossip. But there was warmth and continuity for a large number of people; there was security and much love. Also there was a sense of duty and community – of people's lives genuinely being lived together, whether they liked each other or not – that you didn't get in London. There, those who'd eschewed the family hadn't succeeded in creating some other form of supportive common life. In Pakistan there was supportive common life, but at the expense of movement and change.[91]

All of Kureishi's writings are driven by the contradictions offered in this piece. In his early work, the latter perspective – movement and change – is dominant. This change includes an assertive move by Kureishi away from the subject of Asian identity. But it has also become for Kureishi an ideology of sorts, upholding the central postmodern influences on postcolonial theory, even at the same time that movement away from race appears to reject such associations.

In his most recent work, however, Kureishi offers a more mature appreciation where postmodern liberalism is perhaps not such an easy solution. In his memoir, *My Ear at his Heart* (2004), Kureishi speaks in personal terms about issues of community, individualism, family and religion. What one uncovers at times seems disassociated from the postmodern didacticism of his early work. Indeed, much of Kureishi's belief system is in one passage acknowledged as rooted in anxiety, and surrounded with regret:

> I had girlfriends, but there was always a moment when I had to flee them. The things I've wanted the most, I've fled. I liked to believe I was happiest alone. I even took drugs alone ... I was afraid of being overwhelmed by the other person, of there not being enough of me and too much of them; that they had more words that I did.[92]

There is here, finally, a reluctant move away from the ideals of hybridity, perhaps prematurely gestured towards in his fiction, to the realities of multiculturalism:

The different communities of London acknowledge and mostly tolerate one another; but except when it's compulsory, in state schools, say, they don't mix much. Perhaps they don't know how to, or can't see the benefit. Still, strolling around London I am amazed by how peaceful and friendly it is, how well the numerous individuals and communities get along without attacking one another.[93]

Whereas Kureishi's earlier essays suggest that Islamic fundamentalism could only be a response to racism, his encounters with the beliefs of his own uncle meant Kureishi had to reappraise such views:

To read this shocks me; when I think about it, I lose my bearings. I'd never imagined a liberal and literary man finding a combination of social hope and justice in a religion which, for me, can only seem a betrayal of our family's values.[94]

This shift does not make Kureishi's writing more or less ideological, though it makes his writing more aligned to ethical concerns than the postmodern didacticism of some of his earlier work would allow. It is this change, as much as Kureishi's movement away from explicit concern with issues of race, which ultimately distinguishes his writing from postcolonial literature. Kureishi has moved from being an author whose ideology is very much sympathetic with the central tenets of postcolonial theory, to one who is increasingly calling its preoccupations into question. This establishes him firmly not only as a British Asian author, but as a vital and significant voice in the development of a British Asian viewpoint.

Discussion

- Discussing *London Kills Me*, Kureishi states that 'Roots don't seem to be an absence in their lives. In a way a sort of family is formed in the film of the posse, a parody of Thatcher's idea of the family unit'.[95] How, and why, does Kureishi's fiction offer alternatives to conventional ideas of ethnic and/or familial identity?
- Are there any limits to Kureishi's liberalism?
- How does Kureishi's vision of British-born Asian identity interrogate migrant experience?

Notes

1   Kureishi, *The Buddha of Suburbia*, p. 166. Hereafter *Buddha*. Subsequent references cited parenthetically.
2   Kureishi's very early work is set in South London. The poverty of West London is more evident in Kureishi's drama and film: the Southall of *Borderline,* Hammersmith of *Sammy and Rosie Get Laid* and Notting Hill of *London Kills Me.*
3   Kureishi, *Something to Tell You*, p. 270. Hereafter *Something*. Subsequent references cited parenthetically.
4   Dodd, 'Requiem', p. 10.
5   Stein, *Black British Literature*, p. 115.
6   *Ibid.*, p. 112, p. 142.
7   See Kureishi's comments in Dodd, 'Requiem', p. 12.
8   The occasional short story – 'Touched', 'The Body', pp. 253–66; 'My Son the Fanatic', *Love in a Blue Time*, pp. 119–31; 'With Your Tongue Down My Throat', *Love in a Blue Time*, pp. 61–106; and 'We're Not Jews', *Love in a Blue Time*, pp. 41–51 – does return to ethnicity.
9   For the latter see Ilona, 'Hanif Kureishi's *The Buddha of Suburbia*', p. 94.
10 Thomas, *Hanif Kureishi*, p. 1.
11 See Kaleta, *Hanif Kureishi*, p. 7; Kureishi, 'Rainbow Sign', p. 11. Although he at times complicates this, Kureishi's writing largely upholds the idea of generational difference: 'People think I'm caught between two cultures, but I'm not. I'm British; I can make it in England. It's my father who's caught' (Pally, 'Kureishi like a Fox', p. 53). *Borderline, Laundrette, Buddha,* and *Black Album* all juxtapose a strident younger generation with a more passive older generation.
12 Kureishi, 'Rainbow Sign', p. 38.
13 Moore-Gilbert, *Hanif Kureishi*, p. 18.
14 Pally, 'Kureishi Like a Fox', p. 55.
15 See Yousaf, 'Hanif Kureishi and the Brown Man's Burden', p. 20. For US influences see *My Ear at His Heart*, pp. 1, p. 195, and MacCabe, 'Interview: Hanif Kureishi on London', p. 47.
16 Kureishi, 'Dirty Washing', p. 26.
17 Stein, *Black British Literature*, p. 113.
18 Hollinger, *Postethnic America*, p. 113.
19 *Ibid.*, p. 121; pp. 122–3.
20 Kureishi, *My Son the Fanatic, Collected Screenplays 1*, pp. 279–385.
21 Upstone, 'A Question of Black or White'. See also Ranasinha, *Hanif Kureishi*, p. 88. Stein, *Black British Literature*, too, notes this polarity (p. 124): how it works within his designation of Kureishi's postethnicity, however, is unfortunately not explained.
22 Kureishi, *Intimacy*, p. 132. Subsequent references cited parenthetically.
23 My emphasis, MacCabe, 'Interview: Hanif Kureishi', p. 51.
24 See Pally, 'Kureishi Like a Fox', p. 53.
25 My emphasis, Kureishi, 'The Body', *The Body and Seven Stories*, p. 31.
26 Kureishi, 'Lately', *Love in a Blue Time*, pp. 146–87, p. 151.
27 Kureishi, *My Ear at His Heart*, p. 238.
28 See Sandhu, *London Calling*, p. 263.

29 See Thomas, *Hanif Kureishi*, p. 53.

30 'Cast and Crew', *The Mother* DVD.

31 *Intimacy* is Stein's example of post-ethnicity. The novel includes Asian characters, including perhaps Jay, who has an uncle in Lahore. In 1993, Kureishi became father to twin boys, but, in 1995, left their mother for another woman, with whom he had a son in 1998.

32 See, for example, Sen, 'Re-Writing History', pp. 66–8; pp. 73–5.

33 Kureishi, 'The Flies', *Love in a Blue Time*, pp. 188–212.

34 *Ibid.*, p. 197.

35 Sandhu, 'Pop Goes the Centre', p. 136.

36 Dessau, 'The Buddha of Bromley', p. 11.

37 Pally, 'Kureishi Like a Fox', p. 52.

38 Ranasinha is the only critic to point explicitly towards this: in her chapter on Kureishi's 'Muslimophobia', she stresses Kureishi's unwillingness to 'engage with the possibilities of rethinking a liberal ideology' (*Hanif Kureishi*, p. 83).

39 *Ibid.*, p. 37.

40 Pally, 'Kureishi Like a Fox', p. 52.

41 Kureishi, *My Ear at His Heart*, p. 23, p. 82, p. 158.

42 Jaggi, 'Buddy from Suburbia'.

43 Pally, 'Kureishi Like a Fox', p. 52.

44 Ranasinha, *Hanif Kureishi*, pp. 76–7.

45 See Ranasinha, *Hanif Kureishi*; Stein, *Black British Literature*.

46 Degabriele, 'Prince of Darkness Meets Prince of Porn', para 19. See also Holmes, 'The Postcolonial Subject Divided Between East and West', p. 297.

47 Schoene, 'Herald of Hybridity', p. 112; Sandhu, 'Pop', pp. 142–3.

48 My emphasis, Ilona, 'Hanif Kureishi's *The Buddha of Suburbia*', p. 98.

49 Kaleta, *Hanif Kureishi*, p. 3; Ranasinha, *Hanif Kureishi*, p. 121.

50 See Kureishi, 'Bradford'.

51 Ranasinha, *Hanif Kureishi*, pp. 111–12.

52 For Kureishi, music's liberalism is reflected in its indulgence of sex and drugs. See, for example, 'Eight Arms to Hold You', p. 114.

53 Kureishi, *Laundrette*, p. 66. For the link to Thatcher see Mishra, *Literature of the Indian Diaspora*, pp. 202–3.

54 Kureishi, *Sammy and Rosie*, p. 96.

55 Dodd, 'Requiem', p. 13.

56 Kureishi, 'D'accord Baby', *Love in a Blue Time*, pp. 52–60, p. 52.

57 Kureishi, 'Blue, Blue Pictures of You', *Love in a Blue Time*, pp. 107–18; 'Lately', *Love in a Blue Time*, pp. 146–87.

58 Kureishi, 'Nightlight', *Love in a Blue Time*, pp. 138–45, p. 145.

59 Kureishi repeats this line exactly in *Sleep With Me* (p. 31), offering an interest statement of defiance.

60 Sandhu, 'Pop', p. 140.

61 Kureishi, *My Ear at His Heart*, p. 182.

62 Yasmin Kureishi, 'Intimacies: A Sister's Tale'.

63 Procter, *Dwelling Places*, p. 134.

64 Kureishi, 'Film Diary: Sammy and Rosie Get Laid', p. 75.

65 Quoted in Dodd, 'Requiem', p. 10.

66 Clement Ball, 'The Semi-Detached Metropolis', p. 9. For this view of suburbia see Oswell, 'Suburban Tales'.
67 My emphasis, McLeod, *Beginning Postcolonialism*, p. 219.
68 Modood, *Multicultural Politics*, p. 208.
69 Kureishi, *My Ear at His Heart*, p. 164.
70 Kureishi, *Sleep with Me*, p. 49.
71 *Ibid.*, p. 24.
72 Kureishi, 'Strangers When We Meet', 'A Meeting, At Last', 'The Umbrella', *Midnight All Day* pp. 3–53, pp. 144–56, pp. 180–92.
73 Kureishi, 'The Umbrella', p. 186, p. 192.
74 Kureishi, 'Umbrella', pp. 227–37.
75 Kureishi, 'Esther', pp. 56–62. Kaleta, *Hanif Kureishi* (p. 156) notes that Kureishi chose not to include this in his 1997 stories. The story of adultery is here received from the wife's perspective, and involves the mistress' suicide. Its central protagonist's reflection on 'the difficulty and seriousness of loving' (p. 61) is in contrast to the tone of much of the collection.
76 Kureishi, 'Four Blue Chairs', *Midnight All Day*, pp. 54–63, p. 63.
77 Kureishi, 'Girl', *Midnight All Day*, pp. 92–109, p. 109; 'That Was Then', *Midnight All Day*, pp. 64–91.
78 Kureishi, 'Midnight All Day', *Midnight All Day*, pp. 157–79, p. 179.
79 Kureishi, 'Morning in the Bowl of Night', *Midnight All Day*, pp. 193–205, p. 204.
80 Thomas, *Hanif Kureishi*, p. 119.
81 See Moore-Gilbert, *Hanif Kureishi*, pp. 166–7.
82 *Ibid.*, p. 169. Moore-Gilbert refers here to Taylor's arguments in 'The Politics of Recognition'.
83 Kureishi, *Gabriel's Gift*, p. 8. Subsequent references cited parenthetically.
84 Linklater, 'Death of the Ego'.
85 Kureishi, 'The Body', *The Body*, pp. 1–128, p. 59.
86 *Ibid.*, p. 126.
87 Kureishi, 'Straight', *The Body*, pp. 207–20.
88 Kureishi, 'The Real Father', *The Body*, pp. 233–52, p. 250.
89 Kureishi, 'Remember This Moment, Remember Us', *The Body*, pp. 221–32.
90 Kureishi, *When Night Begins*, p. 47.
91 Kureishi, 'Rainbow Sign', p. 22.
92 Kureishi, *My Ear at His Heart*, p. 25.
93 *Ibid.*, p. 25.
94 *Ibid.*, p. 112.
95 Dodd, 'Requiem', p. 11.

Further reading

Kenneth C. Kaleta, *Hanif Kureishi: Postcolonial Storyteller* (Austin, TX: University of Texas Press, 1998.
Bart Moore-Gilbert, *Hanif Kureishi* (Manchester: Manchester University Press, 2001).
Ruvani Ranasinha, *Hanif Kureishi* (Tavistock: Northcote House, 2002).

Mark Stein, *Black British Literature: Novels of Transformation* (Columbus, OH: Ohio State University Press, 2004).

Susie Thomas, *Hanif Kureishi: A Reader's Guide to Essential Criticism* (Basingstoke: Palgrave Macmillan, 2005).

Sara Upstone, 'A Question of Black or White: Returning to Hanif Kureishi's *The Black Album*', *Postcolonial Text*, 4:1 (2008), http://postcolonial.org/index.php/pct/article/viewArticle/679.

3

Ravinder Randhawa

To find that one is fundamentally unintelligible (indeed, that the laws of culture and of language find one to be an impossibility) is to find that one has not yet achieved access to the human. It is to find oneself speaking only and always as if one were human, but with the sense that one is not. It is to find that one's language is hollow, and thus no recognition is forthcoming because the norms by which recognition takes place are not in one's favor.[1]

At the same time Hanif Kureishi was making his name as a screenwriter, and before he had published any fiction, a female author born in India in 1952 but raised in Warwickshire from the age of seven, and living her adult life in London, was already publishing fiction. While Kureishi quickly became notorious, Ravinder Randhawa operated under the radar of mainstream literary criticism. Well-known, however, within the Asian writing community, and to feminists, Randhawa was essential to the burgeoning British Asian literature. As a founder of the Asian Women Writers' Workshop (AWWW), which she established with Rukhsana Ahmad, Rahila Gupta and Leela Dhingra in London in 1984, Randhawa not only wrote prolifically about the lives of British Asian women, she also fostered the careers of others, including Meera Syal, who used the workshop to develop their own writing, and to publish for the first time in anthologies such as *Right of Way* and *Flaming Spirit*.[2] Randhawa's work, its focus on themes of generational difference, the domestic and economic exploitation of women, and the often dark comedy of women's lives, is highly influential on the women authors who have followed. Moreover, while many critics may declare Kureishi the first truly British Asian novelist, such an accolade is disputed. For Aamer Hussein, for example, it is Randhawa who deserves such a tribute.[3]

If Randhawa was less noticed, then this is perhaps because she focuses more specifically on the Asian community and, in particular, on the lives of British Asian women: her work reflects the 'narrowly focused' writing of the AWWW,[4] but also the literary establishment's neglect of this writing in favour of more 'masculine' projects.[5] Lack of attention on her, and women like her, is testified to by Sharmilla Beezmohun's view as late as 1998 that she finds herself 'searching in vain for any British Asian voices, particularly those of women'.[6] Less obviously international, more particular, and less self-consciously 'post-colonial', her writing reflects her desire to always tell a 'new story', and is difficult to compare to texts by other British Asian writers.[7] Stylistically unique, and structurally complex, it is also less accessible, owing much to modernist stream of consciousness forms. It speaks powerfully, however, to the difficulties of a diverse group which before her writing were unrecognised in British society, and largely unvoiced: the Asian woman born or raised in Britain, negotiating the difficulties of being not only an ethnic minority within one's own country, but also an ethnic minority subject to the additional pressures of patriarchy. Through her writing, Randhawa brought this experience for the first time into novel form, first in *A Wicked Old Woman* (1987), then in the children's novel *Hari-jan* (1992), and later in *The Coral Strand* (2001).[8] Ambivalently oscillating between celebration and despair, Randhawa captures the complexity of being a subject frequently overlooked, focusing on British Asian women who must contend with the dual pressures of ethnicity and gender discrimination, the 'seeming contradictions of being Asian, English and female'.[9]

The paradox of British Asian womanhood: being unreal

In order to explore the unique way Randhawa engages with British Asian identity, this chapter relies upon the theoretical ideas of gender critic Judith Butler. Butler frequently points to the way in which her thinking is affected by race and ethnicity. In particular, while she focuses on how social norms define a politics of inclusion and exclusion in terms of gender, she also points to how judgements are equally made in relation to racial categorisations.[10] Butler argues that the way in which an individual expresses their gender may see them excluded from the idea of the human, and the rights and privileges that come with this: 'If I am a certain gender', she asks, 'will I still be regarded as part of the human?' (2) If this discussion is expanded to the issue of race, one can see how the non-white, non-male individual may be the most socially excluded, alienated on the grounds of both gender and race. This has been the argument, of course, of many in the black feminist movement such as bell hooks and Barbara Smith.

What is useful about Butler's work, however, is that it introduces a framework for considering those individuals whose oppression lies *even beyond* such categorisation. In discussion of gendered prejudice, Butler points to a subject not only oppressed, but rather so disadvantaged and excluded they do not even merit the recognition of negative categorisation. Such subjects, for Butler, are 'the unintelligible'. Existing 'between the norm and its failure' (74) they are neither self nor 'other', but rather that which is denied even negative recognition:

> To be called a copy, to be called unreal, is thus one way in which one can be oppressed. But consider that it is more fundamental than that. For to be oppressed means that you already exist as a subject of some kind, you are there as the visible and oppressed other for the master subject as a possible or potential subject. But to be unreal is something else again. For to be oppressed one must first become intelligible. (218)

It is the unintelligible, I would suggest, that provides the most useful way of considering the representation of British Asian women in Randhawa's fiction. Through construction of British Asian female subjects, Randhawa points to a group who do not even have the advantage of being defined as the negative opposition to an existing social norm. There is no 'writing back' here for, as Patricia Dunker notes in relation to *Wicked*, 'there are no books behind the experience narrated … no texts against which to write'.[11] Instead such women are the silenced, unrecognised and unannounced underclass of British culture.

At the centre of this is the clear separation of British Asian women from an earlier migrant generation. This migrant generation are the more conventional 'other', the opposition to the indigenous. To be foreign, however oppressed, is to be given a position of recognition one can speak from. While the migrant occupies this position, the British-born/raised subject is situated in an ambivalent, undefined space which does not even have the advantage of being recognised in derogatory or prejudicial terms. Instead, it is not recognised at all, not spoken of, and condemned to nothingness. If being a woman is, like being a migrant, to be in a space of opposition, then being a British Asian woman is to not be offered a space at all; to find oneself drifting in a limbo of non-recognition. As Butler points out, being outside the norm does not mean being a subject who has failed to approximate a particular model of identity; it means not being a subject at all (48). It is not a case of being identified as unacceptable, but rather as not even having the luxury of such negative definition.

The British Asian woman, in comparison to her male counterpart, is most unintelligible because her gender makes it more difficult for her to access the social structures making it possible for British Asian men to claim social recognition. Such women, as María Socorro Suárez Lafuente asserts, 'see their own personal values altered – the contrast of East and West exacts the impossible for them: that they remain silent and invisible'.[12] They do not signify, do not even register a reaction, as they are overlooked within the norms determining one's identification. Indeed, the relative lack of critical attention paid to Randhawa when compared to the media frenzy surrounding Rushdie and Kureishi is itself evidence of this different positioning. Despite not being of the same generation as earlier migrant writers, Kureishi and Rushdie seemed to find it possible to gain acceptance. They quickly accessed mainstream publishing opportunities. In contrast, British Asian female writers relied on local government support for their activities and published through anthologies supported by specialist presses. Being male, it can be argued, gave British Asian authors the opportunity to offset the newness of their ethnic experience with an existing position of gender privilege. In contrast, being a woman rendered one already 'othered': to be a British-born/raised Asian (and therefore not a migrant woman either, with its own existing provenance) made one too different to even gain social recognition.

This sense of unintelligibility is woven into Randhawa's fiction. In the untitled introduction to *Wicked* a young Kulwant already recognises the power of recognition. Painting a bindi on her Russian doll, she notes that its red teardrops are 'more real than the salt-tasting water running down her face' (1). As a female Asian child raised in Britain in the 1950s she is already acutely aware of her unreality, of being unrecognised, so that the doll has more presence than she does.[13] This sense of unreality is foregrounded later by a discussion between two women in the Asian centre, Maya and Asha:

> 'We're making ourselves invisible, which is precisely what they want us to be. It's like the old nigger in the book who says "Please massa, you're right massa, I'm not here massa."' Asha scrapes back

the chair, looking ostentatiously at her watch. Warming to her subject Maya is not to be silenced: 'If we have a right to be here, don't we have a right to be human, warts and all!' (105)

In her children's novel, *Hari-jan*, the novel's title speaks for a similar experience: Hari-jan, meaning 'Children of God', was the name given by Gandhi to India's 'untouchables', the lowest Indian caste who were denied basic standards and rights of humanity. By having her central character, Harjinder, take on this name, Randhawa suggests a parallel between this state of nothingness and the experience of being a young British-born Asian woman. Even a box of vegetables has more recognition than Harjinder does:

> This was my quality time, to stand and stare. When I can, that is, in-between picking up suspicious looks, getting pushed, jostled and being moved on by the shopkeeper who was putting out his boxes of vegetables. They took up half the pavement and no-one pushed them around. Even they have a place in the world, I thought jealously. Me? I'm a *wog*, a *female*. An unwanted *Brit-Cit*. An unwanted *daughter*. (106)

Randhawa's characters face the dilemma Butler outlines in which one 'may feel that without some recognizability I cannot live. But I may also feel that the terms by which I am recognized make life unliveable.' (4) Randhawa's women *do* have options: they can gain recognition by subscribing to existing notions of either traditional Asian or white British culture. But in both cases accepting such definition denies part of themselves to the extent that life is, indeed, unliveable. In *Hari-jan*, Harjinder is aware that 'I'd pushed deep away somewhere all the parts of myself that didn't synchronise with the "English Corporate Image"'. The result is negative: 'if you pushed away parts of yourself, they left empty spaces behind' (84). In *Wicked* Kulwant attempts to assimilate, getting a white boyfriend, Michael, only to find that he orientalises her as his 'Indian Princess' (6).[14] She later demands an arranged marriage in an alternative strategy of conforming to her Indian heritage, only to end up divorced. Trapped between Englishness and Indianness, Kulwant finds there is little possibility of negotiation between the two positions and, therefore, little recognition of who she really feels herself to be:

> She'd messed it all up because she had wanted everything, wanted to be Indian and English, wanted to choose for herself what she wanted out of both. Couldn't be done. (29)

These women find themselves continually defined in terms of the norms which they are not, reflecting Butler's sense that 'being outside the norm is in some sense being defined still in relation to it' (42), while at the same time striving for the recognition that acceptance into such norms accords. So they continually search for forms of definition, striving to give themselves meaning in a society which refuses them intelligibility: refuses to offer them a norm to which they can comfortably associate.

As for Butler's unintelligible intersexuals, so for British Asian women the act of giving oneself a name is essential to claiming one's identity.[15] In Leena Dhingra's 'Breaking Out of the Labels' (1987), she explores the ever-changing definitions of Asian women and asks 'Which one fits me? Which one encompasses my reality?'[16] In *Wicked* Kulwant becomes Kuli, but also Coolie; Rani becomes Rosalind; other characters – Sunny, Kami-Kazi – are known only by their nicknames. In *Hari-jan*, Harjinder renames herself in such terms, while her friends have equally abbreviated names: Gazzy, Binny. In her stories, too, Randhawa foregrounds this: in 'Mickey Mouse' (1991) we encounter 'the Black Narcissus', 'Tippy the troublemaker', 'Nimbu my nemesis', and 'Cheeta'; 'Sunni' in the story of the same name (1987) is really Sunninder, the abbreviated form with its meaning of 'left all alone' reflecting the story of the protagonist; the story 'India' (1985) opens 'Inderjit is the name. In-Der-Jit if you're English. Intherjeet with the double ees dragged out if you're Punjabi. India if you're a friend'; India's white boyfriend is known simply as 'Goldfinger'.[17] Butler's theory of performance of identity stresses that it is not the body alone that defines experience, but that body in relation to language (199). So for Randhawa's characters body defines language, but language acts equally to change and transform bodies.

This power of naming moves to the foreground in Randhawa's later novel, *The Coral Strand*. The story of a young woman named Sita, raised in England by an English woman, Emily, and her Indian servant, Champa, it explores the legacy of colonialism for British Asian identity as it moves between present day England and 1940s India. Sita continually renames herself: Sita the Ferret or Sita/Ferret after the names that Emily and Champa give her, then later Mrs Pandey, while with her friend Jeevan she is part of a pairing called Flotsam and Jetsam. In her relationship with Kala both employ a naming game in which the individual letters of words are emphasised – 'C for club ... B for beavering' (28) – so the act of bringing the world into being through language is made explicit. The need to manipulate language only emphasises how it is the way in which one's body is marked: the English women in India have not real names, but rather assignations that define their social function and type: 'Acid eyes and Telegram' (56). In both *Wicked* and *Coral* the self-definition characters engage in is contrasted with a more pervasive definition by others: the inability of the white British to pronounce Asian names, and their tendency to shorten them as a result, is evidence of colonialism still at work, as white culture claims the right to define its 'other'. To engage in naming is thus to reclaim this right: so against her childhood experience of being controlled by others, Sita at the end of *Coral* 'made a baptism, a naming of her own' (247). Renaming Emily, Champa, and her newly discovered mother, Sita is able to assert her own right to define and to fix the identity of others.

Sita is the child of another of Emily's servants: born in England to a migrant mother she has never known. Unlike Kulwant, she is not so much caught between competing identities as she is an unconvincing model of Britishness: 'British born, British bred, British something or other' (25). Performing a traditional Indian identity through reading *Asian Woman* she is disconnected from her Asian heritage, feeling 'rootless and fraudulent' (18). But she is also identified by Emily as a counterfeit Englishwoman, described in relation to a mythical 'Over There' invoked to identify her difference. Like Kulwant and Harjinder, she expresses her unreality: '"There was nothing there," had always been a fear' (57). Taking on employment as a visiting saleswoman for Asian products she 'had salivated at the idea of stepping into others' lives, getting glimpses into homes where regular Indian life happened, of eavesdropping on tradition and culture, brushing against *the real stuff*' (my emphasis, 19). For Randhawa unintelligibility is not only about failing to meet the norms dictated to by society because one inherently falls outside them, but also because one's life experience can alienate one from the self-knowledge needed to find one's place. For Sita and Harjinder, this unreality is added to by their own lack of knowledge about their backgrounds. Harjinder calls India 'the unknown part of me' (69). Sita declares 'Insufficient data ... that's who I am' (37). Her mother is simply 'The Girl': the ultimate unrecognised subject who is denied even the rights of self-definition.

The results of unintelligibility can be dramatic and account for the unique suffering of British Asian women. Part of this trauma is intense mental suffering, which – in a passage which usefully serves to illustrate Randhawa's poetic prose – is summed up in Kulwant's own reflections on her life:

> Her childhood image of herself had been as a gorgeous, multi-coloured bird, soaring through the sky, swooping to the ground, iridescent with each wing shake or bright gaudy in the sunlight, as gaudy as the nail-polish tears on her doll's face; by a cruel twist of fate, this flamboyant rover of the skies had been grounded, its wings clipped; left to fight for survival in the cold climes and grey world of England. No wonder it had lost its colours, shed its feathers, lost its way, become one among the soulless throng. (*Wicked* 118)

In all her texts Randhawa affirms Butler's idea that 'being called real or being called unreal can be not only a means of social control but a form of dehumanizing violence' (*Undoing Gender* 217). In *Wicked*, the character of Rosalind/Rani embodies the concept of unliveable recognisability. Rani transforms herself into Rosalind to assimilate into white culture, but, after two attempted rapes, descends into mental illness. Gender and race act together to oppress Rani, and her mental illness is a physical manifestation of being denied any rights or recognition. Many of Randhawa's characters experience the violence with which intelligibility is enforced, showing the way in which, according to Butler, society acts to 'forcibly define' (57) what is intelligible, through rape, sexual exploitation and physical attack. At one level there is no 'British Asian', there is only foreign or English and Randhawa's women find themselves aggressively driven towards these two identities. On another level, within the non-white community there are other definitions which are equally forcibly defined: black, migrant, postcolonial. Yet these definitions, too, force the British Asian woman into a place that is not comfortably her own.

Performing reality: British Asian women's subversions

Randhawa's engagement with the unintelligible, however, also places her fiction at the centre of assertions of British Asian confidence. As Butler indicates, to be in a position of unintelligibility is not entirely detrimental:

> There are advantages to remaining less than intelligible, if intelligibility is understood as that which is produced as a consequence of recognition according to some prevailing social norms. Indeed, if my options are loathsome, if I have no desire to be recognized

within a certain set of norms, then it follows that my sense of survival depends upon escaping the clutch of those norms by which
recognition is conferred. (3)

The benefits of this strategy in ethnic terms are defined by Paul
Gilroy, for whom 'proteophobia' (the fear of the unclassifiable)
reveals the destabilising threat that existence outside the norm
provides. For Gilroy, the comic performer Ali G – a Jewish man
performing black urban identity – embodies this dynamic.[18]
Randhawa's women exist in a similar unclassifiable state.
Across her fiction, we see Randhawa's characters exploit their
lack of recognition to question the very terms in which identity
is defined and the social norms against which individuals and
communities are judged.

An essential part of this comes in the form of another strategy
outlined by Butler: the subversive and radicalised performance of identity which she first outlines in her groundbreaking
Gender Trouble (1990). The vast majority of commentary on
Butler's now famous theory of performance focuses upon how
the way in which we perform our gendered identities is not a
matter of choice, but is socially determined, a perspective which
is rooted in the influence of Michel Foucault on Butler's work.
However, Butler does also point to situations in which deviance
from expected and socially determined performances is possible, 'radically *incredible*' divergences from social convention.[19] It
is this latter sort of exceptional performance which Randhawa
foregrounds as the possibility of unintelligibility. Against tragic
attempts at mimicry and assimilation are alternative performances of ethnic and gendered identity which threaten to blow
apart the existing assumptions of British society. As Butler
declares that 'the "I" that I am finds itself at once constituted by
norms and dependant on them but also endeavours to live in
ways that maintain a critical and transformative relation to them'
(*Undoing Gender* 3), so Randhawa's women replay existing stereotypes to interrogate them. They embody Butler's connection
between parody and politics, drawing attention to the instability of identities, destabilising existing norms by revealing their
exclusions, and challenging the hegemony of the authentic. For
Randhawa, identity is a matter of 'self-determination and self-
fulfilment', and her characters capture the agency of conscious
and purposeful identity choices.[20]

This critical performance is most evident in Kulwant's
transformation into the old woman that gives *Wicked* its title.
From her youth, Kulwant is a master of strategic identification,

embodying Roger Ballard's description of British Asian youths who consciously code their behaviour according to different circumstances, and for advantageous effect.[21] Such women are, as Felicity Hand argues, not caught between two cultures, but rather 'skilled cultural navigators'.[22] Kulwant develops into 'a newly emergent Machiavelli; soon skilled in circumventing the protective barriers of parents and community, lying with ease to clear her path' (6), and the transformation on which the book focuses, Kulwant's adoption of the personality of Mrs Singh, a bag lady with a stick, is evident of this continued talent. In *Coral*, this process is echoed in Sita's transformation into Mrs Pandey, an Asian widow, in order to assume the recognised form of married woman against the unacceptable form of unmarried yet independent woman. In her new guise, Sita can gain employment, and evade questions about family circumstances. Like Kulwant, she celebrates this ability as a common strategy of survival: 'Camouflage! But a common enough device employed by Asian women living in the West who had to hip-hop between cultures' (30).

As, for Butler, drag shows 'us how contemporary notions of reality can be questioned, and new models of reality instituted' (217) so Kulwant's performance of an old woman serves a similar function; indeed, Butler herself points to ageing as a process revealing the body's potential for transformation and change as it makes explicit the fact that bodies are not static, but continually changing (217). Her description of the body's capacity for change could also be used to explain the effect of Kulwant's assumed identity, where 'the body is that which can occupy the norm in myriad ways, exceed the norm, rework the norm, and expose realities to which we thought we were confined as open to transformation' (217). In becoming an old woman, Kulwant moves from the unintelligibility of the British Asian woman, to the 'otherness' of the old migrant woman. The transformation into an old lady has a particular significance: the privileging of old age in traditional Asian culture is contrasted with the Western neglect of its elderly; so assuming the identity of an old Asian woman in Britain engages with a politics of British Asian perspectives against traditional Asian culture: Mrs Singh is 'othered' in Britain, she would be venerated in India. This perspective is affirmed in Randhawa's short story 'Time Traveler' (2001) where the narrator's mother tells the story of Mrs Desai, who 'doesn't have a family. That is to say, her sons won't have her live with them. Another horror spawned by this strange world! Where your elders are left to a mouldy lonely old age.'[23]

Though this may not seem significant, it is a crucial transformation allowing Kulwant to experience the status of oppositionality, against the non-status of absence. It is not so much, as Tobias Döring argues, that Kulwant 'claims the benefit of unbelonging' in her new guise, but rather that she claims the benefit of recognised 'otherness'.[24] Critics such as Döring, and also Martina Michel, who identify the subversion of Kulwant's disguise as lying in the fact that it allows her to succeed 'in not being recognized (and thus stereotyped) as Indian' neglect the fact that the old lady *is* Indian: but she is a recognisable form, and one therefore not subject to the pressures of being a 'new' British Asian.[25] The scrutiny she avoids as a result is not because of invisibility, or 'unrecognizability' as Michel calls it, but because of a recognised form, which is therefore not subject to the same scrutiny as the British Asian woman.[26] Kulwant's transformation is focused upon being 'authentic' (13): she supplements her stick with NHS spectacles, and adopts the stereotypical persona of a complaining and intolerant elderly person. In doing so, she finds herself able to inhabit a form that, while poorly treated, does have an identified persona which society recognises. An old migrant woman may be ignored, but to be ignored indicates a denied presence: the old woman is the 'other' of youth and the West's preoccupation with youthful bodies, the migrant the recognised 'other' of white Britain.

Yet unlike Gilroy's male performers, Randhawa's women acknowledge that real material survival does depend upon recognition, however creatively achieved, and however unpalatable. For Kulwant her new role, however negatively conceived, allows her to inhabit herself: it is a body that *is* something, rather than one constantly grappling for definition, a body with a 'badge of old age' (3) connoting identification. With her stick becoming 'a stick with which to beat others' Kulwant uses her new form to interrogate and challenge the world within the context of an identity within which such reaction is acknowledged and tolerated.[27] Equally, Sita's performances in *Coral* lead her to ask 'Is this how you change into something else? Is this how you fool the world?' (245); the phrasing offers at once a sense of sadness, but also a site of empowerment allowing the British Asian woman to manipulate a society in which she is otherwise disadvantaged. These moves reflect Butler's awareness that 'the thought of a possible life is only an indulgence for those who already know themselves to be possible. For those who are still looking to become possible, possibility is a necessity' (31). What may appear to be the inhabiting of a worthless form is in fact for Kulwant and Sita a movement forward: from impossibility to possibility, from being nothing to being ignored.

Making oneself recognisable is, for Randhawa, an essentially communal practice and, as Sharon Monteith has argued, her novels can be situated within the context of 'narratives of community' as a distinctly female form of expression.[28] Against Kureishi's didactic individualism, Randhawa foregrounds the value of communal identities. For her, such identifications do not mean capitulating to restrictive practices. This is because the community that she identifies with is a newly constructed one: a specifically British community of Asian women who are united by life experiences even as they represent the diversity of British Asian womanhood. The women making up such a community could not be more different, yet the pressures of unintelligibility supersede such differences in providing the shared basis for communal identification. This is most evident in *Wicked* where, as Chris Weedon notes, 'whatever the internal problems and conflicts in the Asian community, differences become insignificant in the face of White racist oppression'.[29] Beginning a shelter for young Asian girls, not to support the stereotypes held by 'concerned white people who think running away for an Asian girl is some kind of promotion in life' but rather to provide a 'transition place' (172), the women in *Wicked* offer a physical site protecting British Asian women's position between cultures. This becomes a personal project when the women collectively heal Rani at the end of the novel in an act of female solidarity.

Here Randhawa's work needs to be located within the broader context of its production. Randhawa worked for Asian women's groups responsible for refuges and other facilities, actively campaigned against racism and, specifically, for the rights of Asian and black women. Such activity is captured in the story 'Sunni', where the central character is employed by an Asian women's community project in Southall, concomitantly celebrating the town's vibrancy and reflecting upon its exposure to racist violence in the late 1970s. Setting up the AWWW in 1984 Randhawa convinced funding bodies such as the Greater London Council (GLC), Black Ink, Lambeth Council and Greater London Arts of the value of Asian women's writing. The later renaming of the AWWW as the Asian Women Writers' Collective says much about its socialist and communal ethos. The group brought together migrant and British-born/raised writers, and specifically identified an 'Asian' community against broader black, feminist, or socialist politics. They were involved in outreach programmes in local communities and schools, with an explicitly social as well as literary function. The group itself established a position of positive unintelligibility in their attitude to writing: the women exhibited a 'choice not to locate themselves within either an Indian/Asian or an English tradition of literature. There is no sense of working within a history, of looking to common antecedents. Theirs is evidently a decision to start from ground zero, to create a tradition or a place for their particular cultural subjectivity.'[30]

There is the beginning here of an intense community between women. The powerful connection between Randhawa's female characters approaches what Adrienne Rich refers to as the *lesbian continuum*, referring to a world of 'woman identification' that is undermined and eroded by society's anxiety about protecting heterosexual behaviour as a social norm.[31] This physical and emotional connection, not to be confused with same-sex *sexual* attraction, refers to the powerful relationships between women, often vital 'survival relationships', of which sexual attraction is only the most extreme manifestation: 'a range – through each woman's life and throughout history – of woman-identified experience, not simply the fact that a woman has had or consciously desired genital sexual experience with another woman'.[32] Amongst her concern for ethnicity, Randhawa also considers issues of feminist politics, most notably in *Wicked,* where she confronts postnatal depression, divorce, physical and sexual abuse and poor working conditions. In *Coral* this continues with more discussion of domestic and sexual violence, paedophilia and exploitation, universalised by its presence in both the contemporary and historical strains of the narrative so that Sita is forced to acknowledge 'throughout the centuries, women have only had one thing to barter' (254). In *Hari-jan*, the boundaries of children's fiction exclude such themes, but the novel does point to the devaluing of women's roles as mothers and wives (63). Amidst these pressures, strong bonds between women become essential. When Kulwant meets Kurshid, the new wife of her ex-husband, her response is not hostility, but the desire for connection: 'Couldn't they learn from each other? Two women linked to the same man' (72). Indeed this celebration of communal power is *Wicked*'s overall message. Whereas Kureishi ends his novels with independent protagonists, striking out as individuals, *Wicked* ends 'celebrating the return of the prodigal daughters, Kuli and Rani, to the sheltering fold of Asian British life'.[33] That the value of this female community has been pursued by almost all British Asian female writers who come after Randhawa suggests something about the importance of her work. It has made British Asian women's writing a distinctive field in its own right.

As an unintelligible British Asian woman, to identify with feminist concerns is to claim a place within an oppositional community which, although 'othered' by patriarchy, is nevertheless part of an intelligible norm. The women through this place themselves in a position where the norm can be questioned and interrogated: by becoming intelligible women, that definition of women is transformed to include ethnic and racial concerns. The ability of the feminist movement to confront such complexities is highlighted by the fact that the coalition in *Wicked* is genuinely cross-cultural, with not only white and Asian women, but also black women like Angie. In *Coral* the parallel careers in prostitution of Emily and Champa are testaments to the connections between women, the shared oppressions beyond the confines of ethnicity. Equally, *Hari-jan* centres around a beauty contest being held by a multicultural 'Harmony committee' at Harjinder's school. Initially, Harjinder is deeply suspicious of the politics of such an endeavour; she doubts the possibility of Gazzy's desire to 'unite with others' (75), her 'mini-United Nations' (93) of Jews, Greeks, English, Afro-Caribbean, Asian, boys and girls. Yet at the novel's conclusion the contest is revealed as a veil for feminist consciousness raising: 'to demonstrate that colour's no barrier and women, mostly have the same problems' (120). Here are the beginnings of the lesbian continuum: adolescent women's recognition of their shared circumstances.

Randhawa's protagonists employ a cross-cultural intervention that mirrors the action of Randhawa and her fellow writers in the early years of the collective: the feminist movement in *Wicked*, led by 'Big Sister', is involved not only in high-profile issues such as the anti-nuclear weapons Greenham Common protests, but also in the struggles confronting Asian women workers, and Asian women authors. The feminist magazine *Spare Rib* was, in the 1980s, deeply involved in the black and Asian feminist movement: almost every issue in the 1980s includes a feature on 'ethnic' feminism, including reviews of Randhawa's fiction, and reviews and extracts from the black and Asian feminist anthology *Charting the Journey*.[34] Randhawa captures therefore the mutual support of this period: the Asian women are encouraged by the wider feminist movement, but the wider movement is also supported by the Asian women, who are able to identify with the larger causes: 'freedom fighters ... that's what Ammi reckons the Greenham women are' (*Wicked* 75). Such actions at once gave British Asian women a space of inclusion, while at the same time dramatically calling into question the very institution in which they were being included, the beginning of the gradual unravelling of the universalist claims of the second-wave feminist movement, and its critique from the perspectives of race, ethnicity, and class. While such action threatens the universal, it at the same time demands its reconfiguration. It is therefore a 'productive risk', Butler's possibility of changing what the universal stands for:

> To claim that the universal has not yet been articulated is to insist that the 'not yet' is proper to an understanding of the universal itself: that which remains 'unrealized' by the universal constitutes it essentially. The universal begins to become articulated precisely through challenges to its *existing* formulation, and this challenge emerges from those who are not covered by it, who have no entitlement to occupy the place of the 'who', but who, nevertheless, demand that the universal as such ought to be inclusive of them. (191)

Through placing themselves within the universal category of womanhood, from which they are excluded, British Asian women re-structure that universal definition through their demand to be included.

That for Butler movement between this social body and the personal body is possible, that 'the body is only later, and with some uncertainty, that to which I lay claim as my own' (21), is revealed at *Wicked*'s conclusion. Kulwant's transformation is a necessary step towards reclaiming her British Asian female body as her own, outside of public definitions. So at the end of the novel she abandons her old woman persona and returns to the body previously denied, proclaiming that 'she'd have to be a baby and consciously grow herself all over again' (204). Equally, at the end of *Coral* Sita refuses to choose between traditions, instead allowing herself to fall outside such socially sanctioned options:

Sita/Ferret wears flimsy dresses with deep necklines and high hemlines that swish around her thighs, sunglasses and a satin-ribboned straw hat. She melts into the London crowd – but only on alternate days. The other days she wears sheer saris with bikini blouses, displaying her body as never before, revelling in its shape and form, admiring its composition. The body is for display, enjoyment and fulfilment – not for locking away. (298)

Importantly, Sita's celebration of different facets of herself on different days is very different to the hybrid fusions she observes in other young women. Unlike Kureishi, Randhawa here seems to recognise that hybridity, too, can become a normative choice, reflecting her uneasiness about the popularity of the term.[35] As alternative to this Randhawa's women move from uncomfortable unintelligibility, via assumed intelligibility, to comfortable unintelligibility. They choose to live, finally, outside of binary definitions, and refuse to choose between existing social norms, or even the liberal alternatives. Instead, they reflect Butler's 'humans ... who live and breathe in the interstices of this binary relation, showing that it is not exhaustive' (65). This is best expressed by another of Randhawa's Asian protagonists, the narrator of the short story 'Games' (1994), who declares 'I would now be my own puppet-maker and puppet; this here, one Indian girl no longer running, from her inheritance, be it battleground or playground'.[36]

For Michel, this decision on the part of Randhawa's protagonists is, in relation to *Wicked*, evidence of Homi Bhabha's 'third space': a space outside binary definitions, announcing the confidence of the British Asian subject who can exist outside of norms, not so much waiting for recognition as comfortable in the absence of it. Living between binaries, Randhawa's women do embody hybridity, speaking Anglicised Punjabi in *Wicked*, a 'lovely mixture of Hindi, Panjabi and English' in *Hari-jan* (63), in *Coral* employing 'ingenious mixing and matching' (147). Such perspective is sustained in Randhawa's short fiction, where the protagonist of 'Time Traveler' eats '*roti* and baked beans',[37] but is most evident in *Hari-jan* where the focus on a teenage protagonist allows Randhawa to celebrate the exuberance of urban youth culture; if one thought the sort of representation offered by Zadie Smith in *White Teeth* was original then a cursory glance at Randhawa's novel proves such assignations false. Hari-jan wears Reeboks with shalwar kameez; she does not lament her contradictions, but chooses instead to 'use' them (15). Her straddling of two cultures destabilises both of them, reflecting Bakirathi Mani's argument that the hybrid clothing of South Asian youth can be read, in Butler's terms, as an 'ethnic performativity'.[38]

Yet Michel's own modification of Bhabha's theory – that this is 'a space created by women, woven, so to speak, out of the stories of their lives, the histories of Asian women living in Britain' – points to the limitations of such frameworks in feminist contexts.[39] That such a process is not without pain is central to Randhawa's writing, an important re-visioning of postcolonial literature's celebratory nomadism. In the contexts of 1980s right-wing politics *Wicked*'s women are aware that 'they'll be British by birth but never by colour' (144). The young women in *Hari-jan* face racist prejudice, particularly Gazzy, the Muslim character, who is subject to a range of Orientalist stereotypes, even from Harjinder, who assumes her arranged marriage is forced. The concept of 'real' here never gives way for the postmodern idea that such authenticity is an illusion: it is something that can be grasped, if only in the very important, and regrettable, sense that one can attain the norms which facilitate social acceptance and, indeed, that some have easier access to these norms than others, able to take them for granted in a way the British Asian woman cannot. These norms exist; Sita in *Coral* is aware that those around her 'all had a background, whether they bucked against it or not' (90), and her desire for the same experience, her jealousy of Kala with his sense of 'being placed, materially, psychologically, geographically, historically' (224), marks the value of roots, while at the same time critiquing any simplistic nostalgia for an imagined India. The same experience is offered in *Hari-jan*, where Harjinder describes India as 'the unfulfilled, lonely, aching part' (69) of herself.

Living in a hybrid space is therefore an experience of suffering as much as something to be celebrated. So Randhawa's novels reflect the broader field of Asian women's writing, in which difference 'is very far from postmodern notions of free choice, celebration and play' and hybridity is 'far from liberating'.[40] It is for this reason that the conclusions to Randhawa's writings are so often ambivalent. *Wicked* ends with Kuli's acceptance of her difference, but also with Rani's negative awareness of it as she faces prosecution, the world 'still the ghastly place she'd tried to evade' (204). *Coral* concludes with the end of Conservative rule, but also the death of Princess Diana, a sense concomitantly of hopefulness and tragedy. *Hari-jan* ends with Harjinder claiming her Englishness, but claiming with it British racism (160). Perhaps this is because, at the same time Randhawa's women can accept their position, and even prosper in it, so the reader must feel uncomfortable about the perpetuation of such a social reality, which is not Bhabha's abstract world of hybridity as the natural state of affairs, but rather a real world in which hybridity must be nurtured and consciously constructed. As Sita in *Coral* comes to experience, the ideal of hybridity is brought into sharp relief by the 'real' world:

> She had lived with Emily and Champa and grown up thinking that the English and Indian ways were intermingled, that the differences didn't cancel each other out, but cohabited; sometimes with difficulty, sometimes like a seamless joining. However, the 'Byofriends', as she came to call them, thought otherwise and examined her colour, compared, commented, and asked endless questions about culture, religion and tradition. (64–5)

This ambivalence reflects Butler's argument that the chaos of trauma can in fact be, exactly because of this, an experience of revelation: where 'a fractured state, or a state of displacement, can surely be a site of suffering, but it can also be the site for a new possibility of agency' (196). Yet it also means that personal confidence must go hand in hand with a call for social reform and a desire for change.

Conclusion

In *Coral*, Sita's mother remembers how 'once she had scored a furious zigzag into the table' (193). This repeats an image in *Wicked* where Maya tells Rani the story of a 'zig-zag woman ... with zig-zag eyes' (183). The zig-zag woman, so the story goes, was miserable until she stopped looking for acceptance from others, became aware that everyone was different, and, as a consequence, 'lived happily ever after' (184).

Randhawa presents life for British Asian women as a zigzag, with the message that accepting your uniqueness – your unintelligibility – is a source of suffering, but also empowerment. Once accepted, it connects you with a strong community of women who, regardless of race, are to differing degrees caught in this process. The path will never be straight, she assures us, but it will be more exciting as a result.

Discussion

- To what extent is it more useful to consider Randhawa's writing in terms of gender rather than ethnicity?
- How is Randhawa's role as founding member of the Asian Women Writers' Collective evident in her fiction?
- Why do you think Randhawa's work has received less critical attention that her male contemporaries?

Notes

1 Butler, *Undoing Gender*, p. 218. Subsequent references cited parenthetically.
2 Asian Women Writers' Workshop, *Right of Way*; Ahmad and Gupta, *Flaming Spirit*. *Right of Way* includes four stories by Randhawa: 'Pedal Push', pp. 7–13, 'The Heera', pp. 70–83, 'Games', pp. 120–30, and 'War of the Worlds', pp. 155–62.
3 Hussein, 'Changing Seasons', p. 16.
4 Ticktin, 'Contemporary British Asian Women's Writing', p. 72.
5 See Nasta, 'Introduction'; 'Homes Without Walls'.
6 Beezmohun, 'Where are all the British Asian Writers?'.
7 Interview with author, July 2008.
8 Randhawa, *A Wicked Old Woman*: hereafter *Wicked*. *The Coral Strand*: hereafter *Coral*. Subsequent references cited parenthetically.
9 Innes, 'Wintering'.
10 See, for example, *Undoing Gender*, p. 4, p. 13. Butler draws on Spivak (p. 228) and Gilroy (p. 247), and also points to her Jewish ethnicity as an important part of her philosophy (p. 238). Subsequent references cited parenthetically.
11 Dunker, *Sisters and Strangers,* p. 236.
12 Socorro Suárez Lafuente, 'Changing Places', p. 124.
13 Reference to 'pre-time to Beatle-time' (16) suggests Kulwant is a young woman in the late 1950s or early 1960s.
14 Randhawa originally rehearses this racial dynamic in 'India', pp. 27–9.
15 See Butler, *Undoing Gender*, p. 75.
16 Dhingra, 'Breaking Out of the Labels', p. 107.
17 Randhawa, 'India', p. 11.
18 Gilroy, *After Empire*, p. 148.
19 Butler, *Gender Trouble*, p. 193.
20 Interview with author, July 2008.
21 Ballard, 'Introduction', pp. 29–33.
22 Hand, 'Shaking Off Sharam', p. 135.
23 Randhawa, 'Time Traveler', p. 382.
24 Döring, 'Subversion Among the Vegetables', p. 259.
25 Michel, 'Und(der)-Cover', p. 151.
26 *Ibid.*, p. 155.
27 Innes, 'Review of *A Wicked Old Woman*', p. 33.

28   Monteith, 'On the Streets and in the Tower Blocks', p. 27.
29   Weedon, 'Redefining Otherness', p. 233.
30   Ticktin, 'Contemporary British Asian Women's Writing', p. 70–1.
31   Rich, 'Compulsory Heterosexuality' p. 1778.
32   *Ibid.*, p. 1777, p. 1774.
33   Ghosh-Schellhorn, 'Transitional Identities', p. 245.
34   Yasmin Kureishi, 'Review of *A Wicked Old Woman*'; Kay and Parmar, 'Interview with Audre Lorde'; Yasmin Kureishi, 'Review of *Charting the Journey*', p. 33.
35   Interview with author, July 2008.
36   Randhawa, 'Games', p. 130.
37   Randhawa, 'Time Traveler', p. 379.
38   Mani, 'Undressing the Diaspora', p. 128.
39   Michel, 'Und(der)-Cover', p. 148.
40   Weedon, 'Redefining Otherness', p. 233, p. 234.

Further reading

C. L. Innes, 'Wintering: Making a Home in Britain', in Robert A. Lee (ed.), *Other Britain, Other British: Contemporary Multicultural Fiction* (London: Pluto, 1995), pp. 21–34.

Sharon Monteith, 'On the Streets and in the Tower Blocks: Ravinder Randhawa's *A Wicked Old Woman* (1987) and Livi Michael's *Under a Thin Moon* (1992)', *Critical Survey*, 8:1 (1996), 26–36.

Neumeier, Beate (ed.), *Engendering Realism and Postmodernism: Contemporary Women Writers in Britain* (Amsterdam: Rodopi, 2001).

Christine Vogt Williams, 'Rescue Me? No, Thanks!: *A Wicked Old Woman* and *Anita and Me*', in Geoffrey Davis, Peter H. Marsden, Bénédicte Ledent and Marc Delrez (eds), *Towards a Transcultural Future: Literature and Society in a 'Post'-Colonial World*, (Amsterdam: Rodopi, 2005), pp. 389–97.

4

Atima Srivastava

We had leaned into a kiss and that kiss had gone on for hours, a silent rushing journey through the stars. Lost in space. At the end of the kiss, we had come to the heart of each other, gasping for breath, exhilarated with the moon and the world and everything.[1]

Open Atima Srivastava's *Looking for Maya* (1999) and you are not transported into a world of racism, prejudice, or identity crises. Instead, you enter a fairytale world of fated romances, star-crossed lovers and passionate embraces. With such prose Srivastava is the first prominent example of a school of British Asian writing which also includes Preethi Nair, Nisha Minhas and B. K. Mahal: a British Asian romance genre intervention. Born in Mumbai in 1961, and coming to Britain at the age of eight, Srivastava's two novels, *Maya*, and the earlier *Transmission* (1992), feature young women protagonists, working in creative industries, with roles as writers and television researchers that mirror Srivastava's own career path (Srivastava has written screenplays, plays, librettos, and short stories as well as novels). These women are perfect models of the 'chick lit' heroine.[2] As both the first and the most sophisticated example of the rise of British Asian popular romance, Srivastava's fiction simultaneously challenges two core values of the romance genre: whiteness and heterosexuality. Moreover, the favouring of romance plots over concerns with ethnicity make Srivastava's novels a further example of the post-ethnic reality to which Hanif Kureishi's work has gestured. Dominated by confident British Asian women, Srivastava's novels offer a contemporary urban reality in which political concerns have made way for personal engagements: not just romantic, but spatial.

'Will they, won't they?': universal romance

Although the earlier writings of Ravinder Randhawa do not

ignore romantic relationships, these are secondary to issues of cultural identity. Srivastava reverses this hierarchy; her novels, while not unconcerned with cultural issues, make these secondary to presenting romantic dilemmas. Discussions which focus on the racism presented in the texts give the sense of a bleaker reality than is offered by their overall content.[3] This is true of both *Transmission* and *Maya* which offer broadly similar narratives. *Transmission* focuses on the story of Ungelliee, a young British Asian woman whose work as a television researcher creates conflicts between her career and growing romantic involvement with Lol, an HIV-positive man. *Maya* presents a similarly independent British Asian woman, Mira, who becomes romantically involved with an older, married, Asian man named Amrit. Both novels are set in a world contemporary to their publication, and are located entirely in London.

Implicit in the marketing of Srivastava's novels is negotiation: between acknowledging the presence of a British Asian protagonist, and emphasising a universal story. In both texts, the protagonists' names do not specifically identify them as Asian. Ungelliee is called Angie by her friends; Mira is more culturally specific, but nevertheless does not immediately indicate a particular cultural background. While the paperback cover of *Transmission* refers to Angie as a 'second-generation immigrant', the cover of the later *Maya* does not reference the character's cultural background, perhaps as counterbalance to her more ethnically specific name. Equally, while *Maya* shows a young Asian woman, the cover image of *Transmission* is abstract.

The universal nature of Srivastava's stories is represented by the problems faced by her protagonists. In neither novel are these issues principally related to matters of ethnicity. In *Transmission*, Angie's central dilemma is whether to exploit her relationship with Lol to further her television career. In *Maya*, Mira must confront the reality of her relationship with a married man. In both cases a universalised ethical dilemma forms the central thrust of the narrative. In this sense, Srivastava foreshadows other popular narratives of female British Asian experience. Her novels foreground, for example, the same model of British Asian female identity offered in Gurinder Chadha's immensely successful *Bend It Like Beckham* (2002). A similarly comic drama, Chadha's film is the first British Asian cinema endeavour to achieve mainstream box office success. Focusing on the story of Jasminder, a young British Asian woman whose desire to play football challenges the expectations of her Asian community, the film confronts the struggles for young British Asian women attempting to negotiate traditional Asian culture and alternative lifestyles promoted in contemporary British society. Jasminder's career aims are further problematised as they lead her into a relationship with the football team's male coach, Joe. The conventional romance plot is complicated by the theme of inter-racial dating; not only must Jasminder face the tension between conservative Asian attitudes to dating and the dominant liberal values of British society, she must also confront potential problems raised by conducting a relationship outside of one's own religious and racial group. The film, however, universalises these tensions so as to normalise Asian culture as part of Britishness. The problems raised by Jasminder's life choices are contextualised by others around her suffering similar problems *without* sharing her cultural background. It is not just Jasminder struggling to play football, but also her friend Juliet, whose own mother similarly struggles to accept her daughter's questioning of conventional gender roles. Both girls shorten their names – to Jess and Jules respectively – indicating their solidarity. Equally, that such problems are gendered is complicated when it is revealed that Joe, too, has a difficult relationship with his father: another 'J', Joe forms the last member of a trio of alienated youth. The tensions between parents and children are universalised, and the problems that Jess faces are just one cultural incarnation of this issue, rather than a specific conflict between migrant and British-born generations.

Both Chadha and Srivastava exploit the possibilities of recreating Western romance narratives with a British Asian twist. In this, they draw upon an already established Indian romance market. Romances such as the popular US imprint Harlequin and its British equivalent Mills and Boon are imported in large numbers to the developing world, in particular to India, where they are read in English by middle-class Asian women. There has been little research on how the consumption of such Western fictions impacts upon the attitudes of women readers from other ethnic backgrounds in terms of their own self-image. Stevi Jackson asks us to consider that romances 'derive from a specifically Western cultural tradition – if they are being consumed world-wide we need to know why they are being read. It cannot simply be assumed that all women everywhere make sense of them in exactly the same way'.[4] Despite this, the notion that 'the romance novel transcends cultures' is still frequently expressed, for example by Pamela Regis in her book *A*

Natural History of the Romance Novel (2003), whose reading of E. M. Hull's *The Sheik* (1919) dismisses the cultural connotations of the text to declare instead it is 'like any other twentieth-century popular romance novel'.[5] Despite this lack of attention, any ethnic intervention into the romance genre is potentially subversive, given its stereotypically 'Western' heroines and scenarios. Popular romance novels conventionally rely upon a white hero and heroine, and while Western romances appear largely immune from direct criticism, discussions of postcolonial romance novels emphasise how such texts engage with the genre to question the universalising of Western ideals of romantic love and emphasise their roots in colonial myths of ideal womanhood.[6] It is therefore interesting to speculate as to how a British Asian intervention into the romance genre might negotiate its cultural norms – whether, in fact, the same issues arise as in postcolonial readings of the genre, necessitating a re-writing or subversion, or whether the Britishness of British Asian identity precludes such concerns, or at least alters them.

That in both Srivastava's novels the central female protagonist is ultimately confronted by the unsavoury elements of Western norms of premarital sex and promiscuity might be read as comment on Srivastava's part about the limited pleasure to be gained through Western practices, and in particular their feminist discourses. Yet the universalising of the women's experiences calls this into question. Neither Angie nor Mira turn to the values of their Asian community, conventionally portrayed as more conservative, as an alternative. Indeed, in the novels there is little sense that belonging to the Asian community is at odds with the behaviour of women like Mira and Angie. Despite the use of first person narratives in both books, there is little detailed reflection, and the women rarely consider their behaviour in relation to their Asian backgrounds. This questions stereotypical readings of Asian women as less sexually adventurous, more passive, and submissive to traditional cultural practices. Rather it is suggested there is no difference between young British Asian women and other comparable individuals from different ethnic backgrounds.

What then does an ethnic perspective offer? If not an explicit challenge to Western behaviour, nevertheless Srivastava's novels do interrogate Western romantic discourses. Despite their concern for heterosexual relationships, both Mira and Angie are alone at the end of the novels. Or, at least, they are without heterosexual partners. Instead they maintain strong connections based on alternative alliances which supersede, ultimately, heterosexual partnerships. In *Transmission*, this takes the form of conventional female friendship. Angie ends the novel not with Lol, who has returned to his wife, but with Maggie, who counters Angie's depression with the statement "'You're twenty-five, you've got soul, and you're driving a Porsche' ... What do you want?'" (266) In *Maya*, the alternative comes in the form of Mira's closest friend being a gay man, Frank. In the first instance, Srivastava continues the lesbian continuum represented so strongly by Randhawa. In particular, the AIDS context of *Transmission* offers female relationships as a power-ful alternative to the dangers of heterosexual encounters: the friendship between Angie and Maggie hints towards a lower-risk emotional connection which is not simply platonic love but also exists, by extension, within the context of lesbian sex-ual practices. In *Maya*, through Frank, Srivastava extends the lesbian continuum to offer alternative models of non-sexual relationships, in which even male/female relationships work most productively outside of sexual relations, subtly question-ing the heterosexism of romance writing.

In both cases, these endings reject conventional romantic resolutions, centred on the successful heterosexual union, with what could be read as feminist alternatives. According to Regis conventional romance offers eight core elements: social context, initial meeting, barrier to union, attraction, declaration, insur-mountable problem, means of resolution and finally, betrothal,[7] so that the question is 'more how they will get together, than whether they will'.[8] Both of Srivastava's novels offer the ear-lier stages of romance, but both also culminate with the failure of the quest: the books end with the insurmountable prob-lem (what Regis calls 'ritual death') as the hero, who must be transformed in conventional romances if they are to succeed, is proven unalterable.[9] That obstacles such as existing mar-riages cannot be overcome reflects the realism of British Asian novels, offering messy realities in which the entanglements of the central protagonists are complicated to such an extent by contemporary living that they cannot be so easily swept away. More significantly, both novels are ambivalent about whether such resolution is, indeed, a 'failure' at all. A romance may pro-vide alternatives to happy resolution in tragedy, as in *Romeo and Juliet* or *Wuthering Heights*, but neither *Transmission* nor *Looking for Maya* is tragic, and there is in neither Mira nor Angie the kind of angst which preoccupies Bridget Jones.[10]

This is not the place to consider complex readings of the gender implications of romance novels and the status of the genre as both the most popular type of fiction and simultaneously the most maligned.[11] Needless to say, there is no consensus over the ideological impact of romance novels, which have been read not only as encouraging patriarchy, but also as possible statements of female fantasy allowing the expression of prohibited desires: 'more a sign of women's dissatisfaction with their social lot, of their unfulfilled desires, than a confirmation of their passive anti-feminism'.[12] Thus I do not want to suggest something as narrow as Srivastava's novels being more empowering for women (which would require detailed research into reader-response), but rather simply that they offer more explicit models of female independence than are presented by some of their counterparts. Indeed, Srivastava maintains much of the fantasy that is a positive escape for women, and good examples of the strong heroines who in particular have been emphasised in recent positive readings of contemporary romantic fiction. Yet her work also counters potential criticisms of the genre by firmly limiting the eventual role of romance in the lives of her central protagonists. If, for example, we take Regis's identification of two major criticisms of the genre – that, firstly, it 'extinguishes its own heroine, confining her within a story that ignores the full range of her concerns and abilities ... and denies her independent goal-oriented action outside of love and marriage' and, secondly, that it 'binds readers in their marriages or encourages them to get married: it equates marriage with success and glorifies sexual difference' – then clearly Srivastava's novels do neither of these things.[13] While both Mira and Angie are looking for love, this is not to the detriment of their careers; while both follow a desire for heterosexual monogamy, this is framed by, in both cases, involvement with married men who ultimately prove the instability of marriage and a less than ideal reality.

Srivastava's subtle subversions, therefore, come equally from a feminist as an Asian perspective. Such intervention means that Srivastava needs to be noted not just for her representation of Asian identity, but perhaps even more so for her contribution to the romance genre. In particular, when categorised as 'chick lit', considering her work offers an interesting example of the dialogue with feminism identified in this fiction more generally.[14] Whereas 'chick lit' is represented on the whole as having an ambivalent relationship to feminist politics, Srivastava suggests a more active role for this fiction in continuing the role of an earlier 'feminist bestseller'. The elements of abortion and unhappy marriage that were central to these texts are precisely the difficulties Srivastava's protagonists negotiate;[15] like these earlier feminist figures,[16] Srivastava's protagonists, too, relocate themselves outside the home and in the public space, while much 'chick lit' returns them to it.[17] Whereas 'chick lit' on the whole proves that men and domestic success are the true means to happiness, Srivastava's protagonists find their happiness elsewhere.[18] Srivastava's work in this sense again is the natural offspring of the Asian Women Writers' Collective, whose aims bore similarities to the consciousness-raising groups out of which many feminist bestsellers developed. It may be, therefore, that whereas 'chick lit' in general has disassociated itself from obvious politics, the politics of race has meant writers such as Srivastava are the natural inheritors of this role.[19] Avoiding a third-wave feminism which takes politics for granted and produces a blasé attitude towards gender, the continued struggles of race offer a unique perspective of the continued gender inequalities of contemporary British society.[20]

The 'ease of presence'

Srivastava's universal romance narratives at the same time make an important point about the contemporary reality of being British Asian. The identity crises of earlier British Asians – whether migrants or British born – have been replaced by what Darcus Howe calls an 'ease of presence', challenging representations of British Asians as in any sense alienated, disaffected, or caught between competing cultures.[21] It is not that ethnic identity does not feature in the lives of these individuals, but rather that it has become a minor concern within the complex dynamics of urban contemporary living. That romantic desires supersede ethnic concerns indicates a world in which ethnicity no longer looms large on the horizon of British Asian women.

One of the ways in which this ease manifests itself in Srivastava's novels is in playful or irreverent reference to ethnicity. *Transmission* may begin in conventional migrant terms with a discussion of Angie's experiences of racism, the cultural implications of 'black girls with straightened hair' (14), and threats of skinheads. Yet Angie rejects the implications of this world; she dismisses the black power politics that her friend Maggie is involved in. Such a negotiation is a metaphor for the book as a whole. There is a political story to be told, Maggie seems to suggest, a narrative which would reflect the growing black political consciousness of the 1970s and 1980s out of which her actions come. But there is also an alternative narrative which may re-frame ethnic experience outside these terms. And it is this latter narrative that Srivastava presents. That Angie is the only individual not politically involved, preferring instead what is described by her friends as 'a world of superficial manners and trendy people' (9) indicates that ethnic narratives need not necessarily be political and, indeed, that political narratives are not to be found only in the province of the postcolonial. This irreverence towards racism is embodied in Angie's relationship with Lol. Previously a skinhead involved in racial violence, Lol provides the perfect opportunity for an in-depth discussion of racism. But instead, Angie accepts Lol's past with little comment. Romance, and the power of sexual attraction, supersedes politics so that when Lol recounts his racist past, Angie responds:

> I thought about it for a second. Nothing. I didn't know anything about it. And I couldn't have cared less whether this man was an imperialist in the Raj, or a skinhead in the seventies. (64)

Equally, in *Maya* Mira rejects the concepts of ethnic and cultural studies that would connect her to a migrant past. No more political than Angie, she dismisses the relevance of migrant experience. While her parents believe 'there was nothing stronger than the umbilical cord of the past', Mira is instead 'constantly on the lookout for getting swamped by an alien culture' (89): India is 'alien', the past disconnected from the present. This is evident in Mira's discussion with Amrit on the concept of 'Race memory' – the idea that the 'memory of your ancestors lingers in your blood or something like that, engraved in a deep memory'. While Amrit says this 'makes sense', Mira instead declares 'it sounds like nonsense ... You can only remember what happened for real. All the rest is suggestion and fantasy' (41). The idea of a homing desire which unites British-born and migrant under the banner of diaspora is rejected: Mira is not looking to go 'home', she situates herself precisely where she is, and in the present moment. The starkly conventional realist style of narrative chosen by Srivastava embodies this reality: anything outside of the tangible and immediate is fantasy.

In this world, prejudice has not disappeared; rather it has been replaced by an underlying hostility or more commonly a passive disinterest and ignorance, which means in *Transmission* that the neighbours do not understand the fireworks of Diwali but are 'too polite to investigate the ritual' (49). But this ignorance is largely something to be laughed at rather than feared; nicknamed STVs: safe Tory votes (50), these individuals are rendered pathetic.

Such irreverence represents confidence that is the most tangible evidence of an ease of presence. A 'successful television researcher on the way up' (8), Angie is neither alienated not oppressed. Her comment that she 'knows nothing about' the racism Lol describes presents a generation who have been the beneficiaries of earlier struggles, and whose disinterest marks the success of these struggles. This is reflected in Angie's brother: his request to his mother for his 'Paki lunch' (166) betrays a confidence that allows racist terminology to be reclaimed in the service of comedy. In the same way, Mira, we are told, studies postcolonial literature – 'Naipaul and Rushdie and Desai' – yet doesn't attend lectures, and uses the notes on 'Race Deconstruction' she is given only to line her underwear drawers (21). Such detail is explicit comment on the failure of postcolonial frameworks to engage with a British-born generation. One might assume that Mira would be interested in such subjects. Yet, in reality, they hold little appeal, and are less relevant than the more immediate and personal concerns of socialising and relationships. The novel she is going to write, we are told, will not be 'the Great Immigrant novel' (28). This reflects a wider concern in *Maya* with the nature of such 'representative fiction': Amrit, although he is an academic who sympathises with many of the theories that Mira rejects, similarly is negative about the association of fiction with the identity of the author:

> Amrit said that these days victimhood was in vogue, either it was black or female or working class. He said that literature was being written by barbarians, it had become a cheap and shameless public relations racket. (46)

Directly engaging with the burden of representation, Srivastava moves towards a post-ethnic narrative that questions the unproblematic association of author and subject: all of her novels and short stories, too, present characters who move easily in multicultural environments as 'citizen[s] of the world'; the narrator of Srivastava's short story, 'Dragons in E8', is white.[22] Mira herself negotiating this burden adds a more explicit comment. Facing a publishing world in which 'Asian writing was in vogue' (68), Mira's identity as a 'Pukka Indian Writer' makes her feel 'like a pretender on all three counts' (173).

'Love-in' the city

If universalising the romance narrative feeds into British Asian confidence through an assertion of presence, then subverting these narratives feeds into the same confidence in different terms. As love is proved disappointing, what takes its place is geographical affiliation. Against the disappointed promise of heterosexual romance, personal identification with place offers a more powerful relationship, and an easier route to a positive sense of self.

In Kailash Puri's poem, 'Circle Line' (2000), the British Asian claims London through an accurate negotiation of urban space and, more specifically, through knowledge of transport networks:

> I like the circle line:
> whichever way it goes
> the destination is always mine.[23]

The Circle Line, with the impossibility of going the wrong way, stands as a metaphor for a confident British Asian youth sensibility, where whatever choice is made is positive and affirming. In both of Srivastava's novels a romantic engagement with setting – London – is similarly used by the author to indicate the belonging of her central characters.

In Srivastava's narratives, the double-voicing of Naipaul and Rushdie is eroded in favour of characters who share the author's confidence. Her characters display their confident movement around the city: the Finsbury Park of the Victoria Line (*Transmission* 79), the 73 bus to Stoke Newington Church Street (*Transmission* 82), Mira's 'jumping the trains without a ticket' (*Maya* 3), waiting for the number 30 in Tottenham Court Road (*Maya* 21). Mira claims London assertively, declaring it '*my* beautiful city' (my emphasis, *Maya* 2), emphasised later in the novel when she reasserts this: 'rediscovering my city' (*Maya* 68). *Transmission* marks not just the famous landmarks, but the routes between them: between Shaftesbury Avenue and Denmark Street (57), St Anne's Court connecting Wardour Street and Dean Street (88), the route between Wardour Street and Shaftesbury Avenue (259). The same is true of *Maya* – the opening page with Soho with Greek Street opposite, Bar Italia,

Ronnie Scott's Jazz Club, Maison Bertaux (1) immediately announces a deep understanding of the city. Mira traces Soho Square with its four pathways (14), the Charing Cross Road (19) with the Electric Ballroom and Foyles and Burger King, Tottenham Court Road with its Habitat and Heals (20–1, 68).

What Angie and Mira embody through such movement is not simply an ease of presence, but also a legibility of the urban space. In his groundbreaking 1960 study *The Image of the City*, Kevin Lynch outlines a practice for the reading of urban spaces. Cities, he suggests, have a quality of legibility: they can be read through their paths, structures and landmarks. Some cities are more legible than others, and Lynch's aim is to expose for planners and architects features that might allow legibility to most easily occur. Inherent in Lynch's discussion is the sense that legibility comes with belonging and a sense of ownership. It is the citizen, and his or her 'long associations with some part of his city' that best reveals how legible an individual space is.[24] It is not a matter of the outsider, Lynch continually tells us, but of the knowledge of the inhabitant. Legibility can only be achieved, even in the most legible spaces, by being a permanent inhabitant of that space. This is further reinforced by Lynch's assertion that the image of the city held by the individual is the product not only of immediate, but also past, experience.[25] What is of particular interest in terms of the British Asian representation of space is that Lynch identifies having a clear image of the city as holding definite benefits for the individual. Lynch suggests that 'a clear image of the surroundings is ... a useful basis for individual growth' – it allows exploration that offers the possibility of personal development.[26] Equally, it facilitates belonging, and allows entry into a communal identity that would otherwise be denied:

> A vivid and integrated physical setting, capable of producing a sharp image, plays a social role as well. It can furnish the raw material for the symbols and collective memories of group communication. A striking landscape is the skeleton upon which many primitive races erect their socially important myths. Common memories of the 'home town' were often the first and easiest point of contact between lonely soldiers during the war.[27]

Finally, it gives a sense of confidence – an 'emotional security' which allows a 'harmonious relationship between himself [or herself] and the outside world'.[28]

In this sense, legibility offers the British-born citizen, with his or her firm knowledge, a sense of belonging and possibilities of personal development that are denied to the migrant, whose comparatively short-lived experience lacks the same intense relationship to the urban space held by the indigene:

> People with least knowledge ... tended to think of the city in terms of topography, large regions, generalized characteristics, and broad directional relationships. Subjects who knew the city better had usually mastered part of the path structure: these people thought more in terms of specific paths and their interrelationships. A tendency also appeared for the people who knew the city best of all to rely more upon small landmarks and less upon either regions or paths.[29]

Both Maya and Angie exhibit conventional cultural capital that facilitates such confidence, knowledge of popular reference points allowing them to relate to their surroundings. Yet what is owned here might also be described as *urban capital*.[30] Angie and Maya are not just Londoners: they are North Londoners who understand the complexities of London identity, Angie recognising a Kensington accent (124), Mira detailing the geography of her childhood haunts (11). Such insider status is acknowledged in *Transmission* by the contrast between Angie and her boss Madeline, an American:

> 'I came here when I was five ...'
> 'Oh, but you're British now. I mean that's a real cockney accent you've got.'
> 'I grew up in North London. Kathi's a cockney. She's from the East End,' (152)

Madeline, as outsider, can locate a Londoner, but the specifics of this cultural identity are lost to her. In contrast, Angie negotiates such complexities with ease.

Equally, Mira is represented as having far greater urban knowledge than her white boyfriend Luke, who 'didn't know about the Kings Road or the Marquee in Wardour Street' (3). That Mira can feel more at home than the white male – seemingly privileged in terms of both gender and race – announces a reversal of traditional hierarchies, and a challenging of assumptions about what facilitates belonging. One passage of *Maya* exemplifies both Mira's privileged position, and her delimiting of an accurate geography, which is not just generalised London, but a detailed and specific territory:

> I smiled, because it was I who had begun Luke's introduction to London with the famous words about being tired of London and being tired of life. He'd grown up in Brighton, he'd only seen London on day trips and then only the London of tourists. I had shown him

the pockets of London that he had never imagined could be true. The little countries inside the capital. I'd taken him to Wembley full of aspiring Gujeratis in Mercs, to Green Lanes dotted with Cypriots sitting in darkened rooms playing cards, Finsbury Park thrumming with Nigerian taxi drivers who said, 'I dihnk I no you from somewhere, befour.' The Spanish tapas bar in Camden Town, the Jewish bagel bakery in Golders Green, the Irish fish and chips in The Free Republic of County Archway. 'How come we never cross the river?' Luke had asked. 'What river?' I'd said. There was only North London and Soho. All the rest, the West and the East and the South, was all propaganda. (19)

Mira is not ethnic, but the tour guide to those who are. The 'little countries' she introduces to Luke suggest ethnic groups who belong: who have claimed their part of London and reformed it for their own purposes. That there is only North London to Mira announces her own stake in such a project, her existence within a pluralist multiculturalism of complementary but discrete communities. Her confidence to negotiate these areas suggests there is nothing to be feared by such spaces: at the same time that they have their own individual character, they are open to the wider human traffic of London – they are not closed or isolationist, but rather acknowledge a commitment to cultural diversity. This is a more positive rendering of the black British world of exclusive postcodes and ethnic enclaves: rather than gangs or ghettos, here are communities in their most productive sense.[31]

Reflecting Bhikhu Parekh's 'community of communities', Srivastava's vision of the city centre is a space in which the different cultures of the wider city mix effortlessly and the communities of London as a whole fuse – the Soho of *Maya* is 'full of different cultures' (1). In *Transmission* it is Kathi that embodies this fusion: she uses 'the same words as the black girls in Stoke Newington' but her accent is 'pure East End' (85). The mixed-race romantic relationships in both novels are the most physical representation of such cultural combination, however. Mira's relationship with Luke, and Angie's relationship with Lol, are both represented as largely unproblematic: there is little sense of a racist reaction to their public displays of affection, or communal pressure to resist such relationships as are commonly offered in discussions of inter-racial relationships in the romance genre.[32] This lack of hostility is cemented by the actual pleasure of being involved in such a relationship, as Mira and Luke find it 'enjoyable to be looked at together', 'making a creature which was IndianEnglish' (3). Yet it also offers, in the suggestion of not just cultural but potentially racial hybridity, the possibility of a permanent blending of backgrounds through the act of procreation. Indulging obviously in the expression of this mixing represents a conscious desire to challenge and subvert any last remaining racial prejudices, striking at the heart of the fear of 'interbreeding' as the last bastion of racist ignorance from both white and Asian perspectives. When Luke and Mira are photographed for a magazine article on Londoners they are described as 'Interesting looking people' (4), more fashionable than frightening, more representative of a fusion of different kinds of insiders than marginal and dominant cultures. Such binaries are irrelevant in the city, it seems. The nature of this experience can be starkly contrasted with the lives of early migrants, who encountered extreme hostility when embarking on relationships with white Britons.

It is this complexity which means that such cultural fusions do not necessarily sit well with the discourses that postcolonial criticism largely interprets them through. Although Mira's and Angie's relationships announce desire for cultural fusion, their need for location and their privileging of individual cultural identities stresses the firm situating of such experiences within a familiar and claimed territory. Mira, in particular, is not 'much of a traveller' (171) and the detailed London geography of *Maya* suggests an intimate relationship to the city. This is not so much hybridity as what David Hollinger refers to as 'rooted cosmopolitanism', not the unemotional movement of the continual wanderer, but rather a more engaged, located acceptance of difference.[33] Such a model is intrinsically more suited to Srivastava's gendered concerns. As Mira Nava argues, the classical cosmopolitan model is inherently male, while the female cosmopolitan embodies an experience that, in her words, is more 'intimate and visceral'.[34] Whereas cosmopolitanism as a model represents the individual as a 'citizen of the world, free from national limitations and prejudices', the female cosmopolitan only represents the first part of this equation: a citizen drawing from world culture, but not necessarily at the expense of personal spatial identifications and allegiances.[35] *Maya* also reflects the particular quality of London itself as a space of rooted cosmopolitanism: a space of belonging precisely because of its belief in diversity. The relationship between Mira and Luke captures precisely Nava's definition of cosmopolitanism. Mira and Luke indulge positively in their differences: they do not attempt to erase the contrasts between them, but celebrate

them, reflecting Nava's conclusion that while focus on difference may promote racism and prejudice, at the same time it can
also foster 'commitment to an imagined inclusive transnational
community'.[36] Such representation offers an interesting engagement with the debates surrounding Britishness, social cohesion,
and multiculturalism – while multiculturalism often promotes
social exclusion at the expense of cohesion, here the maintenance of discrete differences promotes qualities of tolerance
and cultural vibrancy essential to London's positive atmos-
phere. That pluralism rather than integrationist discourse has
such positive results interrogates those speaking for the latter:
it is in respecting difference, it seems, that London facilitates
space for cultural exchange.

Such confidence has greater significance given the gendering
of Srivastava's narrative. Not only does the self-assurance of her
protagonists challenge representations of migrant experience,
it at the same time interrogates the specifically female migrant
experience as represented in novels such as *Brick Lane*, parallel
in terms of location and time. The gender politics of Srivastava's
novels mirrors their racial politics. The female Mira is not just
an ethnic *flâneur*, but a female one, challenging from a feminist
perspective the spatial exclusion of women and, in particular,
the historical hostility towards women inhabiting public space.
Conventionally, the ideology of separate spheres developed in
the nineteenth century located women in the domestic, private
space, with men given freedom instead to negotiate and enjoy
the public arena. That a female *flâneur*, a *flâneuse*, was historically inconceivable has been well documented, most famously
in the work of Janet Wolff, which stresses the historical impossibility of women wandering, alone, and without purpose, in
the urban space.[37] In this context, the wandering of Srivastava's
central female protagonists marks the contemporary possibility
of this role for women. Mira here is a kind of contemporary *flâneur*, wandering and looking in the urban space, like Baudelaire
using the city to both drive and relieve a 'search for meaning'[38]
but also, in her confidence, making herself 'the self-proclaimed
and self-believing monarch of the crowd'.[39] She can take a
'circuitous route' from Dean Street, to Shaftesbury Avenue, to
Leicester Square (26), announcing herself an insider with the
ability to negotiate the city's non-linear pathways, to consider
walking as leisure and as pleasure, rather than the fraught and
often perilous journey of the migrant.

At the same time, the ethnic female re-works *flânerie* in her own terms. Whereas, like the migrant, Baudelaire's wandering is rooted in the desire to be at home anywhere, for the British Asian female *flânerie* becomes a more located activity which represents precisely the dynamics of rooted cosmopolitanism.[40] The confidence and aimlessness of the *flâneur* may be maintained, but the *flâneuse* is less detached than her male counterpart. Mira and Angie are *flâneurs* in London because they know and identify with its geography. There is no suggestion that they have the same relationship to other urban spaces. Such an alternative exists in both negative and positive terms. On the one hand, it suggests women still are denied the unlimited pleasures of men, their freedom determined by a necessary sense of familiarity. On the other hand, however, it also posits a positive re-working of the more abstract and unemotional masculine undertakings of *flânerie* while, at the same time, revealing that such actions have their less idealised rendering in the dislocated and anxious wanderings of the migrant with which the actions of the British Asian must not be confused.

The gendered and racial aspects of Srivastava's novels directly enhance each other in these spatial terms. Linda McDowell makes this connection between the position of women and ethnic minorities in relation to space:

> This disruption of space through migration, of course, has parallels with women's position in the West, perhaps making more visible arguments from within feminism about women's awkward 'place' in the West. For women, too, were/are excluded by Western philosophical ideals, equally 'out of place' in that discursive space called the West.[41]

In the nineteenth century, urban space was explicitly identified as a space not only of male pleasure, but explicitly white male pleasure.[42] The fact that historically urban space is thus implicitly controlled by patriarchal Western interest means that Mira's subversion is a double one: disrupting the dual dominance of white and male discourses of space. The ways in which both Angie and Mira claim public space defies the colonial masculine discourse in which space is often rendered female, as in discourses of the nation which describe the national territory in terms of a female space to be conquered.[43] Instead of being conquered, both Mira and Angie conquer space: their confidence rejects the implicit association in colonial metaphors between space and the female. Equally, the 'circuitous routes' that Mira takes are a disruption of conventional modes of mapping that embody the white male's dominance of public space as they are 'encoded with a particular gender, class and racial positioning'.[44] Her relation to space renews the specifics, idiosyncrasies, physicality and emotion which are denied by the masculine project, an alternative mapping which stresses the journey over the abstract and static quality of the conventional map.[45]

Conclusion

Through her concerns with confident female protagonists, Srivastava extends the movement towards a more post-ethnic reality begun by Kureishi. Like his work, hers too challenges the assumptions of what constitutes a British Asian text. Yet by also working within the popular genre of romance fiction, Srivastava further destabilises the boundaries upon which literary fiction has conventionally relied. Through subtle subversion of Western romance, Srivastava's novels interrogate stereotypes of British Asian women, announcing a confident and independent contemporary identity.

Discussion

- To what extent, and for what purposes, does Srivastava subvert reader expectations of romance fiction?
- What picture does Srivastava offer of the reality of young British Asian women?
- Does Srivastava affirm or challenge the idea of a 'generation gap' between British-born Asians and their parents?

Notes

1 Srivastava, *Looking for Maya*, p. 3. Hereafter *Maya*. Subsequent references cited parenthetically.
2 Whelehan, *Feminist Bestseller*, p. 210, p. 214.
3 For a discussion of racism in *Transmission*, see Hand, 'How British are the Asians?'
4 Jackson, 'Women and Heterosexual Love', p. 51. The only noteworthy study is Parameswaran, 'Reading Fictions of Romance'.
5 Regis, *Natural History*, p. 109, p. 123.
6 See Bryce and Doko, 'Textual Deviancy'.
7 Regis, *Natural History*, p. 30.
8 Pearce and Stacey, 'Heart of the Matter', p. 16.
9 *Ibid.*, p. 17.
10 *Ibid.*, p. 17.
11 This is embodied in Bloom, *Bestsellers*, that declares romance one of

the two most popular genres, only to make it the only genre which does not receive its own chapter in his book.

12   Eagleton, 'Genre and Gender', p. 254. Radway's *Reading the Romance* is the most frequently cited defence of the genre.
13   Regis, *Natural History*, p. 10.
14   Whelehan, *Feminist Bestseller*, p. 5.
15   *Ibid.*, p. 7.
16   *Ibid.*, p. 151.
17   *Ibid.*, p. 172, p. 195.
18   *Ibid.*, p. 214.
19   *Ibid.*, p. 159.
20   *Ibid.*, p. 169.
21   Cited in Phillips and Phillips, *Windrush*, p. 388.
22   Srivastava, 'Dragons', p. 4.
23   Puri, 'Circle Line', p. 125.
24   Lynch, *Image of the City*, p. 1.
25   *Ibid.*, p. 4.
26   *Ibid.*
27   *Ibid.*
28   *Ibid.*
29   *Ibid.*, p. 49.
30   This term was coined by Philip Cavalier, 'Urban Capital: Henry James, William Dean Howells, and Beyond', Conference Paper Presented at *The Idea of the City: Early Modern, Modern, and Post-Modern Locations and Communities*, Northampton University, 8 June 2007.
31   For discussion see Upstone, 'Negotiations of London as Imperial Urban Space'.
32   See Nkweto Simmonds, 'Love in Black and White'.
33   Hollinger, *Postethnic America*, p. 5.
34   Nava, *Visceral Cosmopolitanism*, p. 8.
35   *Ibid.*, p. 5.
36   *Ibid.*, p. 13.
37   Wolff, 'The Invisible *Flâneuse*'; 'The Artist and the *Flâneur*'; 'Gender and the Haunting of Cities'.
For a contrary reading see Wilson's critique of Wolff, 'The Invisible Flâneur'.
38   Tester, 'Introduction', p. 7.
39   *Ibid.*, p. 4.
40   *Ibid.*, p. 3.
41   McDowell, 'Spatializing Feminism', p. 39.
42   D'Souza and McDonough, 'Introduction', p. 2.
43   See McClintock, *Imperial Leather*.
44   Kirby, 'Re: Mapping Subjectivity', p. 46.
45   *Ibid.*, p. 47.

Further reading

Sheila Ghose, '"Young, Gifted and … Brown!": British Asians Getting Real in Atima Srivastava's *Transmission*', in Neil Murphy and Wai-Chew

Sim (eds), *British Asian Fiction: Framing the Contemporary* (New York: Cambria, 2008), pp. 255–72.

Felicity Hand, 'Shaking Off Sharam: the Double Burden of British Asian Women', in Fernando Galván and Mercedes Bengoechea (eds), *On Writing (and) Race in Contemporary Britain* (Alcalá: University of Alcalá, Spain, 1999), pp. 133–8.

5

Nadeem Aslam

We have seen that Orientalism is very much alive in contemporary cultural practice. All of its main tropes have been seamlessly integrated into modernity. While it is not a monolithic discourse, Orientalism does demonstrate a consistent character throughout history. It has different stylistic moments, diversity of opinions, changing fashions and emphasis. Nevertheless, it has reworked itself from one historical epoch to another.[1]

Nadeem Aslam, more than any other author discussed in this book, represents the complexities of British Asian authorship. In his three novels, *Season of the Rainbirds* (1993), *Maps for Lost Lovers* (2004), and *The Wasted Vigil* (2008), Aslam fuses conventional postcolonial themes and literary techniques with a distinctly British sensibility. Born in Gujranwala, Pakistan, in 1966, Aslam came with his parents to Britain at the age of fourteen, where the family settled in Huddersfield, West Yorkshire. Since leaving, Aslam has never returned to Pakistan. He has described himself as 'a Pakistani man living in Britain'.[2] Yet, elsewhere, he is described as 'Pakistani-British'.[3] This personal history embodies his dual positioning as both British Asian and postcolonial migrant author. While Aslam's first and third novels are largely 'postcolonial' works, his second novel – *Maps* – is a profound intervention that more than any other marks the shift from the 'Asian cool' of the 1990s to post-9/11 concerns with British Muslim alienation.

Substance and style

In many senses, Aslam, rather than embodying the qualities of British Asian fiction, is part of the publishing storm surrounding postcolonial writers which developed in the 1990s. *Rainbirds* was accepted by Andre Deutsch as an unsolicited manuscript in ten days, and won both the Betty Trask Award and the Authors' Club First Novel Award. That the 1993 paperback edition of the novel carries a quotation from Salman Rushdie describing it as 'one of the most impressive first novels of recent years' associates Aslam with the highly lucrative genre of postcolonial magical-realism, and *Rainbirds* was marketed to exploit this association, promising the reader 'an exotic and timeless world'.[4]

Set in Pakistan in the 1980s, *Rainbirds* documents how one small community deals with the challenges of modernity and social change, paralleled with the larger upheaval of national political tensions. It can be read as the successor to Salman Rushdie's *Shame*, bringing the latter's critique of 1970s military rule in Pakistan forward into the 1980s. On this level, it is also an intensely personal reflection. Aslam's family fled to Britain when his poet and filmmaker father, a communist, was threatened by President Zia's regime, which also imprisoned his uncle.[5] Like *Shame*, the novel offers a critique of Zia's totalitarianism from the position of an exile sensibility, documenting amongst its domestic narrative the abuses of the political regime.

Comparisons with *Shame* also bear fruit when considering the very postcolonial style in which Aslam's critique is offered. As *Shame* makes use of a folklore narrative that allows a damning criticism less viable in more direct prose, so *Rainbirds* makes use of a highly lyrical and ornate prose style that not only allows comparisons with the magical-realist genre dominant in postcolonial fiction, but also establishes the influences of Aslam's Pakistani upbringing. Aslam draws heavily on the Urdu literary tradition in which he was raised, and in which he produced his first forays into writing as a young boy. Like many Urdu prose narratives, *Rainbirds* acts to 'protest and challenge the complacency of society'.[6] Echoing prominent tales in Urdu literature such as Ratan Nath Sarshar's *The Tale of Azad* (1880) modernity is juxtaposed with tradition, and the tensions between these positions exposed, producing a story with the same political concerns and moral didacticism as much Urdu prose.[7] Aslam shares with Urdu literature a preference for poetic language, highly detailed metaphors and copious use of imagery. *Rainbirds* is filled with the 'abstract nouns and lush adjectives' integral to the prevalence of poetry over prose in Urdu culture, and the latter's close reliance on the former's mode of expression.[8] One reason why Aslam's language can alienate the Western reader is that, again borrowing from Urdu literature, this highly poetic language is applied to everyday life.[9] Rivers appear 'like a silver thread'; mornings are bright 'as though the walls were draped in sheets of luminous cloth'.[10]

These Urdu influences continue to be dominant in *Maps*. Aslam says 'The book in many ways is about the classic theme of Islamic literature: the quest for the beloved. The book wouldn't be what it is without 1001 Nights, the Koran, Bihzad.'[11] Equally, the novel can be connected to the early Urdu novel form in verse called the *masnavi*, which often tells 'tragic stories of lovers'.[12] The language is even more poetic and ornate than in *Rainbirds*, even in the most violent of circumstances. The death of the lovers, for example, is framed by 'the sky turning the blood-red of anemones in the east'.[13] Moreover, the novel shares with its precursor and thus also with earlier Urdu tales a similar concern for the tensions between the relentless pace of change in modern society and religious values. Aslam's 2008 novel, *The Wasted Vigil*, continues this trend: a tragic and brutal story that traces the effects of a long history of global conflict on the lives of individuals in post-9/11 Afghanistan, the novel recounts scenes of torture with a lyricism that only serves to make the violence more painfully felt.

These properties make Aslam perhaps an exemplary 'postcolonial author'. The subject matter of *Maps*, however, indicates a distinct British Asian perspective, with Aslam himself describing the novel as 'an overview of race in Britain over the past 50 years'.[14] Winning the 2005 Kiriyama Award, the Encore Award for the best second novel of 2004, and longlisted for the Booker Prize, *Maps* continues Hanif Kureishi's concern with the tensions between strong religious belief and British liberal values. It reflects the fact that 'In the post-September 11 climate, British Muslims are at the forefront of questions that turn on what it means to be British or English.'[15] Focused on a Muslim 'honour killing' in a small, isolated British town, *Maps* is a coterminously violent and beautiful engagement with twenty-first-century British Muslim identity, at the same time that it continues to acknowledge Aslam's interest in issues of migration and his Urdu influences. Here, then, the principle of positioning identified in the introduction becomes of great significance: Aslam might be in terms of personal history better placed with Rukhsana Ahmad who describes herself as a 'British-based South Asian writer or a writer of Pakistani origin living in London', but his subject matter and the attitude towards this suggests a more complex cultural positioning.[16] *Maps* has more in common with the internalised focus on the British Asian community in *Brick Lane* and *Life Isn't All Ha Ha Hee Hee* than earlier migrant novels.

Maps of lost love

Maps is a novel about a community in isolation: not a vision of Bhikhu Parekh's 'community of communities', but a community refusing national identification. The setting of *Maps* is a small, unnamed, British town, where 'white-flight' has led to the formation of an entirely Muslim enclave.[17] The community's description of their location as 'Dasht-e-Tanhaii' both linguistically and hermeneutically signals their segregation, a theme which Aslam had already taken up in *Rainbirds*.[18] Named in Urdu, the community is linguistically outside of the British nation; translated as 'Wilderness of Solitude' or 'Desert of Loneliness' (*Maps* 29) the interpretation, equally, identifies a desolate space of remoteness and seclusion.

The oppressive nature of this seclusion is evidence of a representation of British Muslims notable for a distinct lack of subtlety or light and shade. Aslam's description of the honour killing in *Maps*' final pages represents the killers as brutal and unflinching. Two lovers, Chanda and Jugnu, are killed by Chanda's brothers. Yet in their murder this personal relationship is given no acknowledgement, as the brothers pursue what is represented as their religious ideology relentlessly. When she is dying, Chanda's brothers show no mercy or shock – they make no attempts to save her, despite the fact that her killing (unlike Jugnu's), is initially unintentional. Instead, they are emotionless, telling Chanda she must repent before dying, and then going on to brutally dismember her body, 'burning with the help of Sheridan's fuels, dismembering and burying her changeable eyes, her hair, the flesh orchid of her womb' (29).

The novel's predominant focus, however, is not the honour killing itself, but the attitudes of Jugnu's family members, in particular his brother Shamas and Shamas's wife Kaukab, who both migrated to Britain several decades earlier. Like the killers, Kaukab is presented as outside the realms of 'natural' behaviour. Her strained relationship with her children, all of whom have to different degrees adopted Westernised belief systems, posits her religious faith as a barrier to the natural bond between mother and child. This is offered in its most extreme form in a scene in which Kaukab starves her baby son by refusing to breastfeed him during daylight hours of Ramadan (40–1). Mah-Jabin describes her mother as 'the most dangerous animal she'll ever have to confront' (111). While Aslam does not universalise the immigrant experience, he uses Shamas and Kaukab to offer sharply delimited models of alternative world views. Shamas is liberal and westernised, while Kaukab is firmly rooted in strong religious beliefs, and her Pakistani traditions. Against the characterisation of Shamas as gentle, generous and humble, Kaukab's views are represented as uncompromising, harsh and filled with vitriolic hatred. She declares 'England is a dirty country, an unsacred country full of people with disgusting habits and practices' (267), describes her daughter as 'used goods' (110), and condemns the murdered couple as unclean (though she does not support their murder).

Such positing mimics directly media and government stereotypes of Islam: 'tolerance and freedom ... equated with the West, so too is liberalism, while illiberalism is imputed to Islam'.[19] Representation of Kaukab and the killers together means that the practising religious community gives no room to the appreciation of difference. There is no sense of a diverse Islam in *Maps* that would see the potential for the possibility for alternatives to violence *within* strong religious faith, despite the fact that Islam can equally be represented as a progressive and diverse religion.[20] Instead, as for Kureishi, the only alternative is to accept a secular western viewpoint. Against Kaukab's fundamentalism, the positive alternatives offered are her husband Shamas (amongst other things an adulterer) or her westernised children. As Kaukab debates her values with her children, her husband is firmly positioned in favour of the latter:

> it was obvious from the look on his face that he personally had no problem with what the children wanted. Sometimes Mah-Jabin wonders whether her mother knows Shamas at all. Shamas wouldn't object to her visiting America, she knows. (111)

In this respect, the interrogation of British Muslim identity in *Maps* lacks the subtlety of the engagement with broader Islamic belief in *Rainbirds* or *Vigil*. While *Maps* represents religious faith as singular and homogenous, *Rainbirds* offers space to competing versions of religious faith, as represented in the progressive mosque of Maulana Hafeez and an alternative run by the more mystical Maulana Dawood. It also allows for more ambiguity: Maulana Hafeez may want to fortify the town from outside influence, but he is also represented as a gentle and compassionate man. *Vigil* is in many ways similar to *Maps* in its representation of Islam, focused on the abuses of the Taliban and their supporters, which include the denial of teaching and medical treatment, suicide bombing, rape, stoning, the

reworking of Fascism, torture, abduction, and which culminate in the story of the central character of Marcus having his
hand amputated by his wife Qatrina, the latter forced into this
action for being an 'adulterer', her 39-year marriage unrecognised because the ceremony, although religious, was performed
by a woman. As in *Maps*, such acts are characterised by the
broader representation of Islam as a religion of intolerance,
focused on severe repression of women and artists, embodied
in clerics who murder their wives, and supported by reference
to the Koran. Nevertheless, against the fundamentalist support
of violence in the name of religion, Aslam in *Vigil* for the first
time introduces a character, Duria, who is devoutly religious,
and yet against such practices. Duria interrogates the indoctrinated young Afghan, Casa, and also David, the CIA officer: she
declares 'Muslims hate fundamentalism' and interrogates the
assumption that the US invasion was motivated by anything
other than revenge for 9/11.[21] That Duria is missing at the end
of the novel, unable finally to convince Casa of the immoral-
ity of his path, is a more poignant tragedy than that offered in
Maps, speaking as it does to a genuine alternative *within* Islam
that is being silenced by fundamentalist ideology. Moreover,
Vigil shows more awareness of the complexities of the development of fundamentalism; the real-world context of Afghanistan
allows Aslam to situate religious intolerance within the context
of both Soviet violence and American corruption, both of which
perpetrate crimes as heinous – if not as widespread – as those
enacted in the name of Islam. Marcus's awareness that 'the
West was involved in the ruining of this place' draws awareness to the complexities of global politics – shifting allegiances
and self-interest – and their painful consequences for innocent
lives.[22]

It is a lack of this powerful context that *Maps* suffers from.
The positive sense of Aslam's internal focus is that it does, as he
says, achieve his aim of 'not want[ing] to give the impression
– which most novels about immigration give – that interaction
with the often-hostile whites was all there was to an immigrant's life'.[23] The downside of this is that there is as a result
little contextualisation for the extreme behaviour which domi-
nates the novel. *Maps* is much more strongly delineated here
than Kureishi's fiction. By making clear the association between
Muslim violence and racism, Kureishi provides an important
social context, missing in Aslam's novel, which makes only passing reference to racial tensions. Most significantly, Kureishi's

critique is directed not against Islam specifically, but religion more generally. This important distinction is raised by Akash Kapur, who suggests that 'While Aslam will inevitably be compared to Monica Ali and Hanif Kureishi, two other authors who have chronicled the lives of South Asian Muslims in England, the psychological and emotional core of his novel is closer to that of Golding's "Lord of the Flies."'[24] Here, as in Golding's novel, there is a more sharply marked clash of opposing world views, and an apocalyptic breakdown of what is constructed as 'normal' and 'civilised'.

It is in terms of Aslam, therefore, that it would be neglectful not to address concerns about potential literary Islamophobia. This term, first coined in 1997 by The Runnymede Trust's report *Islamophobia: A Challenge for us All*, defines the practice of ingrained prejudices against Muslims rooted in negative stereotypes.[25] While this term in many ways reflects Aslam's representation of religious belief in the novel, it is Edward Said's earlier term Orientalism that perhaps better describes Aslam's attitude, pointing as it does to stereotypes with a historic presence. Although Said's seminal *Orientalism* (1978) initially focused on pre-twentieth-century European discourses, Said himself argued for their contemporary relevance in *Covering Islam* (1981). Aslam's transference of Orientalist attitudes to the Muslim population in Britain might be seen as the latest manifestation and reworking, therefore, of earlier European Orientalist attitudes, an example of 'internal orientalism' in which the imperial centre becomes the focus itself of the imperial gaze.[26]

In particular, Aslam's harsh treatment of Kaukab repeats an Orientalist vision. There is little difference between Aslam's critique of Kaukab for her fundamentalist views, and the attitudes of European colonialists who centred their attacks upon Islamic culture on women, 'colonialists for whom the veil and customs regarding women were the prime matters requiring reform ... saving women from the odious culture and religion in which they had the misfortune to find themselves'.[27] As the female protagonist, Kaukab's voice is as equally lost in Aslam's discourse as it would be in any fundamentalist regime in the Middle East. Like Gayatri Spivak's subaltern woman subject caught between nationalist and colonialist reform, there is little room in the novel for Kaukab to speak her own experience.[28] The solution is for her to give up her principles, it seems, and Aslam shows no awareness of the possibilities for feminist reform *within* Islam.[29] Near the end of the novel, the narrative

offers some insight into Kaukab's consciousness, and the alienation that consumes her as a Muslim in Britain. However, these
moments of sympathy provide little defence against the damning critique. That Muslims must be converted out of their beliefs
only plays to the universalising of Western values as 'normal',
with anything outside of this system deemed abhorrent.[30]

It is not Kaukab's attitudes or the honour killing alone,
it must be stressed, that make the novel open to charges of
Orientalism. Rather, the particulars of its content raise the most
questions. Aslam's representation of the honour killing is not
balanced by positive representations, but rather reinforced
with stories of sexual abuse, domestic violence and exorcism.[31]
As Kapur notes, 'Surrounding this main event [the honour
killing], like a ring of darkness, are other, no less gruesome
ones that appear almost as incidental details.'[32] In one incident,
unrelated to the plot, a holy man conducts an exorcism which
results in a young girl's death (186). In another incident, again
not directly related to the main narrative, the religious community's brutality is added to with a representation of their sexual
depravity, as a Muslim cleric is reported for sexually assaulting
young children under his tutelage (234–5). Here, an additional
Orientalist stereotype of the sexual threat of the Muslim 'other'
re-emerges.[33]

In both these cases, the narrative is keen to point out the failure of the local Muslim community to condemn such acts. The
cleric is supported by a petition, and the exorcism is contextualised by an expression of continued belief in Djinns, removed
from the Koranic context to further Orientalist stereotypes of
irrationality (245). The way in which Aslam describes these
events is also unique and thus of significance: in Kureishi's
The Black Album, the final tragic firebombing is only reported.
Consider, in contrast, how Aslam reflects upon the exorcism of
a young Muslim woman:

> The girl was taken into the cellar and the beatings lasted several
> days with the mother and father in the room directly above reading
> the Koran out loud. She was not fed or given water for the dura-
> tion and wasn't allowed to fall asleep even for five minutes, and
> when she soiled herself she was taken upstairs to the bathroom by
> her mother to be cleaned and brought back down for the beating to
> continue. The holy man heated a metal tray until it was red hot and
> forced her to stand on it ... According to the report in The Afternoon
> the coroner found the arms and legs broken by a cricket bat. The
> front of the chest had caved in as though she had been jumped on
> repeatedly. (185–6)

This singularly brutal representation is reinforced by the framing of Aslam's novel. Not describing a singular place, but rather a mythically referred to British location, means that the 'map' gestured towards in the book's title is a universal one, not linked to any specific community or incidence. It is, rather, a metaphor for the state of Muslims worldwide: 'this Dasht-e-Tanhaii called the planet Earth' (367). On one level, as suggested earlier, this is a statement of profound sadness, as it expresses a universal isolation and suffering. Yet on another level, given Aslam's lack of sympathy for the isolated Muslim community, it is also a statement of the universal, and unavoidable, threatening 'otherness' of Islam.[34] Such segregation is not the situation of most Muslims in Britain, and yet it reflects common perceptions of a Muslim refusal to engage with wider British society.[35]

Aslam's Orientalism has direct relevance to his straddling of British Asian and postcolonial identities. One can define Aslam's perspective as that of the 'Orientalized Oriental', 'one who physically resides in the "East" and sometimes in the West, yet spiritually feeds on the West. S/he announces her/himself to be "post-Oriental," or "postcolonial," yet is a practicing member of the "orientalizing" praxis in its daily operations'.[36] Like Aslam, the Orientalised Oriental associates the West with a 'grand model of civilisation' against which the native is constructed in binary opposition.[37] Such identification, however, relies upon seeing Aslam as a postcolonial author: a 'traitor', as it were, to a Muslim identity and Muslim nation defined as 'home'.[38] Yet Aslam's relationship to such classifications strongly illustrates how the old positions are no longer relevant: as both migrant and British Asian the categories of both 'native culture' and 'Western other' are profoundly complicated.

Maps of lost life

Given then the potentially offensive nature of Aslam's representation, one must ask why he has avoided the hostility directed at other British Asian authors. *The Economist* predicted that Aslam 'may be tempting the same fate as befell Salman Rushdie', and yet no such criticism emerged in the wake of the novel's publication.[39] Most reviews do not mention the potential controversy of the novel at all and, when they do, dismiss this: 'Islamists', we are told, 'would be foolish to try to make political mischief out of it'.[40] In fact, Kapur is the *only* reviewer of note to speak out at all against the novel's representation.[41] Instead, there has been a noted lack of questioning of the singularity of tone of Aslam's narrative. Why, then, is this?

The density of the novel, spanning over 350 pages, is in itself not enough to ensure a lack of attention: this did not help *The Satanic Verses*, often criticised by those who had not ever read the text. Two factors, however, explain such an absence of reaction. Firstly, the magical-realist quality of *Maps'* prose style obscures its intensely violent content, and masks its strong critique. Even in describing the novel, Aslam's style jars with the events he describes; wanting to provide a place for stories of British Muslims 'to coalesce onto like dew on the petals of a flower' presents a poetic framing obscuring the novel's violence, and thus the brutal associations made with Muslim identity.[42]

Secondly, Aslam has both in the novel itself and in commentary on it strongly refused to play the 'representation game' into which British Asian authors, like their black British and post-colonial counterparts, are often lured. Although the novel uses real life incidents, there is no mention of these in the novel's acknowledgements. Equally, in interview Aslam has distanced himself from any ideological discourse: he states: 'Writers have always got into trouble with people who think they know the answer … there's no message in my books. My writing is my way of exploring my own life and the workings of my own consciousness… there is no conscious attempt to be universal or relevant'.[43] Therefore, even though Aslam has made reference to Islamic fundamentalism in interviews, he frames this with an emphasis on the novel being a personal reflection:

> On the very first page of my first novel, I wrote about an adult who takes children's toys from them and hands them back broken. Islam forbids idolatry. Toys can be considered idols and are to be smashed. My uncle did that to me: he snatched from my hands a mask that I had just bought from a vendor in the street and tore it to bits. I can still remember my feelings of shock and incomprehension. My uncle's version of Islam was the same kind practised by the Taliban regime in Afghanistan three decades later. It would be state policy in the Taliban-ruled Afghanistan to ban children's toys, as well as music.[44]

Aslam's use of an unnamed locale gives his novel a mythical element which discourages real-world comparison. Set in the fictional town of Dasht-e-Tanhaii, it is harder for critics to claim that Aslam has 'misrepresented' a real-world community. As Rushdie's narrator declares in *Shame* that 'the country in this story is not Pakistan', so by setting his novel in an unnamed place

Aslam announces it to be removed from real-world concerns.[45] Of course, just like with Rushdie's *Shame*, this is explicitly not the case. Nevertheless, it does seem to have allowed Aslam to bypass the critical attention directed at other representations of Islam, most notably the attacks on Monica Ali after the publication of *Brick Lane*.

One final factor might also be considered, however. *Maps* famously took Aslam eleven years to write. Yet the book in its final form is very much a distinctly post-9/11 text. As Michael O'Connor emphasises: 'There are no terrorist bombs, nor Al-Qaeda links in Aslam's novel. Nothing as sensational, but rather a mosaic of violence on a smaller, local level, of intimidation, and murder.'[46] In Aslam's own words, the same transference is evident:

> Walking around Ground Zero last year the friend I was with asked me how I felt. Being there made me feel angry and disappointed with myself. Had I, as a human being and as a writer, done enough to expose and condemn the smaller-scale versions of 9/11 that go on in Islamic societies every day? If me and people like me had acted earlier, discouraged and prevented those smaller crimes, then perhaps the criminals wouldn't have had enough strength and opportunity to plan and execute the mass murder of 9/11.[47]

To consider *Maps* as Orientalist, therefore, neglects the very specific circumstances in which it was produced. Aslam uses violence at a domestic scale to reflect on the dangers of international terrorism and the threat of fundamentalism on a larger scale; not only its violence and dogma, but the fact that the novel presents a community which will do *anything* for their interpretation of their faith, seems particularly resonant in the post-9/11 period. One might speculate that, before 9/11, the final version of *Maps* might have been somewhat different, with more room for sympathy with its British Muslim protagonists, and more room for a more diverse vision of British Muslim identity.

In the wake of 9/11, media and government representation has been widely noted by critics to have constructed a Muslim 'other', a foreign invader who would challenge the 'safe space' of a Western society represented as embodying ideas of civilisation and humanity. Shamas and Kaukab's oppositions, as westernised liberal and religious fundamentalist respectively, are a direct transference of these oppositions to a personal setting: a world today in which 'Muslims are forced into two set categories – "terrorist" or "apologist"'.[48] In Britain, this discourse surrounding the outsider quickly evolved to become a concern with Britain's own British Muslim population.[49] The British Muslim becomes a figure of what Cindi Katz refers to as 'banal terrorism' in which discourses of the threat of the 'other' are transferred to everyday settings, with a simplistic, stereotyped ethnically and racially different threat emphasised and pervading ordinary life:

> Banal terrorism also produces and reproduces common sense themes about what constitutes a terrorist. The common sense is predictably racist and also ignorant. It conflates Islam and Arabs to embrace all brown men no matter what their national origins or religious beliefs.[50]

In this sense, terrorism is no longer distant: media and government discourses encourage the sense of a direct and all-pervasive threat entering the minutiae of ordinary life, 'everyday, routinized, barely noticed reminders of terror or the threat of an always already presence of terrorism in our midst'.[51] All Muslims, rather than the few, become subject to this stereotype, as in the wake of 9/11 in Britain 'by extension, all Muslims in the West were thus being marked as potential, if not actual, terrorists'. [52]

In Aslam's bleak vision British Muslims are no longer part of the Asian diaspora in Britain. Rather, they are a separate group: alienated, disenfranchised, 'a virtual underclass in Britain'.[53] Here Aslam's focus not on racism but rather on the need for the British Muslim community itself to address the issues of fundamentalism is largely in line with post-9/11 discussion in both the general media, but also in the Muslim community itself. With no focus upon either the misguided morality driving the brothers, or their disassociation from the true teachings of Islam, they become not individuals, but representatives of the faith. This echoes the way in which media discourse chose post 9/11 to identify the crimes' perpetrators as representative of Islam, rather than as misguided, socially alienated, or manipulated individuals.[54] In such circumstances, the humour attached to representations of Islamic fundamentalism in the British Asian community in *The Black Album* or, outside the British Asian authorial community, in Zadie Smith's *White Teeth*, would seem deeply inappropriate. Yet that *Maps* supports the rhetoric of Islamophobic publications is equally unfortunate. Had a similar novel been produced before 9/11, critics might have been less reluctant to criticise its bleak vision. Equally, the Muslim community, in particular, might feel more able to be critical. In the wake of the 7 July 2005 Tube bombings, criticism seems even less likely, as Aslam's association between the British Muslim community and violence seems to have proven itself true.

Such awareness may for some provide a defence of *Maps*: in its particular context perhaps it is closer to the truth than liberal readers might like to admit. Aslam captures a particular moment of crisis, an apocalyptic fear that certainties have been shaken, which consumes not just British Asian literature post-9/11, but situates Aslam within wider literary trends. Turns of centuries are always moments for millennial fears of the apocalypse to gain strength, *fin de siècle* nightmares in which the end of the century gestures in the collapse of civilisations.[55] More directly, the threat of the foreign invader is often at the heart of these fears, as in the nineteenth century when fears of a *fin de siècle* apocalypse, at the height of Imperialism, in part focused on fears of the contamination and degeneration of white Europe.[56]

9/11 has provided the literary community with a solid and tangible event on which to latch such fears. Aslam's transference of violence to the level of the everyday is something he shares with John Updike's *Terrorist* (2006), but perhaps more notably Ian McEwan's *Saturday* (2005), which constructs a comparable parable in which the threat of foreign violence is displaced into a domestic struggle. While McEwan's central character Henry Perowne is an embodiment of supposed civilisation – a man, we are told, who 'likes precision', does not believe in God, and who 'doesn't know how to be reckless' – the man who threatens his home, Baxter, is the 'other' within: irrational, a sexual predator, and a biologically inferior 'savage' with a 'simian air' and a fatal genetically inherited disease.[57] Baxter has no notable race or religion, and it is easy to transfer his behaviour as 'a man who believes he has no future and is therefore free of consequences' to the attitude of the suicide bomber.[58] With Baxter presented as Perowne's own white man's burden who must be disabled and dealt with we are offered the same warning of the 'other' within that Aslam presents in more explicitly defined terms: these characters may not be terrorists in the sense of Updike's characters, but, just as his terrorist figure must 'see the light', so they are equally in need of 'saving' by what is presented as a benevolent and morally superior West.[59]

One does have to question, however, the social role of such representations. In reinforcing the view that 'differences in values have become tantamount to treason (or terrorism?) in

the new world order' how does Aslam feed into existing prejudices?[60] While British Asian fiction should not be pressured
into being 'representative', nevertheless literary fiction has
often been immune from the sort of criticism directed at the
media. This neglects the ideological role of literary texts, and
their place in informing public opinion. One needs to ask what
the effect is of representing a group in a particular way before
there is a legitimate reason for doing so. Although the Tube
bombings of 7 July 2005 did in some ways legitimise the sense
of an 'insider within', both McEwan's and Aslam's novels were
published before this event. To what extent, it might be asked,
does the construction of a group as dangerously 'other' before
an event that would provide motivation for such representation, condemn them to playing out such a role in the future? In
Britain, the vast majority of Muslims are not of Middle Eastern
origin, but South Asian. Yet their Muslim identity sees them
subject to the same representation as those from the Middle
East who have been subject to stereotyping because of 9/11 terrorism and events in Iran, Iraq and Afghanistan, both before
and after the terrorist attacks. These dynamics make the use of
Orientalism to describe the treatment of this group most appropriate: representing as it does the specific focus on the Muslim
'other', but at the same time the identification with the 'East'
integral to the contemporary stereotyping of Muslims (as with
anti-Arab racism), regardless of ethnic identity, as the stereotype of the 'dangerous Arab' is transferred to all who identify
with Islam.

In a large sense, therefore, the positioning that identifies Aslam
most strongly in terms of British Asian concerns, rather than
postcolonial ones, can be viewed as an unfortunate one, sharing the identification of strong religious faith with violence and
oppression offered by Kureishi, but in even more pronounced
and unsympathetic terms. A particularly interesting facet of this
representation is a distinction between the representation of
British Muslims and, alternatively, the representation of a different category which might be termed Muslims in Britain. The
latter offers a very different portrayal of Muslim life in the West,
represented in terms of peace, and certain and positive identity.
Most notable in this regard in works written in English is the
writing of Sudanese writer Leila Aboulela, whose novels span
the literary and the popular with the use of the romance genre
to debate issues of religious identity. Aboulela's first novel, *The
Translator* (1999), presents Islam as a non-threatening force that

'draws Western emptiness into a rooted Islamic-African core.[61]
The central protagonist Sammar's identity as a Muslim woman
is 'utterly vindicated' by the conversion of her potential love
interest Rae to Islam, the faith's significance emphasised by
this conversion being represented as a genuine coming to faith,
rather than a necessity for the relationship to survive.[62]

Equally, in Aboulela's second novel, *Minaret* (2005), the central character of Najwa, an exile from Khartoum, is a devout
Muslim whose faith is not the source of her confusion, but her
respite from it: emotionally lost in London, it is her recitation of
religious verses and the ever-present, ever-welcoming mosque
which provides relief even when she is at her lowest point.
Although the novel's ending is bleak, it is framed by acceptance
of religious principles as guiding one towards positive actions
of compassion, mercy and submission. Moreover, the central
male character, deeply interested in Islam, is distinguished from
the concept of terrorism: his involvement in the mosque and his
desire to study Islamic Studies do not make him a potential terrorist. Nor do those around him, such as his mother, approve of
this possible development:

> Once or twice he did sound fanatical, nagging me and Lamya to wear
> the hijab, making a fuss because I smoked – but he kept his limits,
> he was never extreme ... At times I worried that he was spending too
> much time at the mosque. Maybe, I thought, a terrorist group would
> mess up his mind and recruit him but thankfully he's not interested
> in politics, so that's a relief.[63]

For Aboulela the Muslim community is conscientious and
socially responsible: concerned about the dangers of radical-
ism, but firmly distinguishing this from devout faith. This offers
a much more sharply nuanced and complex sense of Muslim
identity: not simply secular versus terrorist, but with the possibility of devout, yet tolerant, modern, rational, and peaceful,
faith.

Conclusion

Ironically drawing comparisons with Said's *Orientalism*, Aslam
has produced a polemical text for polemical times. While that
might reduce the complexity of his representation, it does
undoubtedly strengthen his message. If Aslam does move close
to Orientalism, then one needs to ask whether this itself is a
problem, or whether the publishing industry, literary criticism,
and even the reading public, perhaps, are at fault for demanding

certain sorts of British Muslim narratives. As Yahya Birt accurately argues, 'In some other recently lauded fiction on British Muslims, the predominant motif of escape from traditional Islamic society and family through personal liberation and freedom only to be truly experienced in wider society, e.g. in Monica Ali's *Brick Lane* or Nadeem Aslam's *Maps for Lost Lovers*, seems to have become **the** story to be told in contemporary fiction about British Muslims.'[64]

Raised in Pakistan but residing in Britain for the entirety of his adult life, Aslam's lyrical narrative voice illustrates how child migrants may potentially repeat the liminal spacing of Rushdie and Naipaul between British Asian and postcolonial worlds. Approaching British Muslim identity from the position of simultaneous insider and outsider in relation to Muslim faith, but also as both migrant and British citizen, Aslam defines the complexities of postcolonial and British Asian positionings, and the lack of distinctness between them, while at the same time announcing a definite British Asian sensibility resulting in what is not simply a repetition of postcolonial narratives. Yet Aslam is also evidence of how to consider British Asian authors simply in relation to an ethnic literature (whether defined as British Asian, Black British, or postcolonial) is to neglect wider paradigms in contemporary literary fiction: not just British, but also international.

Discussion

- How might one construct a defence of *Maps for Lost Lovers* against accusations of Islamophobia?
- To what extent do Aslam's novels – in terms of both content and prose style – suggest that the concept of liminality is still relevant to the discussion of British Asian identity?
- In what ways do *Season of the Rainbirds*, *Maps for Lost Lovers*, and *The Wasted Vigil* represent a 'trilogy' on contemporary fundamentalist ideologies?

Notes

1 Sardar, *Orientalism*, p. 107.
2 Aslam, 'Nadeem Aslam on *Maps for Lost Lovers*'.
3 Weidner, 'Cosmos of Traditionalist Muslim Migrants'.
4 Back cover, 2005 Faber paperback edition. For the demand for an 'exotic' postcolonial literature see Huggan, *Postcolonial Exotic*.
5 See Rees, 'Nadeem Aslam'.

6   Rahim, 'Mirage of Faith and Justice', p. 231.
7   Russell, *Pursuit of Urdu Literature*, p. 87, p. 111, p. 209.
8   *Ibid.*, p. 11.
9   For criticism of Aslam's style, see Robson, 'The deadly honour'. For a positive appraisal of Aslam's style see Bhattacharya, 'Goodbye, young lovers'.
10   Russell, *Pursuit of Urdu Literature*, p. 10; Aslam, *Season of the Rainbirds* (London: Andre Deutsch, 1993), p. 12, p. 27. Hereafter *Rainbirds*. Subsequent references cited parenthetically.
11   'Nadeem Aslam on *Maps for Lost Lovers*'.
12   Russell, *Pursuit of Urdu Literature*, p. 83.
13   Aslam, *Maps for Lost Lovers* (London: Faber, 2004), p. 356. Hereafter *Maps*. Subsequent references cited parenthetically.
14   'Nadeem Aslam on *Maps for Lost Lovers*'.
15   Abbas, 'British South Asian Muslims', p. 16.
16   Author's interview, April 1999. Quoted in Schlote, 'Confrontational Sites', p. 87.
17   Some reviewers speculate the town is Huddersfield where Aslam grew up, however there is no specific indication of this.
18   In *Rainbirds*, Maulana Hafeez's solution to the town's modernisation is to fortify it (p. 130).
19   Esposito, *Islamic Threat*, p. 190.
20   See Sardar, 'Cultivating the Soil', *Emel Magazine*, September 2003, as quoted in Commission on British Muslims and Islamophobia, *Islamophobia: Issues, Challenges and Action,* p. 24; Ansari, *Infidel Within*, p. 2; Lewis, *Islamic Britain*, p. 25; Halliday, 'West Encountering Islam', p. 16; Sharify-Funk, 'From Dichotomies to Dialogues', p. 72, Safi, *Progressive Muslims*; Sayyid, *A Fundamental Fear.*
21   Aslam, *Wasted Vigil,* p. 269, p. 317.
22   *Ibid.*, p. 74.
23   O'Connor, 'Writing Against Terror – Nadeem Aslam'.
24   Kapur, 'Little Murders'.
25   Runnymede Trust, *Islamophobia: A Challenge For Us All.*
26   Malcolm Brown, 'Orientalism and Resistance to Orientalism', p. 184.
27   Ahmed, 'The Discourse of the Veil', p. 324.
28   See Spivak, 'Can the Subaltern Speak?', for the most well-known discussion of this position.
29   See Simmons, 'Are we up to the challenge?', p. 241.
30   See Lyon, 'In the Shadow of September 11', p. 80. Against Huntington's 'clash of civilizations' theory, Lyon argues that post-9/11 discourse suggests only one civilisation, where Muslims 'have either been 'duped' into not opting for the universal values or are being actively constrained from making those choices'.
31   For detailed discussion of media representation see Poole, *Reporting Islam*, p. 15.
32   Kapur, 'Little Murders'.
33   See Ansari, *Infidel Within*, p. 74.
34   See Huntington, *The Clash of Civilizations,* p. 209, for an example of this

view.
35   See Ansari, *Infidel Within*, p. 175: 'Only 20% of Pakistanis and Bangladeshis live in wards where the majority of residents are from ethnic minorities'.
36   Soguk, 'Reflections on the "Orientalised Orientals"', p. 363.
37   *Ibid.*, p. 375.
38   *Ibid.*, p. 374.
39   *The Economist*, 'A Travesty of Honour', p. 94.
40   *Ibid.*
41   Kapur, 'Little Murders'. The only other is Weidner, 'Cosmos of Traditionalist Muslim Migrants'.
42   'Nadeem Aslam on *Maps for Lost Lovers*'.
43   Nadeem Aslam on *Maps for Lost Lovers*'.
44   Aslam, 'God and Me'. There are also notable similarities between Shamas and the personal history of Aslam's father.
45   Rushdie, *Shame*, p. 29.
46   O'Connor, 'Writing Against Terror '.
47   'Nadeem Aslam on *Maps for Lost Lovers*'.
48   Sardar, 'The Excluded Minority', p. 51.
49   See Poole, *Reporting Islam*, p. 13.
50   Katz, 'Banal Terrorism', p. 351.
51   *Ibid.*, p. 350.
52   Allen, 'From Race to Religion', p. 61.
53   Modood, *Multicultural Politics,* p. 103. This shift is noted by comparing pre- and post-9/11 sociological studies: compare, for example, the optimism of Ballard, *Desh Pradesh*: with Weber's *Imagined Diaspora*s.
54   Examples of such inflammatory readings are Sookhdeo, *Islam in Britain* and Phillips, *Londonistan*.
55   Kermode, *Sense of an Ending*.
56   See Greenslade, 'Fitness and the Fin de Siècle', pp. 37–44.
57   McEwan, *Saturday*, p. 22, p. 128, p. 214, p. 88.
58   *Ibid.*, p. 210.
59   Updike, *Terrorist*, p. 310.
60   Lyon, 'In the Shadow of September 11', p. 89.
61   Nash, 'Re-siting Religion and Creating Feminised Space', p. 31.
62   Stotesbury, 'Genre and Islam in Recent Anglophone Romantic Fiction', p. 75.
63   Aboulela, *Minaret*, p. 264.
64   Birt, 'Notes on Islamophobia'.

Further reading

Humayun Ansari, *The Infidel Within: Muslims in Britain since 1800* (London: Hurst and Company, 2004).
Nadeem Aslam, 'God and Me', *Granta 93: God's Own Countries*, www.granta.com/extracts/2646.
'Nadeem Aslam on *Maps for Lost Lovers*', www.faber.co.uk/article_detail.html?aid=23652.

Commission on British Muslims and Islamophobia, *Islamophobia: Issues, Challenges and Action* (London: Trentham Books, 2004).

Ziauddin Sardar, *Orientalism* (Buckingham: Open University Press, 1999).

Ziauddin Sardar, 'The Excluded Minority: British Muslim Identity After September 11', in Phoebe Griffith and Mark Leonard (eds), *Reclaiming Britishness: Living Together after 11 September and the Rise of the Right* (London: The Foreign Policy Centre, 2002), pp. 51–5.

6

Meera Syal

To be sure, whoever realises the senselessness, the hopelessness of this world, might well despair, but this despair is not a result of this world. Rather it is an answer given by an individual to this world; another answer would be not to despair, would be an individual's decision to endure this world in which we live like Gulliver among the giants.[1]

Near the beginning of Meera Syal's second novel, *Life Isn't All Ha Ha Hee Hee* (1999), one of the three central protagonists, Tania, is making a film about the British Asian experience. Her producer Jonathan critiques her with the following:

Well, it's victim mentality TV, isn't it? Let's look at the strange brown people and admire their spunk or pity their struggles. What about the happy stories? What about the Asians who like who they are, who just get on and do it and ... live? Yeah?[2]

In the wake of the rise of 'Asian cool', the desire to meet the image of a confident, self-assured British Asian identity is overwhelming. As the most 'funny' British Asian voice, best known for her roles in the BBC comedy series *Goodness Gracious Me* and *The Kumars at Number 42*, Meera Syal might be seen to play into this demand. I am going to suggest in fact the very opposite, however: Syal's comedy, rather than a mark of new-found confidence, is instead a device used to challenge the prevailing mood of optimism with a stark warning of the continued difficulties of being not only British Asian, but a British Asian woman especially.

The illusion of happiness

Marketing of both Syal's first novel, *Anita and Me* (1996), and its follow-up, *Ha Ha Hee Hee*, identifies her with the 'funny' public image developed through her television work.[3] The choice of reviews used on the paperback editions of both novels emphasise humour: the original cover to the paperback of *Anita* promises 'lorry loads of laughs'; the *Independent* review, quoted on the cover of the paperback *Ha Ha Hee Hee*, says it is 'funny and sharp'.[4] Such selections obscure a broader concern in these reviews with the serious issues that Syal's novels deal with. They are nevertheless representative in the sense that they do capture the prevailing tone of reviews, if not their entireties. Positive emphasis is often made in spite of the acknowledged content of the texts. The best example in terms of *Anita* is the *Times Online* review, which describes a 'drab village' setting and a protagonist 'learning to lie, steal and swear'. And yet the review opens nevertheless with the phrase 'Syal's *jolly* coming-of-age-story'.[5] A parallel is offered in terms of *Ha Ha Hee Hee* by Jennifer Reese's *The New York Times* review, which notes the dilemmas facing the three central characters and yet concludes that the novel is 'gossipy, funny, and thoroughly entertaining'.[6] In such reviews there is a need to see Syal as funny *despite rather than because of* the overwhelming content of her novels.

On one hand, this desire reflects the longing, like Jonathan in *Ha Ha Hee Hee*, to receive images of Asian identity that meet wider notions of British Asian positivity. On the other, however, it comes directly from Syal's image as a comedienne. Even more than usual, therefore, Syal is subject to the burden of representation of the ethnic author. Her fiction is indubitably tied not only to Syal's definition as an Asian woman, but even more definitely to her popular image as a cultural comedienne. Syal has made important contributions in cultural terms, writing the screenplay for the critically acclaimed *Bhaji on the Beach* (1994) in which she also starred, the book for the musical *Bombay Dreams* (2000), and the first ever play by an Asian woman to be produced by the BBC, *My Sister Wife* (1993).[7] As an actress, she began her work at the Royal Court, and has taken up numerous serious roles such as her part in Ayub Khan-Din's play *Rafta Rafta* (2007), and Hettie MacDonald's film adaptation of Jonathan Harvey's *Beautiful Thing* (1996). As an author, she began her career as part of the Asian Women's Writers' Workshop, writing thoroughly serious fiction which bears witness to the feminist aims of the group. She has been publically recognised, by an MBE in 1997, the 2000 Commission for Racial Equality Race in the Media Personality of the Year Award, and the *Asian Voice* Asian Achievers Award 2001. This has led to Syal being seen by some as 'possibly the most influential South Asian woman in the British media'.[8] Yet it is still as a comedienne that she is best known.

What I want to challenge here is not the idea that Syal's novels are funny, but that this is their dominant feature. I also want to question the move often made from reading this humour, to identifying Syal's works as largely positive or celebratory. If Syal's novels are comedies, this is less about seeing the world in a cheery manner, and more about emphasising the trauma of British Asian existence: Syal's use of comedy is more significant for its engagement with the broader conventions of this genre than its evocation of humour.

The problem with comedy, perhaps, is that it discourages investigation of these serious features. That *Anita* won a Betty Trask Award and was shortlisted for the *Guardian* Fiction Prize suggests an awareness of the serious concerns of Syal's fiction. However, there is nevertheless a tendency in critical work and reviews to focus on the humour of the stories and, from this, to make assumptions about their level of engagement with issues of identity. A particularly good example of this is found in Yasmin Hussain's *Writing Diaspora*. Hussain's book is an intelligent intervention into the much-neglected field of Asian women's writing. Her reading of *Anita*, nevertheless, is exemplary of how Syal's fiction has often been approached. For Hussain, 'Syal ... aims to bring out the confusion of British South Asian youth and the culture clashes involved, but she depicts confrontation and adjustment in simplistic terms.'[9] In Hussain's criticism is the suggestion that Syal's fiction offers only surface engagement with the dilemmas of British Asian identity; that the problems Meena encounters are too easily resolved in Syal's narrative, with little depth or conflict.

In contrast to this, it is possible to read Syal's narrative as infinitely more complex than such readings suggest. *Anita* is as Mark Stein identifies an example of a black British *bildungsroman* and, as such, offers a movement from a position of naivety to enlightenment, as Meena develops and comes to terms with her own complex cultural positioning. Syal's first-person narration is taken to reveal the progress achieved between the confused and unformulated child Meena, and the self-aware adult narrator Meena. The reality of *Anita*, however, questions this easy resolution. In the untitled two pages that precede the novel's first chapter, the narrator offers an introduction which, in part, affirms the idea of a confident British Asian female sensibility. Laughing at the common stereotypes of migrant identity, the narrator recounts her early life as 'the early years of struggle and disillusion, living in a shabby boarding house with another immigrant family', her mother 'a simple Punjabi girl suffering from culture shock, marooned and misplaced in Wolverhampton' (9). She then proceeds to tell us that this is merely 'the alternative history I trot out in job interview situations' (9). The familiar traumatic vision of migrant experience is now, it seems, to be ironically played with for humorous effect. In this sense, then, Hussain is right: the problems of racial prejudice, of being a British-born Asian in the 1960s when such an experience is rare, of being a true minority in a world of almost exclusive whiteness, is behind Meena. She has emerged unscathed, with a humour that announces her distance from the stereotypical definitions of Asianness into which she might be placed.

However, the introduction does not end with this irony. Instead, it offers a far more ambivalent, and yet crucial, comment:

> But I have always been a sucker for the double entendre; the gap between what is said and what is thought, what is stated and what is implied, is a place in which I have always found myself. I'm really not a liar, I just learned very early on that those of us deprived of history sometimes need to turn to mythology to feel complete, to belong. (10)

Thus Chapter 1 begins with a warning: don't trust this narrative, our narrator tells us; I am an unreliable narrator of the worst kind: one who disguises their falsehoods with a veil of realism. Even though you will find little conscious narrative distancing in the novel to distinguish narrator from protagonist (only a handful of occasions in the whole book), this doesn't mean such a distance does not exist. Don't fall for the authority of the first-person voice and forget the subjectivity that lies behind it. Remember that the age of verisimilitude is long behind us: that realism is no longer, as indeed it never was, a synecdoche for truth. Don't look at just what is said here, but look beyond it, look behind it, look in between the often breezy, simple story offered. Undertake instead what Edward Said calls a contrapuntal reading: look for what is not said, and – when you discover what is missing – consider why it is absent, and what this absence might in fact stand for. Don't fall for the suggestion that, at the end of the novel, 'Meena understands that the lies she concocted in the past are no longer necessary', for – this introduction explicitly suggests – the narrator's propensity for falsehood is still clearly at work.[10]

At the very least, this awareness asks us to question the undoubtedly most 'mythological' instance in the book: Meena's rescue by Harrinder P. Singh, the local Asian who is transformed at the end of the novel into Meena's Sikh saviour. Harrinder emerges into an otherwise white Tollington, where he has lived in secret for years, and proves to Meena both that she is not alone, and that it is possible to be successful as a British Asian; he announces a history of settlement in Britain, foregrounds a denied diversity even in the seemingly most white of spaces, and, as the owner of 'the Big House', represents financial power against the struggling economy of Tollington. Yet his appearance is couched in terms that immediately express its unreality. Harrinder, we are told, means that Meena's 'miracle was complete' (317); her father equally declares that Harrinder's presence is 'amazing' (323). Expose the fallaciousness of this part of the story, and what is revealed instead is Meena still alone, re-writing her childhood isolation to give her childhood self, in the form of Harrinder, a sense of community that the reality of Tollington in fact never offers. If, as Berthold Schoene-Harwood suggests, Tollington is presented as unaware of this new shift in the English landscape (167) this is because, in fact, such a mythical presence is more of the narrator's imagining than an actual rendering of place. We must face the reality that in 1960s Britain, children like Meena did not find a mythical saviour; they on the whole moved into adulthood with a growing awareness of their difference, subject to an equally illusive projection on the part of white society.

Once such a pivotal event is problematised, further questions of the narrative need to be asked. Throughout the novel Meena re-constructs her world. Her lies are not just 'harmless fabrications', but also include, she tells us, 'major whoppers' (28). Although *Anita* is often identified as autobiographical, the setting is not the village of Essington into which Syal was born in 1963, but Tollington. The latter is not a real place, and this in itself suggests not reality but an imaginative recasting of it. And if we might doubt whether Meena's storytelling could extend to the minute details of the complex narrative she weaves, then she instructs us otherwise:

> My mind drifted into practical overdrive, as it did with all my daydreams. It was never enough to have a vague picture, such as 'I save Donny Osmond from near death and win a medal'. I had to know what I was wearing, whether it was a fire in a top London hotel or a runaway horse in a summer meadow, what the weather was like,

who was watching and how my hair looked at the moment of rescue. (202)

Anita is not a complete postmodern fiction of unreal incidences; we do trust events such as Meena's relationship with Robert, the attack against the Asian bank manager (which offers an important realist counterpoint to the entry of Harrinder Singh), and her own admittance of her duplicity, such as in her theft of the collection tin from Mr Omerod's shop. These moments of sadness and depression ring true, a reflection at least of a partially changed Meena who announces herself in the scene near the end of the novel when she rejects the possibility to take revenge on Sam and Anita and tells the truth about Tracey's accident. But they stand as insights into a life which does not always seem to be fully represented by the narrative's more comic moments. Meena may have changed, but she has not completely transformed.

Such complex use of the realist form is worth distinguishing. The realism commonly employed by many recent British Asian writers can seem less stylistically vibrant than the form employed by an earlier generation, particularly Salman Rushdie, whose ebullient magical-realist style owes much to postcolonial fiction. What Syal proves, however, is that the use of a simple realist form may have its own sophisticated thematic origins – the novel's epigraph asks us to see the realist form the narrator employs as integral to her practice of re-creating reality, of defining an experience that is as tangible and believable as what might actually have happened a way of resisting that actuality. Syal's novel is thus postmodern not in Rushdie's sense but more, like V. S. Naipaul's fiction, in the way of Ian McEwan's *Atonement* (2001), for example. What this points to is not a less sophisticated consciousness, but a more subtle one, yet equally rooted in the complexities that a concern for issues of identity demands. In her earlier writing Syal shows a great interest in the mythical from which her later fiction should not be simplistically divorced. Her short story 'The Traveller' (1988), for example, is a mythical tale. This magical-realist style offers an opportunity to reconsider the assumptions about Syal's realism: it points to an imagination more complex than critics sometimes assume.

In this sense *Anita* is a novel that suggests a restoration of certainty and calm but, in fact, only reinforces anxiety and tumult. In his book *The Comedy of Entropy* (1990), Patrick O'Neill outlines a postmodern comic narrative form which he labels the comedy of entropy because it emphasises 'the crumbling of ordered systems, the breakdown of traditional perceptions of reality, the erosion of certainty'.[11] This for O'Neill is contrasted to an earlier comic form, the comedy of order, which in contrast offers resolution and surety with its 'untroubled simplicity and unshaken self-confidence'.[12] This new form is associated with the idea of the postmodern game, what O'Neill refers to as 'poststructuralist ludism', with a more serious purpose: the narrative play and self-referentiality of the postmodern text reveals a profoundly destabilising disorder and anxiety.[13] In these terms, *Anita* is a comedy of entropy masking as a comedy of order; the supposed 'fictive reintegration' of order gives way to an acceptance of loss.[14] Not the most obvious of postmodern texts (*Anita* may accept loss but it does not, as in O'Neill's most extreme formulation, celebrate this), the novel offers a sense of final resolution but this resolution in fact only indicates a deep uncertainty and instability akin to O'Neill's entropic irony of 'controlled duplicity of meaning'.[15] Its playful epigraph and deceptive realism is not playful in the benign sense, but rather in order to offer a representation of a volatile existence. Meena as observed character is not Meena the observer: a very different figure whose conscious pointing to the essential gap between, in O'Neill's terms, narrated entity and narrative instance, reminds us of the inherently illusory nature of what we read.

What then lies under Meena's humour? If we strip away her narrative flair, what are the bare bones of her experience? We can no longer trust Meena's celebratory statement that 'the place in which I belonged was wherever I stood' (303). Rather, we must read this statement for its ambiguity: that 'wherever I stood' signifies not self-assurance, but only a limited and contingent identification which offers no lasting sense of acceptance. Instead, we witness a rural community riven by racist ignorance, quickly becoming racist prejudice. We see not only a young girl, but also this community, caught up in the immense shifts of 1960s social, cultural and economic change. Indeed, Syal's novel is a rare consideration of this earlier moment in which British Asian communities began to establish themselves. Caught up in this wider history of settlement, Meena sees herself transformed from an individual to an Asian, to a migrant (even though she isn't one), to part of a group which, as the novel points out, she ironically has little physical or emotional connection to. She captures an early example of the now common experience of being led to define oneself as Asian through the attitudes of others.[16] Moving into the 1970s, 'the number and significance of the Asians born and educated in Britain rose sharply; and this gave a fillip to the general confidence of the community', [17] but at the same time racist hostility increased to counter this confidence, reflected most famously in Enoch Powell's 1966 'Rivers of Blood' speech, and the rise in the activities of the National Front. Presenting a world only on the brink of these conflicts, Meena as narrator imagines a world in which these threats are only transitory, to be easily escaped via educational opportunity. Yet on the whole British Asians did not escape their circumstances as Meena and her family do at the end of the novel, and this too is something therefore difficult to trust from such an unreliable narrator. Most did not have the educational opportunities Meena gives herself to escape the narrow outlooks of the world they found themselves in. And, indeed, even if they were lucky enough to have such opportunities, these did not largely allow them to escape prejudice, but rather only to encounter similar attitudes again, only transformed into a more subtle and eloquent racist discourse.[18] While it may be inappropriate therefore to categorise contemporary British Asian experience in terms of the stereotypes of marginality and exclusion, the reality for young British Asians in the 1960s, Syal suggests, is less starkly opposed to these frames of reference.

Anita is a *bildungsroman*; the classic elements of this narrative – generational conflict, school experiences, the conflict between rural and urban life, and an educated narrator are, as Stein rightly argues, all there in Syal's novel.[19] But Syal's comedy does not easily point towards the 'transformative potential held by the protagonists' that Stein argues for.[20] The journey to self-knowledge, according to Eric Bentley, is offered in comedy through 'indirection, duality, irony'.[21] Thus what Meena learns is not what she obviously seems to have done; the joy which comedy brings to sorrow is also a constant reminder of that sorrow's indefatigable presence, and the distance between the comic world of fiction and the reality of experience. Meena's positive sense of self may be less transformation than a more traditional formation of her adult self with an awareness of society's prejudices and limitations. Equally, the sense in which Stein argues for a black British novel of transformation in terms of 'the *transformation* of British society and cultural institutions' is questioned by the fact that the narrator's admission suggests

little in Tollington – or indeed in white Britain more generally – has in fact been challenged or transformed by Meena's
presence.[22]

Stein himself seems to begin an acknowledgement of these
limitations: he describes Meena as an indulger in fantasies, a
girl who actively 'positions herself'.[23] Yet Stein does not take
this as far as its ultimate conclusion: that the narrative itself
is part of this talent for fabrication and conscious positioning.
In the same way, Berthold Schoene-Harwood notices Meena's
tendency for falsehoods, even quoting the part of the epigraph
I centre my discussion around.[24] More interestingly, Schoene-
Harwood points to the questionable nature of many of the
resolutions Meena draws near the end of the novel; her confidence that she has moved from 'acting to being' is derided as
'only yet another inauthentic act'.[25] However, Schoene-Harwood
too does not take this to its eventual conclusion – that such acts
are in fact intentionally inauthentic, marking as they do the
ever-present trace of tragedy, and the narrator's self-conscious
restricting. It is this narrator who needs to re-write her story
as one of successful integration, and her confident assertion of
movement away from conceit only reveals this more strongly
in classic comic terms. If Meena is still acting at the end of the
novel, this is because she is still acting after it as the epigraph
reveals. Thus Meena fulfils neither Stein's *bildungsroman* nor
Schoene-Harwood's alternative of proprioception: an inward
fulfilment rather than a capitulation to social conventions. Stein
and Schoene-Harwood are engaged in a debate over the nature
of *Anita*; Stein's *bildungsroman* is for Schoene-Harwood an *anti-
bildungsroman*. Yet, interestingly, both critics affirm ultimately
the positive nature of *Anita's* conclusion.[26] This obscures the
possibility that Meena as child has, in fact, not yet learnt how
to survive; it is the narrator, rather, who has achieved this, but
only at the expense of a truthful rendering of experiences in
favour of comic fantasy.

In *Anita* we have to read between the lines to uncover this
bleak reality. *Ha Ha Hee Hee* presents it obviously, embodied in
the novel's title. Beginning with the bleak, if alliterative, statement 'not even snowfall could make Leyton look lovely' (9),
events are less likely to be couched in comedy. There is nothing
funny about Deepak's patriarchal attitudes (12) which make
him marry one woman but love another; Chila's childhood
marred by being seen as the 'plump darkie' (14) is not framed
within the comedy of an agony aunt letter as Meena frames her

own similar feelings of low self-esteem, but rather is addressed directly. Her awareness that her unborn baby will be more valued if it is a boy rather than a girl (200) is in no way comic. Tania's loneliness, fatigue and insomnia is recounted without comic relief (56) and there is nothing funny in her recounting of the pressures she faces, as an Asian woman, to assimilate into traditional ideas of Asian womanhood (150). There is nothing humorous in Sunita being told by her uncle that the rules of reincarnation construct the hierarchy cow–woman–man (78), or the stories of domestic violence she hears at the Citizen's Advice Bureau (81), or her own tale of abortion (89), all of which occur in the narrative within eleven pages of each other. There is nothing funny in her self-harm, the 'tiny criss-cross of recent cuts' (170), which are a sign of her psychological turmoil. The racial tensions skimmed over in *Anita* are captured here directly with references to 'border control … the corner which separated the Eastenders from the Eastern-Enders' (40), the poverty revealed explicitly as Tania watches the 'conveyor belt of disaffection' (50) in Sunita's Citizen's Advice Bureau office. References to the real-world case of Jasbinder Singh (213), and also the cases of Leila Khan, Priya Kumar and Jyoti Patel (218), are in stark contrast to the fictional world of Tollington.

Here it is obvious that the escape offered by Meena's fantasy is literally that – a fantasy. To appreciate this is not simply to acknowledge the contrinuance of racism in Britain but – equally – the complex and unique combination of pressures facing British Asian women as the protagonists recount both racist and patriarchal pressures acting against their desires to achieve self-worth; what are described as 'ordained patterns for a woman' (15) within the Asian community are compounded by the continuance of negative racist stereotypes in white society. This dual oppression marks out the British Asian woman's unique circumstances, caught between the competing gender values of British and traditional Asian culture, and at the same time subject to racist prejudices. Such tension is embodied in Chila's experience at the antenatal clinic: the doctors refuse to tell her the sex of her baby, and Sunita complains about the racist hospital policies, while Chila tells her that she has seen the clinics offering sex selection to Asian women, and that she knows the long waiting lists they hold (229–33). So Sunita finds herself in 'the grey area' (233), caught between competing prejudices. That the focus in the text as a whole is more on the internal prejudice than white racism marks the British Asian text out from its migrant forebears, but also indicates the simplistic nature of Meena's solution: she may escape Tollington in the 1960s but, grown up, it's not this simple: the difficulties for British Asian women in the 1990s, Syal suggests, are not simply about being 'othered' by white society, but also about being interrogated within indigenous culture and labelled as what Tania refers to as the 'Bad Indian woman' (21).

Life Isn't All Ha Ha Hee Hee

Yet if *Ha Ha Hee Hee* is less funny than *Anita*, nevertheless both novels share a perspective on how humour functions. That is, it is used by the British Asian female to play down trauma. In the wake of depression and bad experiences, according to Susan Langer, 'comedy abstracts, and reincarnates for our perception, the motion and rhythm of living, it enhances our vital feeling'.[27] Humour, it needs to be remembered, 'is a reaction to pain and destruction which registers their reality in order to surmount them'.[28] Throughout *Anita*, Meena employs humour to counter negative emotions. Consider the following passage:

> My father showed he was sorry by buying me a hotdog on the way home. I sat in the back of the Mini and concentrated on licking the tomato sauce off my fingertips while singing 'Bobbing Along on the Bottom of the Beautiful Briney Sea' in between slurps. Mummy and papa were talking again, soft whispers, sss sss sss, my mother's bracelets jingled as she seemed to wipe something from her face. This was my birthday and they were leaving me out again. I squeezed my hot dog and suddenly the sausage shot into my mouth and lodged firmly in my windpipe. I was too shocked to move, my fingers curled uselessly into my fists. They were still talking, engrossed, I could see papa's eyes in the mirror, darting from my mother's face to the unfolding road. I thought of writing SAUSAGE STUCK on the windscreen and then realised I could not spell sausage. (26–7)

Meena's rejection by her family is countered in the narrative by the transformation of this memory into a moment of humour, giving far more space in the narrative to comedy than to Meena's feelings of alienation. Throughout the book, this power of humour to counter negative emotions is emphasised by similar couplings of tragic events and recourse to laughter: Meena's fears about Mrs Christmas followed by both Meena and Anita laughing their 'heads off' (44), Anita reacting to being cuffed on the side of her head by her mother by laughing (54). The humorous way the narrator recounts events to reduce their trauma is emphasised by the representation of such a strategy as all pervasive, the events themselves becoming a rationale for the tone and emphasis of the novel. The novel will be told this way, we come to learn, because that is how individuals survive the consequences of death, heartbreak and rejection.

With specific cultural resonance, such traumas are often centred on either racist hostility or the prejudices of the Asian community itself as they impact upon those born in Britain. Humour is represented on the one hand as a way to challenge the prejudices of the Asian community:

> Later on, mama, who had been very quiet during this early crisis of faith, declared that she was taking me to the *gurudwara* in Birmingham the very next day. This was something of a major announcement on two counts; firstly, because mama also had never shown signs of being overtly religious. Of course, she invoked the name of Bhagwan in times of pain or exasperation, and had often praised the virtues of Sikhism to me, how it was a very fair religion that believed totally in equality. 'We Sikhs do not believe in the caste system at all,' she said proudly, and then muttered, 'Of course, now we have different snobberies, who has the biggest Mercedes and the fattest gold necklace, as if the biggest show-off is the most holy ...' (94)

At the same time, it can be used to counter a sense of inferiority through an elevation of one's own culture in comic circumstances. Watching television, Meena and her family deal with their sense of cultural difference through comic engagements:

> Glenys was standing on her stoop, wringing her hands, with her characteristic expression of someone who has sniffed impending doom and knows no one is going to believe her. I'd seen a similar *moue* on the face of the mad soothsayer in Frankie Howerd's *Up Pompeii* on the telly. The soothsayer was depicted as an old wild-eyed woman dressed in rags who began every entrance with the litany, 'Woe! Woe! And thrice Woe!' This never ceased to crease me up because *Wo Wo* was our family Punjabi euphemism for shit, 'Do you want to do a *Wo Wo*?' and 'Wipe properly, get all the *Wo Wo* off ...' The first time I'd heard the soothsayer's lament I'd said, 'I think she must have constipation!' Which made my papa laugh proudly and my mother hide her smile under an expression of distaste. (56)

Ha Ha Hee Hee focuses more intently on the former strategy. Chila's reflection on the difficulties for British Asian young people dating is humorously rendered as she states 'when you ask a guy if he's got protection, what you mean is, has he got tinted windows, safety locks and a baseball bat in the boot, in case of passing brothers?' (30); similarly her lack of self-worth is comically revealed in the statement 'they always try and match you up with someone who they think has got similar deformities to you. "Boy with club foot seeks similar"' (32). For the feminist campaigner Suki, the question 'why beat yourself up when you can ask a man?' is 'quipped' (163).

It is difficult, therefore, to see Syal's use of humour as simply a conventional postcolonial humorous response, as do Susanne Reichl and Mark Stein in *Cheeky Fictions* (2005).[29] Stein and Reichl are right to include British Asian texts such as Syal's in their remit, in the sense of postcolonial humour being a device 'to camouflage rather than express emotions, for instance to cover up aggression or the pain of being an outsider or of being considered inferior'.[30] Yet if Reichl and Stein are more interested in laughter as a response to a stimulus than a disposition, then in British Asian fiction it is precisely this disposition (having a sense of humour) that is crucial.[31] Here Syal's comedy reflects what Elder Olson in 'The Comic Object' (1968) refers to as *katastasis*: 'a special kind of relaxation of concern'.[32] For Olson, this transformation means indifference towards a previous subject of concern. So we find not 'the substitution of desire for its contrary, aversion, nor by replacement, say, of fear, by the contrary emotion of hope, which is also serious, but by the conversion of the grounds of concern into absolutely nothing'.[33] The sense of not taking things seriously which is integral to comedy represents a refusal to see issues of identity crisis as being matters of significant concern.[34] Equally, if part of comedy is centred on a corrective function through ridicule, pointing out what is foolish or misadvised, then the confidence of Syal's narratives comes from the willingness to turn this comic gaze away from racism and towards one's own cultural group, particularly in the light of a pre-existing racist comedy in Britain.[35]

Such relaxation might offer a sense of self-belief in this new British Asian generation to not take issues of identity so seriously. Yet both Syal's novels are deeply ironic, where irony is a mode of comedy in which 'we state what ought to be done, and pretend to believe that this is just what is actually being done'.[36] As Bentley reminds us, 'happy endings are always ironical in comedies (like everything that is happy in comedies) ... The tone says: life is fun. The undertone suggests that life is a catastrophe.'[37] Throughout, Syal focuses on serious events with lightness and humour. Such humorous re-visioning is an act of survival: a British Asian act of defiance and statement of the right to inclusion. Comedy here ensures that unavailable in reality: a sense of social integration in the wake of confusion and conflict. Humour in this sense functions to restore power in situations of powerlessness, an opportunity of disruption given to those without conventional positions of superiority.[38] With the possibility to 'provide an outlet for criticism without aggravating the initial conflict', humour allows issues to be raised that otherwise might be simply too confrontational.[39] Laughter can often negatively act to isolate difference – we must remember that 'the laugh of a satirist is often a sneer'.[40] The claiming of the power to laugh, therefore, by a female Asian author marks a reversal of this 'othering gaze' against racist discourses. So Syal's novels focus on the most profound issues facing the British Asian community, yet the critique of both white and Asian communities implicit in these issues can be more effectively transmitted through humour rather than didactic moralising. Here Syal's television career does *genuinely* become relevant; this method of critique is precisely the same strategy employed in *Goodness Gracious Me*, where the prejudices of both white English and Asian communities are exposed in a format that makes the viewer more receptive than they might be to a more direct criticism.[41]

This strategy has particular relevance in a British Asian female context. It is a more specific marker of a strident female British Asian consciousness which is actively involved in a process of re-imagining the manner in which identity is framed. As Hussain tells us, 'South Asian women have redefined the very idea of South Asianness and South Asian womanhood within both the minority and majority cultures as they give voice to their resistance to oppression.'[42] The issue of female solidarity has always been of great importance to Syal. 'The Traveller', for example, tells of women who have lost their wings to the 'land of the wingless', a fable for the eternal and timeless connection between women. Similarly, in her screenplay *My Sister Wife* a British Asian woman, Farah, comes to discovers a solidarity with her 'enemy', her new husband's first wife, in a polygamist Muslim household; another wife in similar circumstances explains this relationship as: 'We look after each other, her children are mine. No difference. If she is hurt, I bleed. One person.'[43] So in *Ha Ha Hee Hee*, humorous incidences address issues specific to female identity.

In her study *British Women's Comic Fiction 1980–1990* (2001), Margaret D. Stetz suggests that female laughter is so powerful because, historically, women have been discouraged from public displays of laughter. Even in the late twentieth century, she argues, female writers must face female stereotypes of modesty which prevent them from freely engaging with humour.[44] Being a comic female writer means questioning the submissive role created for women by patriarchy, a role Syal herself acknowledges in *Anita* where the local women have been taught to avoid the expression of emotion:

> I knew this was the expected Tollington stance, attack being the best form of defence, and never ever show that you might be in pain. That would only invite more violence because pity was for wimps and wimps could not survive round here. (52)

In her final chapter, which focuses on Sunita Namjoshi, Stetz establishes a specifically Asian female comedy in Britain, which she traces back to the beginnings of Randhawa's Asian Women Writers' Collective and comic contributions to its anthologies.[45] For Stetz, the position of Asian females in Britain exemplifies her definition of 'survival comedy'.[46] Whereas white renderings of the Asian experience, such as Sue Townsend's *The Great Celestial Cow*, end tragically, Stetz argues that the same experiences could be rendered more positively: not as descents into madness, as Townsend represents them, but instead as 'women working together, staying noisily sane'.[47] And this, indeed, is what *Ha Ha Hee Hee* offers: three women, not descending into madness, but rather facing their traumatic circumstances with a shared humour that is the basis of their endurance.

A question of comedy

Such creative practice follows precisely Northrop Frye and Bentley's definitions of comedy in which it is not events themselves which are inherently comic or tragic, but rather the approach of the author that defines them as such.[48] This approach is not just a matter of humour, but of comedy in its broadest sense where humour is 'only one of its most useful and natural elements': a worldview which is distinguished from the solemnity of tragedy.[49] The notion of comedy is inherently connected to the idea of a movement away from reality; as Friedrich Dürrenmatt notes, comedy is, in contrast to tragedy, the genre of conceit.[50] What comedy offers is only 'a *temporary* triumph' over a '*surrounding* world': it marks only a brief interlude in a context that is separate from the wider world outside its realm.[51] Comedy and lying go hand in hand. As Henri Bergson outlines, 'A man in disguise is a comic. A man we regard as disguised is also comic. So, by analogy, any disguise is seen to become comic, not only that of a man, but that of society also, and even the disguise of nature.'[52]

For Bentley, laughter is simply another means of registering a denial: 'when a person vehemently denies something that has not been affirmed, we wonder why he goes to the trouble, and we conclude that expressly what he is denying is true'.[53] Just as 'strenuous disclaimers are read as confessions of guilt',[54] so laughter is a mark of denying the reality of a situation; it allows 'us to distance ourselves from the realities of existence'.[55] Yet whereas, in farce, the real world is denied, rather in comedy the bleakness of the actual shows itself as a lingering trace: 'Comedy has this in common with farce: in the end it decides to look the other way. But there is a difference. Comedy has in the meantime looked the right way. Comedy has seen; has taken note; and has not forgotten.'[56] In this context, comedy is 'an affirmation made irrationally – that is, in defiance of the stated facts'.[57] The conclusion is positive, but we cannot forget the trace of despair to which we have been quietly directed.

Syal's novels follow exactly this broader notion of the comic. For the narrator of *Anita* humour covers up sadness, but as the novel's introduction shows it is part of a wider mode of deception, with or without humour, which obscures suffering. The central element of the novel is not humour but deception; it is deception that drives humour, rather than the reverse. Against the power of definition by an anxious white gaze, Meena narrates an alternative in which she can escape such scrutiny:

> It was all falling into place now, why I felt this continual urge to fabricate, this ever-present desire to be someone else in some place far from Tollington. Before Nanima arrived, this urge to reinvent myself, I could now see, was driven purely by shame. (211)

The most poignant example of this strategy comes in Meena's experience out driving with her mother. Hearing for the first time racist abuse directed at her, Meena is prepared to return home and tell her father. But upon encountering him, she decides otherwise:

> Later that evening, papa pulled me onto his lap and asked me what I had learned that day. I wanted to tell him about the old lady, but then I looked at his face and saw something I had never seen before, a million of these encounters written in the lines around his warm, hopeful eyes, lurking in the furrows of his brow, shadowing the soft curves of his mouth. I suddenly realised that what had happened to me must have happened to papa countless times, but not once had he ever shared his upset with me. He must have known it would have made me feel as I felt right now, hurt, angry, confused,

and horribly powerless because this kind of hatred could not be explained. I decided to return the compliment. 'I learned,' I replied, 'that mama is a really good driver.' (98)

Such deception is equally present in the lives of the three protagonists of *Ha Ha Hee Hee*. The need to deceive – to make a tragedy into a comedy – is maintained. Chila tells the reader in relation to her wedding that 'they weren't real tears ... Life isn't all ha ha hee hee so if you know there's going to be a few tears you might as well enjoy them' (27), rendering ironic Deepak's belief that 'Chila was no actress' (71); she later lies to her mother when she suggests Deepak's infidelity in order to protect her (202), just as Meena protects her father. Sunita reflects upon the bullying of her childhood with the comment that 'even though I felt the pain as much as I ever did, I learned how to disguise it' (74). Here such obscuration is given specifically gendered connotations, as it becomes less about protecting others, and more about protecting oneself. As Tania tells Deepak:

> Getting to know someone and trying to own them is not the same thing. If she says yes because you've got bigger muscles than her, what she probably means is no. Why do you think women have to be such good liars? Especially our women? And how are you even going to know the difference? Scared people never tell the truth. Do they? (136)

For Tania, this is part of a broader experience of denying the truth in order to make life, in pure comic tradition, more pleasant as she proclaims 'I never bought into that truth is beauty and vice versa crap. I'm waiting for proof that telling it like it is makes anyone feel good or better.' (138) Like the narrator of *Anita*, Tania challenges realist authority with her awareness that 'the biggest lie is that we claim to have the real answers' (136).

This focus on the need for illusion is essential to female British Asian novelists in general. Syal's work is foreshadowed by Ravinder Randhawa's and Atima Srivastava's novels. In *Transmission* the legibility of London which is so important to Angie's sense of self is assumed: coming from a confidence that means one may claim the local territory as one's own:

> Talking about the Dog and Trumpet as if I knew the place inside out. I had only been there half a dozen times and already I had it down in my pool of knowledge. Like reading a book review, then talking about the book as though you'd read it. I mentioned it to Phil, once in the restaurant, and Phil laughed and said that everyone did it. Talked bullshit.[58]

Equally, in *Looking for Maya* Mira's search for the authentic is ultimately abandoned for the acknowledgement that 'We need to believe. Even when we know beyond a shadow of doubt that what we believe in is an illusion'.[59] Such a concern, moreover, has been taken up by Monica Ali in *Brick Lane*; the love affair between Karim and Nazneen is dominated by their need to imagine each other in the wake of their own personal crises; it is only with a realisation of how different reality is to these imaginings that both individuals are able to move on.

So Syal illuminates a wider strategy of survival being acknowledged in British Asian fiction, what Susheila Nasta refers to as a new generation of writers who 'strategically invent a series of alternative locations'.[60] It also resonates with the wider concerns of black British fiction, where the power of agency is privileged, a world in which 'ethnicity is partly chosen'.[61] In this sense, British Asian fiction offers an insight into the strategies which, it has been suggested in sociological studies, are now central to the contemporary British Asian experience. In his study of British Asian identity, *Desh Pardesh* (1994), Roger Ballard argues that 'Both the older generation of settlers and their British-born offspring are continuing to find substantial inspiration in the resources of their own particular cultural, religious and linguistic inheritance, which they are actively and creatively reinterpreting in order to rebuild their lives *on their own terms.*'[62]

For female experience, comedy is ultimately problematic. Interestingly, Stetz's first example of this in her book is Syal's cinematic collaboration with Gurinder Chadha, *Bhaji on the Beach*, where 'comedy is fleeting and always threatening to dissolve into its antithesis'.[63] Stetz sees a pattern of authors 'succumbing to growing doubts about the viability of the genre', growing stronger as they move away from youth towards maturity.[64] This, in fact, is the distinction between *Anita* and *Ha Ha Hee Hee*: the young Meena is warned in the former that 'if you tell lies too often, no one will believe you when you are telling the truth' (70). Yet her lies are for her the only way to survive. For the women in *Ha Ha Hee Hee*, however, this strategy is largely unravelled by the end of the novel. It is clear that humour is not enough. In *Ha He Hee Hee* humour is most directly associated with cruelty, as in the comic taunts of Deepak's friends directed at the innocent Chila (115, 176) or with fake emotions, such as the forced reactions of Tania's colleagues (249). At the end of the novel, the comic tendency to obscure truth is directly connected to the romance narrative which the novel parodies – such stories are all comedies, their truth obscured by the illusions of romantic imagery. Sunita speculates that 'Maybe that's why they were all so constantly disappointed, disillusioned, disenchanted, that was the word. Because fairy tales always end with a wedding. Whoever began a love story with "They had just got married ...".' (310) The comic form of re-writing is revealed ultimately to be in the service of patriarchal interests: it divides women from each other, and furthers male interests. This is embodied in Deepak's lying to both Chila and Tania in order, ostensibly, to make their lives less painful, but in reality to make his own life more comfortable (223).

It is only with the breakdown of deception at the end of the novel that all of the women find some sense of resolution:

> 'Oh, stop it! Chila shouted, her voice bouncing off the white high walls. 'No more sodding fairy tales! No more stuff you've picked up in books! It doesn't help when it's really happening!' (295)

Comedy doesn't offer the whole story, only an illusory beginning. Instead, Syal suggests, it is imperative to face the real – the life beyond the romance narrative. Hiding in the world of fictitious narratives only makes it more impossible to step out of this strategy of deception and find contentment in the real world. Moving into the 'real', Syal's women ultimately abandon strategies of deception that perhaps connect them to earlier migrant modes of alienation for a more openly assertive British Asian perspective.

Conclusion

Syal's comedy is less about being funny than about a survival mechanism that re-creates events so that their negative aspects are not entirely disabling. If there is sometimes laughter in this, then it only signifies that the emotion being obscured is perhaps particularly negative, as comedy is taken to its most powerful form in humour. Our popular image of Syal is a woman who makes us laugh. But we need also to look beyond this laughter. This looking underneath is perhaps difficult when the obvious content is so dynamic and engaging. Yet, as James Wilcox – in perhaps the only truly accurate review of *Anita* – notes, 'the reader must search patiently through ... bustling verbiage for the quieter, more subtle revelations'.[65] Undertake this searching and we discover how close laughing is to crying.

Discussion

- How does the introduction to *Anita and Me* help us to re-evaluate the use of realism in British Asian texts?
- How do the strategies employed in Meera Syal's television and/or film work help us to understand her fiction?
- How is the idea that 'we laugh because it is no longer acceptable to bite' useful when considering Syal's representation of British-Asian identity?[66]

Notes

1   Dürrenmatt, 'Comedy and the Modern World', p. 133.
2   Syal, *Life Isn't All Ha Ha Hee Hee*, pp. 63–4. Hereafter *Ha Ha Hee Hee*. Subsequent references cited parenthetically.
3   Syal, *Anita and Me*. Hereafter *Anita*. Subsequent references cited parenthetically.
4   Reichl and Stein, 'Introduction', p. 2.
5   My emphasis, Koning, '*Anita and Me*'.
6   Reese, '*Life Isn't All Ha Ha Hee Hee*'.
7   Syal has also written other unpublished plays: see Ranasinha, *South Asian Writers*, pp. 255–7.
8   Hussain, *Writing Diaspora*, p. 15.
9   *Ibid.*, p. 129.
10 Neti, 'Siting Speech', p. 115. As my discussion below of Stein and Schoene-Harwood indicates, Neti is not alone in this reading.
11 O'Neill, *Comedy of Entropy*, p. 8.
12 *Ibid.*, p. 65.
13 *Ibid.*, p. 69.
14 *Ibid.*, p. 107.
15 *Ibid.*, p. 138.
16 Fisher *et al.*, *South-Asian History of Britain*, p. 160.
17 *Ibid.*, p. 164.
18 A Handsworth study showed strong academic achievement of Asians (*Ibid.*, p. 162). However, early experiences were consumed with encounters of prejudice: see Carby, 'Schooling in Babylon'.
19 Stein, *Black British Literature*, pp. 25–6.
20 *Ibid.*, p. xiii.
21 Bentley, 'On the Other Side of Despair', p. 145.
22 Stein, *Black British Literature*, p. xiii.
23 *Ibid.*, p. 52.
24 Schoene-Harwood, 'Beyond (T)race', p. 161.
25 *Ibid.*, p. 163.
26 *Ibid.*, p. 166; Stein, *Black British Literature*, p. 52.
27 Langer, 'Comic Rhythm', p. 124.
28 Palmer, 'Introduction', p. 20.
29 Reichl and Stein, 'Introduction', p. 1.

30 *Ibid.*, p. 31.
31 *Ibid.*, p. 4.
32 Olson, 'Comic Object', p. 152.
33 *Ibid.*, p. 152.
34 *Ibid.*
35 See Palmer, 'Introduction', p. 9; Meredith, 'An Essay on Comedy'.
36 Bergson, 'Laughter', p. 143.
37 Bentley, 'On the Other Side', p. 139, p. 148.
38 See Brulotte, 'Laughing at Power', p. 11.
39 Reichl and Stein (eds), *Cheeky Fictions*, p. 30.
40 Sypher, 'The Meanings of Comedy', p. 242.
41 For discussion of *Goodness Gracious Me* see Schlote, '"The Sketch's the thing"', p. 181.
42 Hussain, *Writing Diaspora*, p. 1.
43 Syal, *My Sister Wife*, p. 135.
44 Stetz, *British Women's Comic Fiction*, p. ix.
45 *Ibid.*, pp. 116–17.
46 *Ibid.*, p. 118.
47 *Ibid.*, p. 123.
48 Frye, 'Argument of Comedy'.
49 Langer, 'Comic Rhythm', p. 126.
50 Dürrenmatt, 'Comedy and the Modern World', p. 131.
51 My emphasis, Langer, 'Comic Rhythm', p. 127.
52 Bergson, 'Laughter', p. 87.
53 Bentley, 'On the Other Side', p. 135.
54 *Ibid.*
55 Brulotte, 'Laughing at Power', p. 13.
56 Bentley, 'On the Other Side', p. 137.
57 *Ibid.*, p. 145.
58 Srivastava, *Transmission*, pp. 16–17.
59 Srivastava, *Maya*, p. 218.
60 Nasta, *Home Truths*, p. 186.
61 Stein, *Black British Literature*, p. 122.
62 Ballard, 'Introduction', p. 5.
63 Stetz, *British Women's Comic Fiction* p. xiv.
64 *Ibid.*, p. 135.
65 Wilcox, 'Hairy Neddy and the Mad Mitchells'.
66 O'Neill, *Comedy of Entropy*, p. 46.

Further reading

Leila Neti, 'Siting Speech: the Politics of Imagining the Other in Meera Syal's *Anita and Me*', in Neil Murphy and Wai-Chew Sim (eds), *British Asian Fiction: Framing the Contemporary* (New York: Cambria, 2008), pp. 97–118.

Berthold Schoene-Harwood, 'Beyond (T)race: Bildung and Proprioperception in Meera Syal's *Anita and Me*', *Journal of Commonwealth Literature* 34 (1999), 159–68.

Mark Stein, *Black British Literature: Novels of Transformation* (Columbus: Ohio

7

Hari Kunzru

> Expressive individuation has become one of the cornerstones of modern culture. So much so that we barely notice it, and we find it hard to accept that it is such a recent idea in human history and would have been incomprehensible in earlier times ... We still instinctively reach for the old vocabularies, the ones we owe to Enlightenment and Romanticism.[1]

In 2004, the BBC screened a documentary entitled *The Power of Nightmares: the Rise of the Politics of Fear*. Written and produced by Adam Curtis, the documentary controversially argues that Islamist terrorist groups such as al-Qaeda are self-realising myths, encouraged by the West (particularly US neoconservatives) in order to construct identifiable enemies resonant with the popular imagination. At the centre of Curtis's argument is the assertion that terrorists cannot be conceived as individuals; they must be imagined as part of a global organisation, 'A powerful and sinister network, with sleeper cells in countries across the world'.[2] Curtis does not deny the reality of terrorism; what he denies is a well coordinated and hidden organisation as the source of this threat. His working title for *The Power of Nightmares* was *The Elements of the Self*.[3] His previous project for the BBC was *The Century of the Self* (2002), a documentary which began with Freud and traced the development of ideas of selfhood as they have been exploited by mass culture in the modern world. Terrorism, from Curtis's perspective, is, like capitalism, a manipulation of who we are; it is a manoeuvring of individual identities, both by those who perpetrate terrorism, and those who claim to protect us from it.

Reading Hari Kunzru's work, it is valuable to keep Curtis's documentary at the front of one's mind. Like Curtis, Kunzru sees an explicit connection between terrorism and selfhood. Curtis's documentary feeds into a wider discourse surrounding the terrorist and ideas of the self. Being an inward-looking individual facilitates ethical behaviour; turning introspectively inwards is what conventionally is interpreted as facilitating closeness to God and, more recently in more secular contexts, an awareness of right and wrong.[4] The terrorist, we often assume, lacks this individual consciousness; he or she must be, so popular discourses suggest, a member of a group, a cult mentality, which has overtaken the individual power of reflection and disabled moral functioning. The notion of mass destruction not being at odds with the individual's consciousness is a profoundly disturbing idea, which can itself only be made palatable by alternative explanations such as mental illness. In Kunzru's second novel, *Transmission* (2004), the central protagonist of Arjun himself becomes subject to this myth. A single individual who spreads an international computer virus, he is imagined instead as part of a terror network, a 'technological fifth column'.[5] His very personal act, a response to an individual grievance, is transformed into an event in which his own subjectivity is lost: 'he had tried to act but instead had made himself a non-person' (159). An alternative rendering of this scenario is equally central to Kunzru's third novel, *My Revolutions* (2007), focused on a middle-aged man who has covered up his terrorist past by taking on an assumed identity: the man who was 'Chris', a terrorist, becomes 'Mike', a devoted family man. His terrorist group are identified as 'mindless'.[6] Yet, at the same time, the terrorist must strip others of their humanity to rationalise their actions: for Chris/Mike and his revolutionary comrades, those they attack are 'Pigs', not people. 'As individuals' his targets have 'no substance for me at all' (197).

This chapter begins in such a way to explicitly encourage a particular reading of Kunzru's work. By humanising the terrorist through the figures of Chris/Mike and Arjun, Kunzru suggests that individuals with justifiable motives find themselves co-opted into less ethical schemes with a group mentality that strips them of their individual subjectivity, whether such groups are imaginary (in the case of *Transmission*) or real (as in *My Revolutions*). Group identity supersedes the complexity of individual selfhood. Moreover, if revolutionaries may dehumanise themselves and others, this is only in reaction to a system which has already dehumanised them. This, of course, has important parallels to the events of 9/11, even though both novels are set before 2001. Media discourse surrounding the attacks on the World Trade Center has focused on how vulnerable individuals were manipulated by international terrorist organisations.

More controversially, critics have also identified the potential justifications for the emotions behind these actions, if not the actions themselves, in terms of the neo-colonial role of the US in world politics and trade, a role which is emphasised in *My Revolutions* through reference to Vietnam and, in *Transmission*, by the inequality of globalisation. In interview, Kunzru has controversially said that 'I can understand why young Muslims are putting posters of Osama Bin Laden in their bedrooms. He's a fucking rock star. He's the only person who appears to be standing up to a ruthless, homogenising identity'.[7]

Yet how this individual self is lost in the terrorist world is equally a device employed by Kunzru to explore the notions of selfhood central to all his fiction. When considering Kunzru's focus on the terrorist, we should think less about obvious connections to post-9/11 discourse or debates about the current age of anxiety, and more about what the terrorist symbolises for Kunzru in terms of identity. The fact that two of Kunzru's three novels have terrorist elements means most readings of his work have focused on this, with Kunzru's first novel, *The Impressionist* (2002), often seen as divorced from his later concerns. Only a handful of reviewers and only one critic, Alan Robinson, have noted this additional concern which in fact unites *all three novels*: 'Kunzru's abiding preoccupation with the making, and dismantling, of personal identity'.[8] The diversity of Kunzru's writings – he was Young Travel Writer of the Year in 1999 – reflect the career of a writer with global interests. The similarities, however, offer a detailed and developing vision of selfhood.

The politics of selfhood

Philosophers of selfhood such as Charles Taylor draw attention to the fact that 'we naturally come to think that we have selves the way we have heads or arms, and inner depths the way we have hearts or livers, as a matter of hard, interpretation-free fact', but that, in reality, such assumption is a modern phenomenon.[9] While the notion of the unified self can be traced back as far as Plato, the idea that this self has an interior existence is far more recent. As Taylor illuminates, 'the very idea that we have or are "a self", that human agency is essentially defined as "the self", is a linguistic reflection of our modern understanding and the radical reflexivity it involves. Being deeply imbedded in this understanding, we cannot but reach for this language; but it was not always so'.[10] In essence, what Kunzru's fiction attempts is a questioning of that very modern sensibility: not to return the reader to a pre-modern reality, but rather to proffer a post-modern (yet not always postmodernist) alternative.

Kunzru is generous with his own words, and it is not difficult to establish his interest in ideas of consciousness, identity and self. He acknowledges that he is 'obsessed with shape-shifting'.[11] More specifically, he has expressed concern that society has become trapped in models of identity no longer relevant to contemporary circumstance. He locates this in one particular moment of European philosophy: Romanticism. Kunzru is 'very interested in our reliance on a Romantic conception of character', believing 'We're being asked to deal with a very complicated networked world using a set of 18th century beliefs about ourselves'.[12] Importantly, he states that it was this 'romantic notion of personality or character', rather than 'the race thing about identity', which motivated him to write.[13] Identity, then, is different from selfhood. The former concept speaks to communal identification of the kind manipulated by terrorism, what Paul Gilroy refers to as the fact that 'to share an identity is to be bonded on the most fundamental levels: national, "racial", ethnic, regional, and local. Identity is always bounded and particular.'[14] The latter, in contrast, speaks to the sense of individual, profoundly subjective, and personal qualities.

Kunzru's critique of Romanticism comes from what he sees as its belief in a fixed, permanent sense of self. While these notions existed before, Romantics reaffirmed the status of the individual as a unique subject, with an inner voice distinguishing him/her from others.[15] Equally, the Romantics elevated inward looking as a means of developing moral and ethical imperatives to a new level of importance.[16] Romantics for the first time established a self which 'is no longer some impersonal "Form" or "nature" which comes to actuality, but a being capable of self-articulation'.[17] Focus on self-expression established a new level of individuation where the nature of individuality determined the path of life. Within everyone is an originality which they are obliged to do justice to: 'Each person is to be measured by a different yardstick, one which is properly his or her own.'[18] For Taylor this is the first time that the individual self has such a crucial role: it is for the first time, more than social circumstance, *who we are*. Each human maintains a 'radical individuation' which makes originality the cornerstone of existence.[19]

All of Kunzru's protagonists refuse, in different ways,

Romantic self-articulation. They interrogate the idea that there is a unique subjectivity which means that each individual experiences their activities, pursuits, emotions and ideas differently to anyone else: that each person is an original, with what Taylor refers to as an 'unrepeatable difference'.[20] The notion of the individual first person voice as indicative of a supreme individuality is called into question. In *The Impressionist*, the central character of Pran undertakes several transformations, taking on new personae so completely that his former selves are no longer referenced or reflected upon. Born an Indian male, Pran becomes both a woman and an Englishman on the course of his journey. His lack of fixed self can be attributed not to the postcolonial condition, however, but to a kind of multiple personality disorder. Denied the communication essential to the formation of self during childhood, Pran goes on to experience hideous sexual abuse. These experiences resonate with the identified origins of multiple personality disorder, often associated with extreme childhood abuse. It is in the wake of this experience that Pran's self unravels:

> 'Him', in fact, is fast becoming an issue. How long has he been in the room? Long enough for things to unravel. Long enough for that important faculty to atrophy (call it the pearl faculty, the faculty which secretes selfhood around some initial grain), leaving its residue dispersed in a sea of sensation, just a spark, an impulse waiting to be reassembled from a primal soup of emotions and memories. Nothing so coherent as a personality. Some kind of Being still happening in there, but nothing you could take hold.[21]

While the classical division of mind and body which preoccupies European philosophers – Plato and, later, Descartes most famously – suggests we have a sense of self that is separate from our bodily form (often referred to as Cartesian dualism), Kunzru challenges this assumption with an alternative reality in which changing the body may fundamentally alter the self. There is no Cartesian mind here, no Romantic authentic self that is inherent and unique. There is only the physical: a 'primal soup'.

Such modelling may seem little different from the postcolonial notions of a hybrid identity as outlined by Rushdie. Yet Kunzru's ideas extend beyond such frameworks because, more controversially, Kunzru's fiction at times seems to suggest, in fact, that there is no self beyond these bodily mutations. While one may strategically associate oneself with others from a multiplicity of cultural backgrounds, for Kunzru there is nothing underneath such identifications: there is no self on which identity is based.

Through his various transformations, Pran never expresses the idea that he has come closer to his 'true self' or, even, that his 'true self' is a hybrid combination of all the communal identities he has performed. It is not a matter of coming to terms with a heterogeneous identity, but more of accepting the futility of such endeavours, accepting that 'identity' is a false holy grail when the individual self has no fundamental basis. It is this that makes Kunzru more postmodern than postcolonial; it is not that essential identities are hybrid, but that the notion of an essential self on which such identity might rest itself is being called into question. It is a subtle, but significant, distinction.

In these terms, Pran offers an important revision of the post-colonial model of mimicry. While it is tempting to see Pran as the classic mimic, an early twentieth-century version of Naipaul's Ralph Singh, the notion of a mimic is of an individual who has a selfhood which is *denied* by their aspiration for white imperial culture and who makes a 'false' communal identification. Pran, however, has no denied self. There is no original behind his acts of mimicry. There is nothing to deny. From his birth, Pran is defined as an individual without a fixed selfhood: his astrological chart is 'a shape-shifting chart. A chart full of lies' (26). When Pran watches the impressionist (giving the book its title), he has a profound revelation about the nature of selfhood, seeing that 'In between each impression, just at the moment when one person falls away and the next has yet to take possession, the impressionist is completely blank. There is nothing there at all.' (419) Strip away the social construction, Kunzru tells us, and there is nothing authentic underlying it. There is only a nothingness on to which our performances can be, ironically, adhered, a nothingness which makes all expressions of identity – whatever communal allegiance they take for their inspiration – equally inauthentic.

Equally, in *My Revolutions*, the title refers not only to physical revolution in which Chris/Mike is involved, but also his own personal negotiations of selfhood, the going around in circles that is both his experience in the prison yard (70) and his circling around different subjectivities, 'the circular, self-reflective movement of a mind remembering itself'.[22] Yet the emphasis here is slightly different from *The Impressionist*. Is Chris/Mike more 'himself' when he is a terrorist, or a family man? Kunzru shies away from making either of these identifications more 'true'. However, rather than this indicating the lack of self exemplified in Pran, here the possibility of embodying more than one subjectivity is favoured. Chris/Mike initially identifies his two personalities as separate beings: 'after living so long as Mike Frame, it's sometimes hard to find my way back to Chris Carver' (219). However, at the end of *My Revolutions*, Chris/Mike does not choose between his two roles but identifies himself as both of these simultaneously. Choosing to return to Miranda and Sam – his 'Mike' life – when he calls Miranda he announces himself as 'Chris' (277). In this moment he is both people: both selves existing simultaneously.

Such complex selves mean that, in Kunzru's world, Descartes' notion of the self-sufficient individual withers away.[23] In *Transmission* we see how the body, attached to the mind but not of it, can form, in fittingly technical terms, an interface which means that the concept of inside and outside is broken down in favour of a fusion between the individual mind and the social world. That such fusion is centred on the technological confounds another hangover from Romantic thought: the idea that nature is central to human development. Instead cyberspace has become as real as real space: the physical world has lost its power and we have become alienated from the natural world.[24] For Arjun, the world of the computer is just as real; as 'a secret garden. A laboratory' (28) his private area of the network, hidden from all other users, has its own physicality. Yet it is this physicality that alienates him: existing in a space in which he is the only inhabitant distances Arjun from human contact.

One might speculate here that this might be Kunzru's point: that technology has led us away from the self; that, in Romantic terms, 'Nature is fundamentally good, and the estrangement which depraves us is one which separates us from it'.[25] Yet there is no Romantic call here to abandon industrialisation and return to the ecological; rather Kunzru emphasises the redundancy of such frameworks as the urban life rejected by the Romantics has proven itself the most defining feature of contemporary existence. According to Erik Davis, there is not a lack of spirituality in the movement towards machines; rather it is within them that we now 'catch our reflections, even our spirits'.[26] Davis's study of the spiritual aspect of computing, *Techgnosis* (1999), reveals a world in which the pursuit of the sublime has not been eroded in the movement away from nature, only displaced.[27] Kunzru picks this up in his beautiful short story 'Deus Ex Machina' (1998), where a guardian angel saves a woman's life via a computer, expressing that such machines are 'the tools which replaced apparitions and holy relics'.[28]

In all these texts, the debates about the self need to be read as comments on contemporary circumstances. Although Pran is a severe case, his mode of being bears similarity to how Kunzru sees contemporary identity more generally, part of a novel motivated by a desire to create a character 'interrogating whether we are actually immutable or are we much more context driven than we care to believe?'[29] Cases of multiple personality disorder have risen dramatically alongside increasing experimentation with identities in society and,[30] while he is an extreme, Pran also acts for Kunzru as a model:

> All of us have a sense of social range and we tend to maybe modulate our voices differently depending on who we are talking to. We might behave in slightly different ways in different social contexts. I wondered just how far that goes and how much drift is possible?[31]

Throughout *The Impressionist*, other characters display a similar lack of self: the Kwaaja-sara is almost invisible (92), Sir Wydham is a stand-in for England (156), the imperial presence consists not of individuals, but of projections which must stand for the Viceroy, himself standing for the King-Emperor (152). This metaphorical usage of an extreme case to exemplify a broader concern is equally evident in *My Revolutions*. Anna engages in 'an authentically communal experience. It was as if she subsumed herself entirely into Thirteen ... It was as if she had no inner life at all' (171). The revolutionaries declare 'It's not about the self. The self is reactionary crap. It's about mass mobilisation' (88). So, again, while identity may exist, there is no individual subjectivity underlying its construction.

Whether or not the Romantic model worked in its own time is not of concern, although Pran's lack of self even in the nineteenth century suggests a certain scepticism. It is simply that it no longer has relevance in the contemporary world. As a result of this, there is an ambivalent inevitability woven into Kunzru's novels. If we take *The Impressionist* as an example, we can see how this functions. Conventional understanding of self asks us to interpret Pran's loss of self in negative terms, as the terrible loss in which mimicry results. Yet it may not be so much negative as simply the state of things as Pran's mimicry exists within a context in which 'he is copying people who are hollow already'.[32] Kunzru himself has pointed towards this reading:

> Rather than being a sad story of a boy who loses his home and can not find a place in the world, which is often the way people give the outline of this story, but it is more of a kind of way of exposing

the homelessness that, I think, is the human condition. I think the
idea of a natural connection to a place or a natural connection with
a society is false.[33]

At points, Pran's lack of self does have negative consequences:
the final irony in his relationship with Star, where he is rejected
for being too English, points to the limits of performance in the
wake of a world that continues to be preoccupied with authenticity. His performances in the wake of colonial power, abuse
and exploitation, bear little relation to the actions of Kureishi's
exhilarated metropolitan protagonists. Indeed, Kunzru actively
interrogates this representation. Consider, for example, the following passage:

> You may think you are singular. You may think you are incapable of
> change. But we are as mutable as the air! Release yourself, release
> your body and you can be a myriad! (82)

This may seem like the archetypal celebration of fluidity. And
yet the speaker of these words is the Kwaaja-sara, a man who
would prostitute Pran for political purposes.

Yet while Pran's extreme may be undesirable, his ability to
'stitch a personality together' (250) *is* attractive. When a new
self takes over, the former is forgotten. This means that when
Pran transforms into Jonathan Bridgeman he does not so much
mimic Englishness as actually become this, as it 'seeps a little
deeper into his skin' (307):

> He is becoming what he pretends to be, realizing that the truth is
> so unlikely that, despite his occasional oddities and lapses, no one
> would ever divine it. He is starting to coincide with his shadow.
> (317)

It is no coincidence that it is at this point that Pran finally finds,
in his tutor Dr Noble, a voice that expresses a positive alternative to ideas of inherent selfhood. His name giving away
Kunzru's opinion of him, Dr Noble informs Pran that 'we are
not born, Mr Bridgeman. We are made.' (332)

This same reality is expressed more poetically in Kunzru's
short story 'Sunya' (1999):

> I add a tenth. The sign of nothingness. The sign of the nothing that is
> something. The sign of that which has no qualities except existence.
> The sign of myself.
> I could have told you my name, but what would be the purpose. I
> could have told you my age, my sex, my caste. I could have numbered
> and named my children, my city, the titles of the dynasty of kings to
> whom I once owed allegiance. All these things are illusion.

The empty self offers escape from the prejudices surrounding the idea of normative identities. Performance allows Pran to escape Privett-Clampe; it means he can get an education; it allows him to obtain money to live; it facilitates a certain amount of influence. Gradually, it becomes a matter just not of economics, but of fun (245). We may not approve of the ethics of his actions, such as his treatment of the 'real' Jonathan Bridgeman, but we must situate them within the direness of the alternatives for Pran, and on this level can applaud his survival: the fact that at the end of the novel Pran is the only one left standing, marked out from the imperialists who surround him.

As *My Revolutions* tells us, a revolutionary may become a communist, giving up the wants of the individual for a collective identity. Or he or she may become a terrorist. The abandonment of self is inherently neither good nor bad, but rather an essential part of contemporary life. Kunzru may not believe in the Romantic idea of an innate, unified self. He may not believe that the self we construct has a basis in reality. But, nevertheless, this process of imagining who we are is important: it is what allows us to distinguish ourselves from others. And that is why we need, he suggests, new ways of considering selfhood in the contemporary world.

Reconfiguring selfhood: the politics of consciousness

After being educated first at the public school Bancroft's, and then completing his English Literature degree at Oxford University, Kunzru took an MA in Philosophy and Literature at Warwick University. This is not unimportant in that Kunzru's thinking on the self is influenced by debates in philosophy beginning in the early 1990s that attempted to redefine human consciousness. In particular, Kunzru is influenced by the work of Daniel Dennett, who he interviewed while at *Wired* magazine.[34] Dennett's *Consciousness Explained* (1991) has been profoundly influential in both science and philosophy, but has achieved a mainstream cross-over presence; his ideas are often the foundation for contemporary theories of consciousness and subjectivity (Susan Blackmore's *Consciousness: A Very Short Introduction* (2005), for example, is largely a re-writing of Dennett's position for a more mainstream audience). Dennett's theories reject Cartesian dualism in favour of a materialist positioning in which the mind is simply the body: it is matter, rather than anything separate from this, and it is only through a combination of complex processes, rather than through the action of a unique faculty, that understanding is achieved. Dennett exposes how even those theorists who claim to reject Cartesian dualism maintain it on some level: they continue to believe in a 'special' location of consciousness which can be identified, what Dennett terms 'the Cartesian theater'. In the processes of the brain which make up consciousness, there is no role for the pre-existing differentiation – the unique kernel of self-awareness – favoured in Romantic notions of selfhood. Equally, there is no place for a single subjectivity: for one coherent self. This is because Dennett's alternative to the Cartesian theater is the 'multiple drafts model', where competing streams of consciousness exist in parallel to each other. While only one thought or action may eventually emerge, nevertheless the brain is full of multiple impulses.

With the idea of a Cartesian theater rejected, Dennett speculates on the possibility of one body with multiple selves, capturing the notions of selfhood offered in both *The Impressionist* and *My Revolutions*.[35] Pran in particular is used by Kunzru to debate Dennett's ideas. He is a mind, and a body, but largely seems lacking in consciousness. According to Dennett, consciousness is not inherent, but something that exists only if belief in consciousness exists.[36] This belief is transitory, and the self exists only in this moment of belief, transformed with each new moment of awareness. Without this belief, Pran has no self. He is one of Dennett's zombies: a body that appears to have consciousness, but in fact does not.

When Pran *does* show a sense of self it is on Dennett's terms: transitory and fleeting, existing only in that moment and not transferred to other situations, without narrative or continuity. As Pran moves on to a new role, the previous incarnation of his self is seemingly forgotten, no longer referred to. There is no reflection on previous incidences, as Pran experiences events 'at one remove, the pain-messages arriving at his brain like holiday postcards' (98). Pran is more likely to act, or to be acted upon, than to decide consciously upon an action or reflect upon one. At points in the novel, focus drifts away from him, almost as if he can no longer hold the attention even of the narrative. What is revelatory here is Dennett's claim that in fact we all are like this classic model of the zombie: people do not have any special access to the motivations behind their actions. Humans are simply rebuilding themselves and evolving, whereas zombies are not, creating the illusion of a unique human consciousness.[37] It is thus not that Pran's lack of awareness denies him a self, but that his lack of awareness reveals the lack of self inherent to all.[38] There is nothing missing in Pran other than the illusion that there is something missing.

Kunzru's fiction is populated by such individuals. Consumed by mental illness, Chris/Mike's mother in *My Revolutions* is 'only performing her newly learned happiness' (61) on return from the mental hospital. Equally, although Guy Swift in *Transmission* may appear to exemplify the notion of inspired unique individuality, there is in fact nothing behind this veneer. He may appear a self, but is in fact little more than a zombie:

> The music trickled into Guy's brain, slowly clearing his mental space, like an elderly janitor stacking up chairs. He had a sense of angelic contentment. Here he was, existent, airborne, bringing the message of himself from one point on the earth's surface to another. Switching his laptop on, he tried in a half-hearted way to compose a mail to Gabriella, but, confronted by the blank white screen, he could think of nothing to say. (13)

Even the seemingly deepest consciousness may be an illusion. So we are reminded:

> In a world of illusion you have to ask questions. You have to doubt, systematically. Other people may act real. They may behave as if, like you, they are animated by internal processes. But you never know. Some of them are just machines. (104)

As people believe Pran, so Guy is equally convincing: a zombie is more common than we might think.

Essential to the idea of consciousness in Western thought is the concept of agency, or free will. As early as Augustine, the idea exists that through an act of will one can choose to embody a particular selfhood.[39] This is not a matter of postmodern performativity, but rather an emphasis on the fact that all humans, as a result of the Fall, must take responsibility for their actions. It has extended into the present concern for choosing a 'true self' in an act of self-definition which comes about as a result of introspection.[40] The critical reaction to *The Impressionist* is particularly interesting in these terms. When the novel was published, reviews commented negatively on Pran's lack of warmth.[41] Perhaps the reason that reviewers respond with such coolness to Pran is that he never asserts his will, rather accepting the control of others that tells him this is of 'no consequence' (81). He does not choose what self to be in most circumstances, but allows his self to be shaped by others. In this way, he does not exert the power of conscious decision that is held by many to be central to selfhood.[42] Rather, he affirms the philosophical position that free will is an illusion: a product of a mind that likes to believe it has made a conscious decision to act. In *Consciousness Explained*, Dennett asks us to consider whether consciousness should make a difference to how we treat life forms. If desires aren't conscious, does it matter if we crush them?[43] Dennett suggests that such discussions have important consequences for ethical and moral behaviour. The reaction to Pran suggests worrying consequences about our attitude to consciousness. We would care more about Pran if he cared more about himself, it seems.

Being human

Dennett's argument about consciousness has its most profound implications in terms of notions of humans as unique. Throughout philosophy, centring on the human self distinguishes the human both from the external material world, and from other living things: 'the mind is life' and, conversely, the universe of matter is 'not a medium of thought or meaning ... is expressively dead'.[44] Dennett suggests, however, that humans are only unique in their ability to consider themselves unique, rather than because of any fundamental difference. While basic computers may not be able to undertake the learning processes that distinguish humans from zombies, more advanced models that are being built can. Telling us that 'conscious human minds are more-or-less serial virtual machines implemented – inefficiently – on the parallel hardware that evolution has provided for us', Dennett argues that human consciousness is just the result of a rather badly designed computer system.[45] Both humans and computers have evolved beyond their basic capabilities.[46] In these terms, how is computer consciousness any different from that of a human? Both are equally unbelievable, so that if we believe a human brain can evolve into a conscious mind, so we must believe the same is possible for a computer.[47] Kunzru's interest in these ideas means it is much more that his previous occupation as associate editor of the British edition of technology magazine *Wired* (1995–97) that determines his choice of focus for *Transmission*. The principles of computer networks and their implications are essential to his engagement with selfhood. What Kunzru asks his readers to debate is the precise nature of the relationship between human and machine in respect of the increasing similarity between them. Are machines increasingly like humans because humans have designed them in their own image, perhaps subconsciously with the desire of proving these re-creations inferior, and therefore re-establishing the value of humanity? Or, more disturbingly, are machines becoming increasingly like humans because, at a fundamental level, humans are no more than machines?

This blurring is evident from the very first pages of *Transmission*. The virus speaks in the first person: 'I saw this and thought of you.' (3) The relationships it establishes are akin to those between humans: personal and emotional: 'It's not as if you had asked for Leela to come and break your heart.' (3) From this opening, *Transmission* continues developing such connections. Arjun's brain is like a computer: his dreams can be reconfigured, 'outcomes built in as required' (15). Leela appears in human form, but there is 'machinery at work under her skin' (4). The golf course in the Dubai desert is transplanted grass, where veins and arteries are fed by plastic tubing (176). Virugenix's workers are successful because they are 'wired differently' (59), where existential questions are rejected as 'uncomputable' (63). The comparisons work in both directions: one of the computing networks at Virugenix is referred to as 'the Petri dish' (54). Against the Romantic notion of a unique humanity, Arjun sees in computers the potential for an equally animated vitality. 'By the age of thirteen', we are told, 'Arjun had long discounted the theory that there were actual living things inside computers. But something mystical persisted, a hint, the presence of a vital spark' (106).

Here the influence of Donna Haraway – who Kunzru has both interviewed and written about – is profoundly evident.[48] Kunzru's description captures Haraway's world of technoscience in which 'fibers infiltrate deep and wide throughout the tissues of the planet, including the flesh of our personal bodies', creating a cyborg culture in which man and machine are interwoven.[49] At the centre of this is Kunzru's meditation on the nature of the computer virus. If, as Haraway suggests, disease is a kind of language then,[50] with language essential to selfhood,[51] the virus is essential to the breakdown of boundaries between human and machine. It is a 'virtual disease' with the possibility to 'migrate' (*Transmission* 55): it is alive. As Haraway rejects the notion that humans reproduce (unless through cloning) for the idea that they generate themselves, so the multiple replications of the virus replicate the act of procreation.[52]

Arjun's first encounter with a computer virus as a teenager is an awakening to this possibility, a 'string of code that had hidden itself in an innocuous floppy disk and had used his computer to make copies of itself. Every restart had given birth to another generation. Life.' (108)

The diseased computer network represents a threat to the uniqueness of humanity: a technology out of human control, and thus close to the boundaries of consciousness which allow humans to mark themselves out from both matter and other life forms. Equally, if the immune system is in itself essential to selfhood – the identification of something foreign means the body knows what it is – then the fact that a computer might be attacked by something foreign and recognises it as such again represents a blurring of human and machine.[53] So the computer, with its emerging consciousness, asks us to question our individuality. As we are connected online via the Internet we become networked, our individual selves becoming fuzzy as we are continually subject to seemingly endless flows of information. The individual gives way to a collective consciousness. At the same time, online personae allow individuals to re-make themselves with new selves, calling into question the notion of essential selfhood.

This blurring can be a frightening prospect, as Erik Davis outlines:

> With the continued ideological dominance of reductionist science and the sociocultural dominance of its technological spawn, the once glorious isle of humanism is melting into a silicon sea. We find ourselves trapped on a cyborg sandbank, caught between the old, smouldering campfire stories and the new networks of programming and control. As we lose our faith in free will or the coherence of personality, we glimpse androids in the bathroom mirror, their eyes black with nihilism – the meaningless void that Nietzsche pegged over a century ago as the Achilles' heel of modern civilization.[54]

Kunzru, however, sees such blurring as essential to deconstructing outdated notions of selfhood:

> Being a cyborg isn't just about the freedom to construct yourself. It's about networks. Ever since Descartes announced, 'I think, therefore I am,' the Western world has had an unhealthy obsession with selfhood. From the individual consumer to the misunderstood loner, modern citizens are taught to think of themselves as beings who exist inside their heads and only secondarily come into contact with everything else ... Unless, that is, you're a collection of networks, constantly feeding information back and forth across the line to

the millions of networks that make up your 'world.' A cyborg perspective seems rather sensible, compared with the weirdness of the doubting Cartesian world.[55]

Leela's experience exemplifies these two possibilities. Her initial experience of the Leela virus affirms how cyberspace is read negatively to diminish humanity, as she feels her unique personality has been stolen.[56] Yet, by the end of the novel, Leela's online personality has ultimately liberated her, opening up an alternate personality previously stifled. Being reproduced online complicates Leela's sense of her own fixed selfhood, to the extent that she ultimately rejects the media image that has dominated her sense of self since adolescence. Seeing herself endlessly replicated destroys the myth that Leela the actress is a unique, and therefore important, self. And it is this vision that frees her.

The fear of the virus represents not only a fear of the blurring of human and machine, but the possible contamination between them: it is evidence of a cyborg culture as the ultimate challenge to unique human consciousness. In *Transmission*, each of the central protagonists find their lives inextricably connected to the virus's activity and, by extension, to the machine. The central characters positively affirm the fact that 'postmodern bodies do not exist outside, or beyond, information, but are rather one of the two virtual poles (along with information) between which embodiment occurs'.[57] It is this that provides further evidence that Kunzru does not ultimately desire a return to the Romantic pre-cyberspace world. 'Better paranoid through too much connection than dead through none at all', in Haraway's words.[58]

Identity versus self

Kunzru is an intensely political writer: he is on the executive of London PEN, is patron of the Guantanamo Human Rights Commission, and, in 2003, he rejected the John Llewellyn Rhys Prize for *The Impressionist* (which had already won the 2002 Betty Trask Award and the 2003 Somerset Maugham Award, and been nominated for the 2002 Whitbread First Novel Prize) because of its sponsorship by *The Mail on Sunday*, a newspaper notorious for its right-wing views and anti-immigration headlines.

In the wake of this activity, Kunzru's work should not be separated from its political component. Kunzru rejected a prize sponsored by *The Mail on Sunday* because '*The Impressionist* is a novel about the absurdity of a world in which race is the main determinant of a person's identity'.[59] These events remind us of the contemporary relevance of the novel's message: for Kunzru, this race-determined world exists every day in British tabloid newspapers, and the novel is 'a coded way to unpick all the weird debates about race and identity that are floating around'.[60] Named along with Ali one of Granta's Best of Young British Novelists of 2003, Kunzru earned the highest ever advance for a first novel for *The Impressionist* on the promise of being a writer who would take 'his place in the constellation of important young British novelists writing about a very new, multi-racial, multi-ethnic Britain'.[61]

At first glance, none of Kunzru's novels seem to fulfil this particular description. His work, however, is the most evolved form of the post-ethnic reality first explored by Kureishi. Kunrzu's post-ethnicity bears comparison with Haraway's post-gender theory: utilisation of postmodern identity theory in the service of deconstructing existing hierarchies, with powerful consequences for racial/gender identity, *that may not always be obvious*.[62] Such an approach must be used with caution. In relation to the burden of representation, it risks trapping authors like Kunzru in an ethnic framework which discourages wider – and potentially more interesting – readings of their work. Kunzru himself has expressed such concerns, saying 'you're only allowed to talk about and relate to certain ethnic and race issues'.[63] To in this chapter focus on the broader implications of Kunzru's work is to question such tendencies, supporting Kunzru's own sense of himself as part of a group of writers who will not tolerate such restriction.[64] Nevertheless, it must be noted that, for those whose primary interest *is* ethnic identity, Kunzru's work does still have an important contribution to make. To examine the consequences of Kunzru's reflections on selfhood, subjectivity, and what it means to be human is to uncover conclusions with direct relevance to issues surrounding ethnic identity. Kunzru's meditations are not simply about engaging with popular postmodern deconstructions of selfhood; they are also about challenging some of the preconceptions about ethnic and racial identity which haunt ethnic minority communities in Britain.

In particular, Kunzru can be seen to use the idea of selfhood to reflect upon how the idea of ethnic identity – in essence a selfhood constructed in relation to communal notions of belonging – can be destabilised by undercutting its fundamental basis in the idea of a stable self. Kunzru's rejection even of a hybrid authentic self is a reflection of a British Asian confidence that is no longer preoccupied with asking the question 'Who am I?' The reason the model of inherent selfhood is for Kunzru rejected is that it means a 'fascist type of blood and soil connection'.[65] In *The Impressionist*, Pran exists in a world in which he can adapt to any circumstance, comfortable in diverse environments. In *My Revolutions*, the identity of Chris/Mike is a celebration of competing influences on personal identity. The lives of Mike and Chris could not be more different, and yet Chris/Mike ultimately chooses to be *both* these people. This choice resonates with a confident British Asian sensibility that is comfortable fusing, sometimes strategically, often very different cultural influences.

Kunzru's mixed-race perspective – born in Essex in 1969 to an English mother and Indian father (his mother was a nurse, his father a doctor who came to Britain in the 1960s) – here informs his approach. The mixed-race character of Pran expresses concerns with trying to resolve identity confusion that represent the questions often raised for mixed-race individuals:

> You are what you feel. Or if not, you should feel like what you are. But if you are something you don't know yourself to be, what are the signs? What is the feeling of not being who you think you are? If his mother was his mother and his father was the strange Englishman in the picture, then logically he is half-and-half, a blackie-white. But he feels nothing in common with those people. They hate Indians. (52)

Yet although Pran may be confused and alienated his eventual positive utilisation of this experience announces the mixed-race individual's ability to positively reclaim the lack of a firmly delineated racial identity in which selfhood might be rooted for their own purposes. The novel reminds us, through Macfarlane's craniometry, of the usage of hybridity in colonial discourse: in his incarnation as Robert, Pran's 'peculiar disguised form of hybridity' for Macfarlane 'might conceal all manner of antisocial tendencies' (198). To reclaim the hybrid is thus to counter this discourse of biological purity in which the self lies innately in the body. Questioning the notion of the self strikes at the heart of racist discourses of biological purity. Pran's form of mimicry, as in Bhabha's description of this, destabilises the idea not only of a pure self, but of a racially pure self. These racist alternatives profoundly alter the context in which we read Pran's actions: although his continual willingness to change may make him less human, nevertheless his actions must be preferable to the

alternative of an authenticity rooted in racist prejudice. Privett-
Clampe's idea that you can 'listen to what the white is telling
you' as it is 'calling to you through all the black' (109) shows
a connection between consciousness and biology that Pran
rejects: race is *not* character.

Despite their differing contexts, Kunzru's novels are united
in these terms. To be a cyborg is to be a hybrid, reflecting the
idea that 'human beings have been cyborgs from year zero'; the
notion of cyborg is simply the most recent way of imagining
the complex, heterogeneous nature of humanity.[66] Haraway
takes this up most commonly in terms of a feminist agenda,
suggesting that the cyborg is threatening from a perspective
of patriarchy. This is because cyborgs challenge conventional
ordering and hierarchies, questioning traditional definitions of
what it means to be human which have privileged masculine
culture. Yet despite this interest Haraway frequently also draws
upon discourses of racial politics in her work, often using the
work of African American women to exemplify her arguments.
The notion of the cyborg, it seems, is threatening not only to
established gender hierarchies, but also to established racial
ones. This is because challenging the distinctions between
machine and animal, for Haraway, is a way of questioning the
binaries which have dominated the Western view of self with
all their racial and patriarchal prejudices.[67] As Haraway argues:

> From the eighteenth to the mid-twentieth centuries, the great his-
> torical constructions of gender, race, and class were embedded in
> the organically marked bodies of woman, the colonized or enslaved,
> and the worker. Those inhabiting these marked bodies have been
> symbolically other to the fictive rational self of universal, and so
> unmarked, species man, a coherent subject ... You and I (whatever
> problematic address these pronouns have) might be an individual
> for some purposes but not for others. This is a normal ontological
> state for cyborgs and women, if not for Aristotelians and men.[68]

Haraway's connection here between the eighteenth-century and
present-day cybernetics is a mirror of Kunzru's own chronology: the technological 'other' is simply the latest manifestation
of the racial 'other', dehumanised and denied selfhood.

To question the rational, unified self, therefore, is a project
with an inherent racial politics, to be aware that 'judgements
concerning what is or is not a human body sometimes have led
to large injustices'.[69] In *The Impressionist* the Amritsar Massacre
is recounted to emphasise the lack of humanity given to the
Indians by the British generals; not individuals but simply 'the

dark-skinned races' (183). In the novel's discussion of craniometry, Macfarlane comes to believe in polygenesis and the
existence of 'monkey people' (233): non-white races are denied
humanity, miscegenation producing people *'perfectly comparable
with our street-dogs and roof cats'* (231). This is more than simply
saying, as do postcolonial theorists such as Robert Young, that
colonialism and racism are founded on discourses of racial
purity, though this is part of it.[70] It is suggesting, beyond this,
that the idea of a unified self is what is ultimately at stake in
such discourses. What happens in Kunzru's later-set fiction is
simply an extension of this. *My Revolutions* points to the racist
dehumanising and exclusion of others that partly precipitates
the drift towards communal identities in revolutionary practice, as Chris/Mike's group join forces with ethnic communities
to oppose the rise of the National Front (152). *In Transmission*
Arjun is perceived more as machine than human as he finds on
losing his job that he is 'no longer a real person' (127), echoing
the workers of earlier eras, but also the workers as they are perceived in *My Revolutions*, where 'bourgeois individualism' (111)
is central to socio-economic inequality.

Indeed, one should not see Kunzru to be offering a technological alternative to Romantic discourse. *Transmission* makes
clear that the technological revolution may be central to how
we now consider what it means to be human, but it is nevertheless deeply problematic. Arjun's experience is a fictional
rendering of the vast inequalities in global industries exposed
by critiques of globalisation: the shrinking of the world is for
him a 'deflating beach ball' (6) rather than an expansion of possibilities; his exhilaration on departing for the US is crushed in
the novel only six pages later (33, 39). Global connection is par-
odied in the parallel stories of Arjun and advertising executive
Guy Swift. The idealised postmodern notion of interconnected-
ness is firmly dismissed:

> Did Guy Swift sense some occult connection with the boy on the bus
> [Arjun] 30,000 feet below? Did he perhaps feel a tug, a premonition,
> the kind of unexplained phenomenon that has as its correlative a
> shiver or a raising of the hairs on neck or arms? No. Nothing. He was
> playing Tetris on the armrest games console. He has just beaten his
> high score. (12)

Arjun's difficulty infiltrating the computing industry illustrates
Ziauddin Sardar's argument that the new frontier being colonised by the West is cyberspace.[71] The notion of the borderless

world is critiqued by a world in which that border has been transformed into a mental construct that will be equally policed while, at the same time, Guy's final failure at the hands of immigration police is a powerful satire of the Western celebration of free movement. That Guy ultimately is a victim of the very scheme he has supported announces ironically the painful inequalities his advertising rhetoric has obscured. His loss of identity sees him mistaken for an illegal immigrant, powerfully reminding the reader once again that the postmodern notion of fluid identities should not be idealised; as for Rushdie's immigrants, here a stable, recognised identity is something to be craved, where the alternative (as Guy experiences) is to be dehumanised and treated as an animal.

Such reading also places new emphasis on the millennial fears so often surrounding technology. Kunzru reflects an age of anxiety that has preoccupied thinkers in the post-9/11 world. In his only book set in the post-9/11 period, *Transmission*, Kunzru defines the virus as 'future terror' (109). At the centre of this is a resurrection of fears of the 'other', and its unseen presence in contemporary society, the same *fin de siècle* anxiety Aslam's fiction reflects. If terrorism is ultimately a fear of death and destruction, cyberterrorism emerges as this threat in new terms: challenging what it ultimately means to be human, waging a war of destruction that may be virtual, and yet equally destabilising. But the racial politics of such anxiety offers a troubling spin on things. What is more 'other' than the non-human: the technological presence which resurrects the fear of miscegenation in postmodern form? If we fear the computer, Kunzru asks, are we not displacing our anxieties about racial and ethnic purity around which so much post-9/11 paranoia revolves? For this reason, Arjun and his virus are perfect allies: two 'others' attacking the global capitalist system that would reject both of them through a fear of contamination. This is Arjun's 'writing back', but the virus is the synecdoche for his own status, and also – in more gendered terms – for Leela's. It is a non-self that, like the racial 'other' before it, will challenge the province of humanity as it is defined in the limited and exclusive terms of white male privilege.

Conclusion

As Alden Mudge rightfully notes, Kunzru 'has questions about the whole idea about what it means to be a person': he is less preoccupied with the communal identities that consume most discussions of ethnicity than with the more philosophical questions underlying this, the concepts of selfhood which determine the very basis of our assumptions about what it means to exist.[72] The 'free, self-determining subject' developed from Romantic notions of self is absent in Kunzru's novels.[73] Indeed, there is an undercurrent of Foucauldian ideas in all of his work that betrays Kunzru's interest in French poststructuralist theory, a mode of thought deeply influential in the technological and scientific discourses to which his texts refer. Kunzru's fictional endeavours in the early 1990s played on this interest, yet he quickly found that publication opportunities in relation to this sort of writing were limited: in interview with Rushdie the older author gives Kunzru the benefit of his experience by telling him that 'you don't get anywhere in England with French theory'.[74] Despite this, Kunzru has continued, more subtly, to embrace theoretical concerns often largely rejected by British Asian authors; while Aslam, for example, may have a character state 'We don't have souls, we have cells', it takes Kunzru to explore the complexities of such an assertion.[75] This makes him the natural successor to Kureishi and Rushdie. Kunzru's rejection of consciousness in its conventional manifestation means not simply communal identity but also the individual self that underlies it is impossible: not just in essential, but even hybrid, form. This common thread across Kunzru's writing has important implications for how we consider race and ethnicity but also, perhaps more importantly, it offers an insightful contribution into considering who we are, *whoever we are*, in the contemporary world.

Discussion

- In *My Revolutions*, Chris/Mike roots himself in Buddhist belief systems. How might the Buddhist rejection of the concept of the soul be useful when considering Kunzru's fiction?
- Bearing in mind their diverse subject matter, to what extent is it useful to consider Kunzru a 'British Asian' author?
- How might Kunzru's notions of selfhood be problematic for those who believe in ethnic identities?

Notes

1 Taylor, *Sources of the Self*, p. 376, p. 393.
2 Adam Curtis, *The Power of Nightmares*, BBC 2, 20 October 2004, 9 p.m. Transcript available online at www.daanspeak.com/TranscriptPower OfNightmares1.html.
3 Koehler, 'Neo-Fantasies and Ancient Myths'.
4 Taylor, *Sources of the Self*, p. 132, p. 184.
5 Kunzru, *Transmission*, p. 154. Subsequent quotations cited parenthetically.
6 Kunzru, *My Revolutions*, p. 201. Subsequent quotations cited parenthetically.
7 Rachel Cooke, 'I'm the Bloke who got the Big Advance'.
8 Mattin, 'My Revolutions'. See also Robinson, 'Faking It: Simulation and Self-Fashioning in Hari Kunzru's Transmission'; Mudge, 'Identity Crisis'; Sooke, 'Signs of the Times'. For readings focused on terror see Beckett, 'Don't Call Me Comrade'. For those focused on race see Adams, 'Many Unhappy Returns for a Teenage Terrorist'.
9 Taylor, *Sources of the Self*, p. 112.
10 *Ibid.*, p. 177.
11 Sooke, 'Sign of the Times'.
12 Mudge, 'Identity Crisis'.
13 'Interview with Hari Kunzru', www.book-club.co.nz/features/ harikunzru.htm.
14 Gilroy, *Between Camps*, p. 98.
15 Taylor, *Sources of the Self*, pp. 368–9.
16 *Ibid.*, p. 362.
17 *Ibid.*, p. 375.
18 *Ibid.*, p. 375.
19 *Ibid.*, p. 376.
20 *Ibid.*, p. 182.
21 Kunzru, *The Impressionist*, p. 65. Subsequent quotations cited parenthetically.
22 Mattin, 'My Revolutions'.
23 Taylor, *Sources of the Self*, p. 156.
24 Davis, *Techgnosis*, p. 194.
25 Taylor, *Sources of the Self*, p. 357.
26 Davis, *Techgnosis*, p. 129.
27 *Ibid.*, p. 306.
28 'Interview with Hari Kunzru', www.book-club.co.nz/features/ harikunzru.htm.
29 Davis, *Techgnosis*, p. 222.
30 'Interview with Hari Kunzru', www.book-club.co.nz/features/ harikunzru.htm.
31 Mars-Jones, 'East Meets West'.
32 'Interview with Hari Kunzru', www.book-club.co.nz/features/ harikunzru.htm. For a review that casts Pran in such tragic terms see Mendelsohn, 'Karma Chameleon'.
33 Kunzru, 'Futurism'.
34 Dennett, *Consciousness Explained*, p. 419.
35 *Ibid.*, p. 132, p. 309.
36 *Ibid.*, p. 310, p. 375.

37 For this relationship see Persson, 'Self-Doubt', p. 28.
38 Taylor, *Sources of the Self*, p. 137.
39 *Ibid.*, p. 450.
40 Meadows, 'Son of a Sort of Goddess'; Mendelsohn, 'Karma Chameleon'.
41 Schechtman, 'Self-Expression', p. 47.
42 Dennett, *Consciousness Explained*, p. 450.
43 Taylor, *Sources of the Self*, p. 148.
44 Dennett, *Consciousness Explained*, p. 218.
45 *Ibid.*, p. 225.
46 *Ibid.*, p. 433.
47 Kunzru, 'You are Cyborg'.
48 Haraway, 'PRAGMATICS: Technoscience in Hypertext', p. 130.
49 Haraway, 'Biopolitcs', p. 203.
50 See Dennett, *Consciousness Explained*, p. 417.
51 Haraway, 'Promises of Monsters', p. 69.
52 Haraway, 'Biopolitics', p. 203.
53 Davis, *Techgnosis*, p. 131.
54 Kunzru, 'You are Cyborg'.
55 Sardar, 'alt.civilisations.faq', p. 28, p. 37.
56 Thurtle and Mitchell, 'Introduction', p. 14.
57 Haraway, 'Introduction: A Kinship of Feminist Figurations', p. 4.
58 Kunzru, 'Society: Making Friends with the Mail'.
59 'Hari Kunzru, Penguin Authors'.
60 Mudge, 'Identity Crisis'.
61 Haraway, There are Always More Things Going On Than You Thought!', p. 329.
62 Aldama, 'In Conversation', p. 14.
63 *Ibid.*
64 'Interview with Hari Kunzru', www.book-club.co.nz/features/harikunzru.htm.
65 Davis, *Techgnosis*, p. 10.
66 Haraway, 'A Cyborg Manifesto', p. 174.
67 Haraway, 'Biopolitics', p. 210, p. 216.
68 Thurtle and Mitchell, 'Introduction', p. 11.
69 See Young, *Colonial Desire*.
70 Sardar, 'alt.civilisations.faq'.
71 Mudge, 'Identity Crisis'.
72 Taylor, *Sources of the Self*, p. 395.
73 Kunzru, 'Art, Writing: Salman Rushdie'.
74 Aslam, *Wasted Vigil*, p. 202.

Further reading

Alan Robinson, 'Faking It: Simulation and Self-Fashioning in Hari Kunzru's *Transmission*', in Neil Murphy and Wai-Chew Sim (eds), *British Asian Fiction: Framing the Contemporary* (New York: Cambria, 2008), pp. 77–96.

Sardar, Ziauddin, 'alt.civilisations.faq: Cyberspace as the Darker Side of the West', in Ziauddin Sardar and Jerome R. Ravetz (eds), *Cyberfutures:*

Culture and Politics on the Information Superhighway (London: Pluto, 1996), pp. 14–41.

8

Monica Ali

I found it astonishing that it took young Muslims born and brought
up in Britain, but socially excluded and alienated, so long to riot,
and that it required so much provocation from the National Front.[1]

In the summer of 2001, young British Asians took to the streets
of Oldham and Burnley in the North of England to protest
against perceived racial inequality in their neighbourhoods. In
the popular British press, these events were reported as illustrative of the disconnection of young British Asians from wider
British society, driven by outside 'foreign' influences.[2] For Ash
Amin, however, the actions of these young men were characterised as:

> a counter-public making a citizenship claim that cannot be reduced
> to complaints of ethnic and religious mooring or passing youth mas-
> culinity. The anger expressed a demand to own and mould these
> towns of racialized space allocation on their own terms. The Asian
> youths have unsettled those who want to keep them in their own
> minority places, as well as majority opinion that minorities should
> behave in a certain way in public ... Their frustration and public
> anger cannot be detached from their identities as a new generation
> of British Asians claiming their right to own Oldham or Burnley *and*
> the nation, but whose Britishness includes Islam, halal meat, family
> honour and cultural resources located in diaspora networks.[3]

For Amin the protests by young British Muslims mark the
emergence of a subcultural force refusing to remain hidden.
Importantly, they do not mark distance from Britishness, alienation, or confusion. Rather, they are evidence of the very secure
sense of citizenship held by this British-born/raised generation.
Similarly, for Ron Geaves, young British Muslim responses to
the war in Iraq and involvement with the Stop the War Coalition
presents a fluid and hybrid group of protesters where 'the dem-
onstrations have forged alliances with social-liberal values and
shown many young British-born Muslims that a dissenting

voice is also a time-honoured method of showing citizenship'.[4] In these terms, Britishness is not denied by protest, but embodied by it: young British Muslims' 'Britishness', Geaves suggests, 'rose to the fore only in the context of their feeling that their nation of birth provided them with the right to be Muslims and publicly express their democratic right to oppose government policy'.[5] The increasing visibility of young British Muslims in these accounts is not a marker of increased marginality, but rather a defiantly British section of society finding its public voice. Such interpretation relies upon re-visioning certain readings of the significance of protest. While both peaceful protest and rioting are on a number of levels markers of alienation and dissatisfaction, they are also public protests that can *only* be undertaken by those who feel a sense of belonging. Protest relies upon a sense of entitlement: assumption of certain rights of citizenship, and a legitimate claim to representation, both at local and national levels. To protest is not to deny belonging, but to claim a right to it.

Monica Ali's first novel *Brick Lane* is imbued with this spirit of defiance, both on the very public scale that Amin and Greaves document, but also on the small scale which Amin's cultural reference points – halal meat, family honour – point towards. Through protest, Ali's novel challenges alternative representations of British Asian identity, as these are offered both by the popular British media, and by the very genre of contemporary British Asian fiction in which Ali's own work is situated.

Claiming Britishness

Like Nadeem Aslam, Ali seems to straddle worlds of postcolonial fiction and contemporary British Asian writing. Born in Dhaka, Bangladesh, she came to England with her family in 1970 at the age of three, and has spent her adult life in London. *Brick Lane* tells the story of Nazneen, a Bangladeshi migrant who comes to London in 1985 as the result of an arranged marriage to Chanu, himself a migrant to Britain in the 1970s. Received to great critical acclaim (along with Zadie Smith and Hari Kunzru, Ali was named one of *Granta*'s twenty best young British writers in 2003, on the basis of only the manuscript of *Brick Lane*), the novel is celebrated for re-imagining the migrant narrative from a female perspective, providing both counterpoint and accompaniment to the large number of male-centred migrant narratives.

Focusing on Nazneen's migrant experience draws attention to the inherent gendering of both movement and settlement. *Brick Lane* also presents, however, a powerful engagement with concepts of Britishness. At the end of the novel, two generations of British Asian women declare their right to be full British citizens, as Nazneen decides to remain in London without Chanu, making the defiant claim that *'I will decide what to do. I will say what happens to me'*, as her best friend Razia proclaims 'This is England ... You can do whatever you like'.[6] Focusing on the spirit of protest in the novel is a way to recuperate this aspect, and to consider how Ali's perspective – though rooted in a consideration of the migrant experience – also emerges from a distinctly British Asian sensibility. While Nazneen is a Bangladeshi migrant, the novel's other key figures include members of a British-born generation: most notably Nazneen's young lover, Karim, and her eldest daughter, Shahana. This interaction is central to the narrative's construction of a tone of defiance, which pervades the novel as a whole, and is not restricted to Nazneen's actions or attitudes. The relationship between these characters, and their shared experiences, ultimately challenges the distinction between postcolonial migrant and British Asian experience, in favour of a shared identity. Defiant behaviour both in private and public space becomes symbolic of an assertive claim to British citizenship and ethnic confidence. The novel is ultimately optimistic, about not only the future of the Asian diaspora, but also its ability to be accepted as part of British society without a sacrifice of cultural or religious values.

Claims for *Brick Lane* in terms of self-assurance, buoyancy and national conviction pose a challenge to readings which have been unconvinced by its optimism. For many critics, the ending of the novel jars. Yasmin Hussain in *Writing Diaspora* is uncertain about the novel's ending: 'Nothing is resolved, Ali's characters are still living in a transitory state.'[7] For James Procter, Nazneen's agency 'has little to offer in the way of political alternatives', as she continues to work in partnership with a 'white-run clothes store'.[8] Equally, for Natasha Walters the ending 'felt as if Ali was trying for a more definite fictional closure than, by that time, her complicated characters can bear'.[9] For Delia Falconer, there is an 'overdetermined plotline which seems ... to push the narrative in a feel-good feminist direction'.[10] Michael Gorra offers an analysis that is more profound, but of similar character: '"Agency" isn't a word from *Brick Lane*;

it intrudes and jars and is then forgotten – at least until a brief narrative coda, when the book finally slips into soft focus', producing final pages that 'are squishily affirmative'.[11]

Such readings obscure the assertions of self which the novel develops that define a distinct progression towards a more hopeful, positive future. What critics such as Hussain rightfully recognise, however, is an unresolved tension in Ali's narrative. The majority of the novel echoes the conventional – and somewhat clichéd – model of alienated migrant subject most associated with postcolonial fiction. Dealing with the relatively late mass migration of Bangladeshis to London, which only reached its peak after the 1962 Immigration Act, such similarity is on some levels not surprising, as Ali's text is dominated by similar tropes to an earlier generation of narratives of migrant arrival. The novel employs an elaborate use of figurative language in its first half to reinforce this tone. Looking out from her council flat window at her neighbours, Nazneen sees the tattoo lady's boredom as 'a state [that] was sought by the sadhus who walked in rags through the Muslim villages' (13), while walking through Brick Lane traffic is described as being 'like walking out in the monsoon and hoping to dodge the raindrops', as 'a horn blared like an ancient muezzin' (43). These metaphors and similes are employed as part of a larger strategy which secures Nazneen's emotional survival in her first year in London, but also marks her out as archetypal diasporic subject, with one foot in present location, another in the geography of the past. With her relationship to the environment defined by a desire for return and a sense of isolation Nazneen accurately reflects the split between the location as 'home' for the migrant, and their place of settlement, what Mark Stein characterises as the distinction between the location of residence and the location of belonging in migrant literature.[12]

Resistance to celebratory readings is also reinforced by the fact that this depressing tone does, despite the ending, constitute the predominant mood of the novel. *Brick Lane* gives little sense of the progress of time as an active force in changing the position of migrants, either in terms of their own self-development, or changes in government policy and the attitudes of the white population. Jumping from 1985 to 2001 little appears to change in Nazneen's personal circumstances. Indeed, in many ways the experience deteriorates. In 1985 Brick Lane is a bleak environment for the migrant population: Chanu recounts, '*it's a Tower Hamlet's official statistic: three point five Bangladeshis to one room'* (39). Yet it only declines over time as it becomes 'four or five' in Chanu's estimation by 2001 (273). Any change that has occurred, it is emphasised, has not benefited the migrant. The changed landscape in 2001 is one that reflects the increased investment in East London, with 'money, money everywhere' (208), expensive fashions and overpriced coffees. The impact of gentrification on the indigenous population offers not the improvements governments so often promise, but instead a widening gulf between rich and poor and, for those in the migrant community who form part of the latter, an added layer of alienation from their immediate surroundings. This is echoed by Atima Srivastava in her story 'Dragons in E8': while Hackney is gentrified to include health-food and designer jewellery stores the narrator becomes hooked on smack.[13] As a result, not only is there a sense of stasis which projects the migrant as being incapable, perhaps unwilling, to integrate, but – additionally – British society as a whole comes to reflect what James Procter refers to as the nation's status as 'a stable bland monolith'.[14]

Ali's British-born characters are also imbued with a sense of personal confusion which seems to contradict the novel's positive conclusion. This again reflects recent discourse – particularly in relation to British Muslims post-9/11 – which has defined young Muslims as culturally and socially isolated. Karim has a stutter which is a physical symbol of his anxiety and lack of confidence: seeing Nazneen as the 'real thing' (320) he is represented as searching for a perceived lost authentic ethnic identity. Shahana, equally, offers typical adolescent aggression and rejection of parental authority, yet her retort 'I didn't ask to be born here' (298) betrays the cultural conflicts informing her rebellion. At the novel's ending, attempts to challenge white racism have deteriorated into intra-community violence. In Razia's final statement Nazneen seems to be being offered unproblematically the possibility to reconcile her personal desires and a wider, national identity. There is no suggestion that Nazneen's religion might form a barrier to national acceptance of the kind of expression of individuality that she desires. Yet in the wake of the novel's implication of state-sanctioned racism, as Karim declares that 'people only take on a job themselves when their leaders aren't doing it for them' (398), such a solution seems unrealistic. In this context, the positive conclusion of the novel presents an idealistic and incomplete resolution. Nothing has changed materially for Nazneen or her community, yet she has undergone a profound change in circumstances nevertheless.

That Razia not only reaches for such a future but declares assertively its existence in the present tense implies that the expressions of both the individual Muslim migrant woman and the wider community to which she belongs are not incompatible with notions of rootedness and, given Razia's reference to Englishness, more specifically with national belonging. Yet this is against what much of the narrative has suggested.

However, one must carefully read the chronology of *Brick Lane* to fully consider why this novel is as bleak near its conclusion as near its beginning and why, in fact, this does not prevent the novel's ending expressing celebratory sentiment. Three-quarters into *Brick Lane*, 'a piece of New York dust blew across the ocean and settled on the Dogwood Estate' (305). What results is not in keeping with this poetic image, but instead violent and extreme: young girls have their hijabs pulled off; Razia wears her Union Jack sweatshirt and is spat at. That the violence suggests repetition of earlier urban tensions is a depressing representation, as London's historic exclusion of difference is resurrected. Yet if a contextually and ethnically specific reading is pursued, an alternative possibility emerges. Things indeed may have changed, but 2001 – perhaps – presents its own unique circumstances that raze progress far more quickly that it has been achieved. In these terms, the depressive nature of much of *Brick Lane* seems understandable. While there is a generalised optimism, this is tempered not by a depressing reflection of black British identity in general, but by an awareness of a more specifically British Asian, indeed British Muslim, reality. In general, there may be the opportunities of cross-cultural interaction. But for the British Muslim, this reality has been undercut: not by a continuance of the racism and prejudice faced by the migrant, not by continued feelings of alienation stemming from a migrant sensibility, but rather by a new and insidious form of religious discrimination. More than any other novel discussed in this book, *Brick Lane* therefore indicates the importance of substituting a generalised reading through the concepts of black British writing for a more culturally and historically specific British Asian consideration. It is only in reading the novel through such specifics that the complexities of *Brick Lane* are fully appreciated.

Not only 9/11 but also post-Iraq War tensions consume the 2001 section of the narrative. Even before 9/11, police are visiting the mosque and questioning the imam (169). Shahana turns the television on to find images of 'hooded young men, scarves wrapped Intifada-style around their faces, hurling stones, furious with cars that they set alight' (228). These riot scenes, distanced from the Brick Lane community as being in 'a place called Oldham' – where 'called' indicates a place unknown – contextualises the mentioning of 9/11 within a wider discourse of race relations in Britain involving events in Iraq, Palestine, and the growing moral panic inspired by the Western media's Islamophobia. By referencing Oldham directly, the novel gestures towards the claims for social inclusion and representation being made by young British Muslims. Within this context, Karim's growing fundamentalism is not the failure of integration in terms of the maintenance of a migrant 'outsider' sensibility in the British-born citizen, but indication of the rejection of those citizens as British by the state and its white majority, a continuance of earlier challenges to the acceptance of racial minorities where 'Islamophobia ... is less a new phenomenon that a translation of earlier concerns around the presence of black communities in Britain or Europe'.[15] In these terms, the depressive tone to *Brick Lane* prior to its conclusion is not a rejection of British-born reality, but an engagement with it in very specific circumstances. Defiance grows steadily through the novel as a marker of Britishness; that the development of this consciousness may not always be reciprocated in social attitudes does not, the novel suggests, destroy what has become an inherent claim to citizenship and inclusion. The pessimism of Ali's novel, if contextualised, is in fact ironically a discourse of British-born belonging, as it marks a defiant spirit of national assertion.

I want to suggest, therefore, a reading of *Brick Lane* through the concept of protest, in which movement into public space is the central metaphor of Ali's novel. Echoing the events of Oldham in less violent form, Nazneen moves out into the streets to make a definite statement of self-assertion, denying what Amin refers to as the 'claims for minor spaces of recognition' which migrants have often been limited to.[16] By moving outwards, Nazneen challenges the discourse of invisibility surrounding ethnic minorities in the public sphere. This is particularly relevant in terms of British Asians: while they may have emerged as the 'new folk devil' in more recent post-9/11 discourse, they have also been constructed conventionally in passive terms.[17] In the novel's final chapter, Nazneen makes her most definitive entry into public space as a result of an anti-racist protest, when the Bengal Tigers, a local Muslim community group, organise a demonstration against a local racist group called the Lion Hearts who are spreading Islamophobic material in the wake of 9/11. In doing so, she not only challenges the oppression and stereotyping of Muslim women from both within her own community and outside it, she also becomes part of a wider Muslim alliance bridging the distance between migrant and British-born subject.

Entering public space in such a way is a well noted method of ethnic defiance. The streets are one of the most essential sites of identity formation. In terms of ethnic identity, in particular, the location of the street has been emphasised, most notably outlined by Procter who devotes an entire chapter to the subject in *Dwelling Places*, his study of black British literature, but also in sociological studies. For Claire Alexander in her study of British-Muslim youth identity, for example, 'the trope of "the Street" is deeply encoded as a metaphor for gender and for "race"; it is black men who are seen to own "the Street"', making it a powerful site of identity contestation and challenge.[18] Brick Lane as a street has a history of such a role, and the incursions made by the Bengal Tigers resonate with a past in which refusing to be moved along, making the street a site of temporary inhabitancy, is a statement of citizenship rights.[19] In ethnic terms, this precedent had already been established in Britain by the social unrest in the wider black British community in the 1970s and 1980s. Yet what Procter draws our attention to is the specific role of British Asians in what otherwise is seen as a largely Afro-Caribbean-driven protest movement, events such as the 14 May 1978 protest march by 7000 Bengalis in Brick Lane following the murder of Althab Ali, or the united march of the Anti-Nazi League and the Bengali Youth Movement Against Racist Attacks on 18 June 1978, attended by an estimated 4000 people. While we would do well to heed Procter's warnings not to romanticise such struggles, nevertheless Ali's novel engages with such metaphorical associations. By moving into Brick Lane and its surrounding streets and making themselves visible, Ali's characters are claiming a space analogous to claiming the wider public space with which it can be identified. The street thus stands as synecdoche for the British nation, and a right of occupation. Although the protests are most notably about racism on the Dogwood Estate, they also become connected to anti-war demonstration: in expressing both local and national concerns they make explicit the connection between local action and social comment on the scale of national politics.

For all three of Ali's characters involved with the protests,

their presence is symbolic of forging an inclusive British identity. Shahana is running away to avoid relocating to Bangladesh
with her father. Karim, as protester, is staking his claim for a
British Muslim identity with full rights of citizenship. His personal development is as profound as that of the women in the
novel: despite his stutter, he becomes the public voice of the
community, speaking in front of several hundred people. The
local allegiances these youths are involved in may be violent –
'in their gangs, and they fight the posse from Camden or King's
Cross. Or from the next estate' (215) – but they do mark the
British-born Asian's right to belong. For Hussain, representation of public protest through these male characters offers not
Amin's mood of engagement, but rather – akin instead to wider
media representations – a negatively defined uncontrolled
and senseless violence. 'In the novel', she claims, 'these men
roam around, treating Brick Lane and its surrounding streets
as military zones to be occupied and fortified, territories worth
annexing; anxiety and resentment are in the air as they attempt
to rid the estate of the racism that has infiltrated it. They are
presented as merely competing for control over territory, under-
mining attempts to unify them.'[20] However, within Amin's
terms, their actions need to be seen as more complicated. Rather
than accepting racism, this generation has the confidence to
subvert and reclaim its terms of reference:

> Someone had written in careful flowing silver spray over the wall,
> *Pakis*. And someone else, in less beautiful but confident black letters,
> had added, *Rule*. (194)

In this context the depressing tone can be re-read ironically not
as a denial of the possibility of confident British Asian identity,
but a further affirmation of it. Protesting against racism can be
read not as the rising up of a minority, but rather of a British
Asian generation finding their voice.

This defiant claim for recognition is most noted, if less
physical, however, in the case of Nazneen herself, who has a
much longer journey to make towards Britishness than Karim.
Looking for Shahana, Nazneen is described as putting 'her face
right up to the policeman's face. *Do you see me now? Do you hear
me?*' (392) Like the marchers, she demands her recognition by
the British establishment, here signified by the policeman, the
official symbol of Britain's law and order. That it is Nazneen
who most noticeably embodies the spirit of street protest, rather
than Karim, challenges the usual masculine associations of

such strategies, particularly in the black British context. Early migrant narratives not only express the migrant experience in terms of alienation, but represent this also as doubly oppressive in terms of the female migrant who, as Sukhdev Sandhu notes, has always been denied the easy wandering of the city so often recounted in male migrant narratives.[21] More specifically, the female Muslim subject is interpreted in much Western feminist discourse as silenced and oppressed. Yet Nazneen's presence challenges both these representations. On this level, too, *Brick Lane* marks social change and transformation. The protests are not only a challenge to the invisibility of the migrant, but also to the gendered construction of the Bangladeshi community.

Equally, the vocalising of Karim and Shahana's generation is itself a transformation. For Geaves writing about the anti-war protests, the distinction between the space of this engagement and that of previous Muslim connections to politics is particularly significant: 'It is a far more public space; they are less invisible that their elders, whose political activities took place in the relatively anonymous realm of ethnic relations and intra-community affairs.'[22] Traditional Islamic organisational structures, embodied in the mosque, hold little right of access for women or the young, but protest allows them a space to define the community's agenda. As Geaves notes, 'new organisations provided British-born generations with their own political space, to include not only the young but women – both traditionally denied access to the leadership of the mosque' (72). This adds an additional dimension to the fact that public visibility in itself is a departure, as riot represents for Muslims 'not only a rejection of white majority practices, but also of the "ethnic" politics practised by their own community leaders'.[23] Alongside the patriarchs at the march in *Brick Lane* is the *'Bethnal Green Islamic Girls' Group'* (386), representing precisely the sort of new religious formations forged in British communities against the conventional structures of top-down religious organisation.[24] The next generation is transforming British society not just in terms of its ethnic make-up, but in terms of the practices defined by their own ethnic group: Nazneen's incorporation into these events marks a transformation of the entire community driven by its young people. For Amin, it is this act of freedom that proves young Muslims are making 'the claims of full British subjects'.[25] What Ali suggests is that such claims filter upwards towards an older generation who are themselves therefore equally motivated to demand citizenship and social change.

That such claims are made through protest is not without significance. The riots of 1981 in Brixton were in part a reaction to that year's Nationality Act. In Nazneen's claiming of her own Britishness through this same method of protest, she reaffirms the lost right to belonging based on locality. Nazneen may not have been born in Britain, nor are her parents British, and yet she asserts herself in defiance of Thatcher's legislation as an indigenous citizen. Protest is reclaimed against its use as fuel for definition of the British subject in racial and ethnic terms, turned instead – and more successfully than in 1981 – back towards an assertion of broader notions of belonging. Ethnic alienation is temporary, proving that with time and personal motivation, the ethnic citizen gains engagement with public space equal to its indigenous or ethnically dominant citizens, leading to a coterminous sense of identification and optimism. Citizenship is defined by a fluid set of self-styled and voluntary allegiances, which even post-9/11 prejudices cannot indefinitely disrupt. The sense of protest as citizenship means that the novel, through its violence and discontent rather than in spite of it, defines a new multi-ethnic Britishness.

Reducing the scale

Such public emphasis is not at the denial of the domestic spaces so central to conventional feminist claims for autonomy. Ali's novel is as much a feminist as a British Asian text. This means that while Nazneen, as a migrant, must subvert the discourse of invisibility, as a woman she must combine this with a reworking of private and familial space. At the beginning of the novel, Nazneen's comments that she is 'trapped inside ... this concrete slab of entombed humanity' (61) illustrate that she sees her flat on the Dogwood Estate in Tower Hamlets as marking the limits of her existence. Yet as the novel progresses, her movement outwards is reinforced by a reconfiguration of the domestic space, too, into a site of gradual empowerment. In the novel's penultimate chapter, Nazneen asks the question, 'What kept her tied to the corner of the room?' (376). While claims to citizenship are reflected in growing public visibility, they are also entrenched in the relationship to personal environment, as the home, like the streets of Brick Lane, must be finally claimed. This relationship is reinforced through the character of Razia, whose confident Britishness and independence from patriarchal structures is marked in her domestic investment:

> Razia called it a 'breakfast bar' and lined up cereal packets like cer-
> emonial soldiers along the back. When her husband was alive, when
> the flat was filled with junk, every spare pound (and many that were
> not spare at all) went back home to buy another brick for the new
> mosque. After he died, Razia spent her money on her children, and
> her flat. She never talked about going home. (357)

Engaging in what Perla Korosec-Serfaty defines 'appro-
priation', Razia claims her domestic space as evidence of her
'investment'.[26]

Refusing either to remain constrained by her role as wife or
to maintain a similar role with her lover Karim, Nazneen too
assumes this association as she rejects both Chanu's plans to
go to Bangladesh, and also Karim's marriage proposal. With
her decision instead to assert her right to remain in Britain, her
personal space bears the signs of her commitment to citizenship, and to dwelling, rather than to the diasporic discourse of
return. Instead of her earlier happy acceptance of clutter (114),
Nazneen expresses the need for a state of order echoing her own
growing sense of stability and reflecting the mentality of one no
longer locating themselves elsewhere. This begins as recognition of the desire to claim domestic space as part of a claim to
belonging:

> She should have bought plants and tended and loved them. All those
> years ago she should have bought seeds. She should have sewn new
> covers for the sofa and the armchairs. She should have thrown away
> the wardrobe, or at least painted it. She should have plastered the
> wall and painted that too. She should have put Chanu's certificates
> on the wall. But she had left everything undone. For many years
> all the permanent features of her life had felt temporary. There was
> no reason to change anything, no time to grow anything. And now,
> somehow, it felt too late. (283)

And becomes realised once Nazneen decides to stay in Britain:

> The plane left tomorrow and she would not be on it ... Down on the
> floor she looked at the shelves beneath the girls' desks. The books
> were tumbled and askew, and the corners dented by feet. She looked
> up at the wallpaper, shyly turning in on itself. Nothing would stick
> to those walls. They would have to be scraped clean and begun
> afresh. (365)

It is because of such private positioning that Karim's protest,
unlike the events of Oldham and Burnley, must ultimately fail.
It is not, significantly, because Ali offers the same unproductive

vision of protest as earlier authors. Kureishi and Rushdie critique violent protest as ultimately the action of the outsider: as John McLeod insightfully comments: 'In a similar fashion to Kureishi, Rushdie cannot envisage riotous protest as significantly different from the violence of the persecutor turned back on itself, with oppressor and oppressed locked in cyclical and uncreative dialectic.'[27] Yet, for Ali, protest is only the *first* marker of an assertion of citizenship that must be concluded on a more quotidian, commonplace basis. As part of her gendered re-visioning Ali announces that the solution to a coherent British Muslim identity is not to be found in the sort of assertions to be made through large-scale events or notoriety. This echoes the recent sociological studies of Bangladeshis in Tower Hamlets which, rather than the extremism presented in the mass media, suggest a community in which strong local ties have bred not isolation but confidence, and where extremism and support for violence is exceptional.[28] Citizenship will be claimed not through violence, but via the fusion of public and private defiance offered by the lives of both migrant women and the British-born offspring, standing defiantly through the everyday, rather than large-scale events. While the men follow violence, Nazneen quietly encourages confidence in everyday life by fostering the English speaking of her daughters. Having moved from the public as national and local space, to the domestic, the novel concludes with assertions of confidence on the smallest scale of Nazneen's own physical form, as she ice-skates for the first time. Ice-skating in her sari on the novel's final page, Nazneen's own body defines a fusion of British and Bangladeshi influences: the vibrant colour of traditional dress against the cold whiteness of an English winter day. This personal confidence, literally embodied, identifies against the readings of Hussain and others a stable and assured subject.

The use of the term 'stable' here is evoked with full awareness of its connotations. Against Hussain's reading of the 'transitory' states of Ali's characters, reading the novel through protest encourages instead a consideration of the novel in terms of more fixed and rooted identities. In her final act of ice-skating, Nazneen embodies two traditions, brought together without hierarchy or prejudice. But the sense here is not of endless transformation, but of resolution. Yes, you can do 'whatever you like' in England as Razia suggests, but what Nazneen 'likes' comes distinctly from the two material spaces defining her life thus far. She is content, it seems, and there is not to be the global travel or endless reworking of the self as statements of diasporic identity celebrate. Nazneen remains a Muslim. She remains a heterosexual woman. She remains a mother. She remains a wife, even in the absence of her husband. And although she may not remain a migrant as she becomes British Asian, she does firmly become this dual identity, rather than abandoning such determinants.

This is therefore not so much a postcolonial hybridity, as what might be referred to as a *contingent hybridity*, in which cultural practices are fused, but with a sense of finality rather than continuing transformation. New identities are not being continually moved between here, contaminating each other. Nor will the process of change be endless. Rather, one stable identity is being formed from direct – and therefore limited – first-hand experiences and personalised, family traditions. There is a choice here in terms of what practices to fuse, and whether to involve oneself in such a process. Chanu, for example, never accepts such possibility. There is not, however, once this choice has been made, it seems, the continual movement between different identities that seems to produce confusion. Instead, confidence can be gained by certainty in one multiple-sourced identity that becomes subsumed, because of its very awareness of multiple influences, into a definition of Britishness itself. For Tariq Modood, British Muslims are indeed expressing such an identity: 'Muslim' seen 'less as an oppositional identity that as a way of being British', and it is this 'way of being British' rather than a rejection of such national identifications that the definite cultural combinations made by Nazneen reflect.[29] Part of this shift is a de-poeticisation of the mythical diasporic homeland, and a more balanced weighting of present location and past geography, as Nazneen comes to see South Asia (both through awareness of her mother's suicide, and the struggles of her sister Hasina) in less idealistic terms. It is a much more literal and material engagement with migration than the postcolonial text often allows. While the novel begins with figurative floweriness, it has by its final pages reverted to a more simplistic style announcing an indigenous confidence through directness of expression. Nazneen no longer needs to stretch for poetic devices; instead the English language is gradually becoming hers to define herself in the more straightforward terms of everyday encounter. This rejection of a diasporic discourse of outsider status through the language in which the book is written means re-evaluating what might seem like a somewhat simple narrative style.

Moreover, there is no sense that the next generation's experience will be any more or less defined. As Nazneen skates on ice
in her sari, so her daughter accompanies her with sandwiches of
'cream cheese and mango pickle' which, crucially, she has made
herself (411). Shahana begins as the assimilationist's dream:

> Shahana did not want to listen to Bengali classical music. Her writ-
> ten Bengali was shocking. She wanted to wear jeans. She hated her
> kameez and spoiled her entire wardrobe by pouring paint on them.
> If she could choose between baked beans and dal it was no con-
> test. When Bangladesh was mentioned she pulled a face. She did not
> know and would not learn that Tagore was more than poet and Nobel
> laureate, and no less than the true father of the nation. Shahana did
> not care. Shahana did not want to go back home. (147)

However, by the end of the novel her sandwiches suggest she
has achieved the enculturation which Humayun Ansari privileges as the successful fusion of the British Muslim subject,
fusing together different traditions with which she is equally
comfortable, and which – in contrast to hybridity – she claims
as inherently her own.[30] The next generation too, therefore, will
combine elements from the cultures they have experienced, the
novel suggests, but they will fuse these elements to make a
singular cohesive product: this is a sandwich, we are asked to
remember, and not a smorgasbord.

In terms of this book's aim of distinguishing a distinct British
Asian literature, then, Ali is central. In particular, Ali offers the
most notable claim for the possibility of a specifically British
Muslim identity. Nazneen's rooted and religious identity,
fixed in one place even if it is not her place of birth, is not the
story of diasporic metropolitan wandering and plural identities. It echoes not Kureishi's entirely plural subjects, but rather
Ansari's reflection of the combination of religious absolutism
with ethnic flexibility, where 'young Muslims have come to
feel that while the religious element in their identities remains
relatively stable, the ethnic boundaries are malleable and per-
meable, and have the potential for intermingling and change'.[31]
While texts such as Aslam's *Maps for Lost Lovers* and Kureishi's
The Black Album (and, equally, from a Black British writer, Zadie
Smith's *White Teeth*) do define a confident British Asian youth,
their secular versions of British Muslim identity leave little
place for the devoutly religious Muslim individual to find a
place in British society. In contrast, *Brick Lane* suggests that religious faith and Britishness are indeed compatible. Nazneen's

faith is clearly maintained as her journey towards involvement in British society progresses. As Gorra notes, 'Ali's characters are all believers, and one of the original things about her work is the way in which she uses Islam. The Koran provides the lens through which her characters see their own lives; it gives them strength. Indeed, its importance for Nazneen and her friends matches that of the Bible for the characters in a Victorian novel.'[32] It is only in moving away from the unbridled hybridity of the postcolonial literary text that such a possibility emerges. It is ironic that, in being more tied into such discourses of openness and cultural translation, Aslam and Kureishi do not find the same possibilities for successful cultural fusion that *Brick Lane* embodies.

That what are presented largely in the novel as competing needs – national ideology and personal or communal expression – can be reconciled has particular significance given the literary and extra-literary contexts of Ali's novel. Rather than present 9/11 as a watershed, the conclusion to *Brick Lane* instead hopefully suggests it as a temporary setback in the development of an otherwise rooted British Muslim population. Rather than presenting British Muslims as the threat to national cohesion as in so many media reports following the events in New York, *Brick Lane* instead represents the discourse surrounding 9/11 itself as the most fundamental challenge to national stability, offering as it does a destabilisation of what is otherwise not a hostile and alienated Muslim community, but rather a community making a valuable and integral contribution to post-millennium urban Britain. The novel's conclusion announces in these terms an optimistic refusal to allow such events to derail permanently the project of an inclusive British identity. While further alienation may come from the ostracising of the Muslim community in the wake of such events, this will not be allowed to re-marginalise British Muslim citizens. After the bus and tube bombings of July 2005, the idealism of such representation is even more pronounced. Yet, at the same time, the resonance of Ali's account increases coterminously. Read again in the light of such events, *Brick Lane* offers a stark warning as to the danger of allowing the actions of a minority to define the characterisation of religious or ethnic groups.

Post-script: *Alentejo Blue*

In a comic yet telling scene in *White Teeth*, the young central Asian protagonist of Millat finds that expressing a musical preference when one is Asian is not as simple as he, in his schoolboy naivety, assumes:

> 'Sometimes we find other people's music strange because their culture is different from *ours*,' said Miss Burt-Jones solemnly. 'But that doesn't mean it isn't equally good, now does it?'
> 'NO, MISS.'
> 'And we can learn about each other through each other's culture, can't we?'
> 'YES, MISS.'
> For example, what music do you like, Millat?'
> Millat thought for a moment, swung his saxophone to his side and began fingering it like a guitar. 'Bo-orn to ruuun! Da da da da daaa! Bruce Springsteen, Miss! Da da da da daaa! Baby, we were bo-orn –'
> 'Umm, nothing – nothing else? Something you listen to *at home*, maybe?
> Millat's face fell, troubled that his answer did not seem to be the right one.[33]

Smith herself would become subject, ironically, to this same cultural judgement in the reception of her second novel, *The Autograph Man* (2002), with which Smith refused the framing expected of someone labelled as a 'black British writer'. Comparison with Smith is productive in that Ali's own career has followed a similar pattern. Her own second novel, *Alentejo Blue* (2004), can like Smith's be read as a conscious attempt to refuse to allow simplistic associations between ethnic authors and particular subject matter.

For Ali, the possible politics behind such a departure needs to be contextualised within the reception of *Brick Lane*. Although the novel was critically celebrated, it did not receive the blanket approval Smith's first novel seemed to achieve. In her focus on internal struggles within the Bangladeshi community, Ali may have been situating herself as central to a new British Asian literature that refuses to be defined in opposition to white society, but she was also offering a critique of patriarchal attitudes within Asian culture. In some sectors of the Bangladeshi community, such critique was not always well received.[34] This rose to the fore not when the book was published, but when the filming of its cinematic adaptation began.

These criticisms, which drew comparisons with the Rushdie Affair, illustrate the extent to which British Asian authors suffer the same struggles to be viewed in literary terms – the same burden of representation – which have plagued their postcolonial and black British counterparts. Ali herself, undoubtedly, might take some responsibility for this: entitling one's novel after a real-world street invites comparisons that might have been avoided had – like Rushdie – Ali used imaginative locales. Ali has stated that *Brick Lane*'s title was at the request of her publishers, whereas she had planned *Seven Seas and Thirteen Rivers*, a more lyrical phrase which has been attributed to Tagore, but is also widely used in Bangladeshi literature. Nevertheless, the novel's content itself makes real-world associations that a change of title would only have partially obscured. These prominent real-world connections, and Ali's acknowledgement of sociological sources for the book, offer to the reader a promise of representation which jars somewhat with Ali's subsequent refusal of such a mandate.

Such associations lie more in the hands of critics than authors, who read the book as offering 'a city that is largely foreign territory for most of its citizens, heralding a welcome new "state of England" novel' and which, for Geraldine Bedell, 'opened up a world whose contours I could recognise, but which I needed Monica Ali to make me understand'.[35] Moreover, many of the criticisms of *Brick Lane* misunderstood the book's position, echoing the Rushdie Affair again in the sense that the nuances of the text were obscured. Most notably, critics of Ali's representation of the Sylheti community failed to notice that such criticisms in the novel are voiced by Chanu, himself a figure to be critiqued. Equally, as criticisms were directly explicitly not only at Ali's representation, but her own 'non-representative' status, a dangerous homogenising of what it means to be British Asian was evident. Hussain, for example, argues that 'Ali's positioning as an author outside of the community that she attempted to represent limits the novel's authenticity', where being a 'daughter of a White English woman and a relatively privileged member of the Bangladeshi intelligentsia who had to leave Bangladesh for political reasons' with a 'social positioning outside of the core British Bangladeshi community originating from Sylhet, colours her representation of both Bangladesh and the British Bangladeshi community'.[36] The familiar divisions between ethnic British authors and their white counterparts were again drawn into stark relief:

> The perplexity one feels on finishing it is not the author's fault: it derives from the ecstatic response to the book and the expectations this has aroused. It is claimed to have mapped out a new, invisible London. It is treated as a direct portal into the minds of Bangladeshi East Londoners. One Sunday newspaper ran two reviews, the shorter by a Muslim comedienne who was asked to confirm the novel's

authenticity: she liked the book and thought it true. It's hard to imagine Notting Hill residents being asked if they consider themselves to have been fairly represented in *London Fields*, or the inhabitants of Chelsea Marina being questioned about their portrayal by J.G. Ballard as psychosexually troubled paranoiacs. Is the public recognition of ethnic communities across the United Kingdom dependent on their valorisation by literary fiction?[37]

It is in this context that Ali's movement to an entirely different setting for *Alentejo* is a strategic refusal to accept such definition in 'representative' terms, and to make the claim for a more definitively 'literary' reading of British Asian texts. The poor reception of the novel, unfortunately, suggests such a strategy in the short-term was unsuccessful: *Alentejo* is Ali's Bruce Springsteen. Self-referentially, the novel marks the difficulties of Ali's position through the character of the writer Stanton: a British writer abroad looking for inspiration and acknowledging in relation to his first novel 'How much easier it was to write then, thinking he knew about life.'[38] Like Stanton, *Alentejo* is recognition of the loss of this authority: whereas *Brick Lane* proclaims its non-fictional sources in the acknowledgements, those to *Alentejo* begin 'This is neither a history book nor a travel book, but only a work of fiction.' The use of 'only' bears the scars of *Brick Lane*, marking as it does Ali's awareness that to write 'only' a work of fiction, when one is a British Asian author, is a difficult process fraught with the turmoil of representative status.

At the same time, reviews of *Alentejo* neglect the novel's features which do represent an important continuation of the British Asian sensibility developed in *Brick Lane*. *Alentejo* is more involved in the debates surrounding British Asian authorship than its subject matter might suggest. It is a powerful statement of the need to consider texts by British Asian authors in terms of literariness rather than social comment and, paradoxically, to see that such refusal of the familiar terms of engagement is in itself its own kind of social comment. More than this, its British Asian sensibility is woven into its very location and style. In terms of setting *Alentejo* assumes the classical location of the postcolonial magical-realist novel: a small Portuguese village that is reminiscent of the influential Latin American texts of Marquez and Carpentier which inspired postcolonial magical-realist authors such as Rushdie. However, stylistically, the novel is a radical departure from this model. The novel's sparse realist prose style begins where *Brick Lane* ends: it offers a continuance of the rejection of the postcolonial vocabulary which Nazneen gradually comes to assume.

Equally, Ali's representation of the importance of identity is similar in her second novel to her first. The small community presented in *Alentejo*, like *Brick Lane*'s Tower Hamlets, is filled with a host of diverse characters, many of whom see themselves as outsiders, and the novel is structured as a series of vignettes providing insights into the lives of each of these variously 'marginal' figures. It is, equally, a place 'outside' the power structures controlling individual lives: the 'poorest region in the poorest country in the European Union' (118). Here, the experience of *Brick Lane* is universalised: an English mother realises that she has become the 'bloody foreigner' (204) she associated with Asian families in Britain. Like *Brick Lane*, the novel celebrates heterogeneous communities, and documents the continual movement of peoples: not only those who arrive in the village, but those who leave for elsewhere. But also like *Brick Lane*, it does not subscribe to a model of cultural hybridity. The real warmth of the novel is reserved not for those who are transient, but those who remain: whether the indigenous inhabitants of the village such as João and Vasco, or those who have made their homes there, such as the dysfunctional Potts family. Throughout *Alentejo* there are indications that identity is something that must be questioned, but also something to be protected. Is Jay Potts Portuguese because he lives there, the young boy asks his mother: 'yes' his mother tells him, only to be contradicted by his father (102); the same mother celebrates the Alentejo village as a community when 'there's no community in England any more', yet feels nevertheless socially excluded when her own traditions fail to attract the local population (208–9). Even when its created nature is acknowledged, nevertheless, the imagined community has a coherence in the minds of its inhabitants which is precious:

> He said to Bruno, 'What language do you think your grandchildren will speak?'
>
> Bruno pushed up his cap and grunted. Bruno is not a great thinker.
>
> 'English, my friend,' Vasco informed him. 'With an American accent.'
>
> Vasco sighs a long, wheezing sigh. Oh, he says to himself, what do I know? Not as much as Bruno, even. His grandchildren and their grandchildren will speak Portuguese. Such a beautiful language will never die ... Why does he say all these things? Such a beautiful language. Even when he said it he didn't believe it. (86)

While Vasco acknowledges his invention of an idealised language and heritage, at the same time the novel points to very real, personal and tangible traditions that risk being lost:

> The high airless voice followed her to the door. 'Teresa,' it said, 'when I die I will leave this place. My nephews will come from Porto and Lisbon to sell it and they will not remember my mother's salad, the right proportion of ear and tail and a little dash of red wine vinegar. But maybe you will tell them, maybe you will say, 'Oh, Senhor Vasco, he had such plans.' (175)

As Teresa plans to go to London to work as an au pair, we know that such stories are unlikely to survive. Identity, as for *Brick Lane* held in small significances – the Portuguese equivalent of Shahana's sandwich – is not something to be easily cast aside. Equally, as Nazneen's religion is central to her existence, so the story of a young engaged couple illuminates the need for religious faith, this time in the context of Christianity: 'All the church stuff, he hated it. To him it was just lies. She couldn't argue with that but she wanted to; she realized now that she wanted to. *How do you know*? She wanted to say.' (242) Identities may be lost: but this loss is not the road to a more liberating hybrid existence, but a source only of confusion and doubt.

On a wider scale, too, change is not always a process towards growth. Just as gentrification does nothing for Brick Lane's migrants, so globalisation offers the village only a Vodaphone shop, and an Internet café with no Internet. The young people have mobile phones but João has no electricity (145). Yet when one of these young people, Teresa, visits João she realises he 'did not need her pity. She almost envied his simple life'. (147) The 'old ways', slow and tradition-filled, are not critiqued here in favour of the hyper-real of postmodern fluidity, but rather relished and even nostalgically yearned for. Once again, this is most pronounced at the end of the novel when a local inhabitant, Marco, said to have made a fortune abroad, returns. Marco, however, is proved to be a fraud and a charlatan, and the massive development it is rumoured he will bring to the village never emerges. Instead, the village remains largely untouched by the global forces of market capitalism that Marco represents. A coherent identity, however multi-ethnic, has been saved. The same stories, the novel concludes, will continue to be told. The old ways continue to survive.

Discussion

- What is the relationship between *Brick Lane* and earlier fictions of migrant experience?
- Does the realist setting of *Brick Lane* and its title justify criticism of the novel by the Bangladeshi community?
- What is the role of her sister Hasina in Nazneen's emerging consciousness?

Notes

1 Sardar, 'The Excluded Minority', p. 54.
2 Poole, *Reporting Islam*, p. 6.
3 Amin, 'Unruly strangers?', p. 462.
4 Geaves, 'Negotiating British Citizenship', p. 74. See also Gilroy, *After Empire*, pp. 134–5, for similar sentiment,
5 Geaves, 'Negotiating British Citizenship', p. 75.
6 Ali, *Brick Lane* , p. 337, p. 413. Subsequent references cited parenthetically.
7 Hussain, *Writing Diaspora*, p. 98.
8 Procter, 'New Ethnicities', p. 118.
9 Walters, 'Citrus Scent of Inexorable Desire'.
10 Falconer, 'Brick Lane'.
11 Gorra, 'East Enders'.
12 Stein, *Black British Literature*, p. 69, p. 95.
13 Srivastava, 'Dragons', p. 3.
14 Procter, *Dwelling Places*, p. 1.
15 Alexander, *The Asian Gang*, p. 15.
16 Amin, 'Unruly Strangers?', p. 460.
17 Alexander, *The Asian Gang*, p. xiii.
18 *Ibid.*, p. 237.
19 For this history see Procter, *Dwelling Places,* pp. 108–17.
20 Hussain, *Writing Diaspora*, p. 101.
21 Sandhu, *London Calling*.
22 Geaves, 'Negotiating British Citizenship', p. 76.
23 Amin, 'Unruly Strangers?', p. 462.
24 This is reflected in the Muslim female periodical, *Sultan*, the Women Against Fundamentalism group, Young Muslim Sisters UK, the Manchester Muslim Women Society, and the London-based Muslim Women's Association and by British Muslim student organisations such as the Federation of Students Islamic Societies, Muslim Students Society UK & Eire, and Young Muslim Organisation UK.
25 Amin, 'Unruly Strangers?', p. 462.
26 Korosec-Serfaty, 'Experience and Use of the Dwelling', p. 71, p. 75.
27 McLeod, *Postcolonial London*, p. 156.
28 See Begum and Eade, 'All Quiet on the Eastern Front?'
29 Modood, *Multicultural Politics*, p. 199.
30 Ansari, *The Infidel Within*.

31   Ansari, *The Infidel Within*, p. 19.
32   Gorra, 'East Enders'.
33   Smith, *White Teeth*, p. 135.
34   See, for example, Hussain, *Writing Diaspora*, p. 93: 'the Bangladeshi community in Britain is presented by Ali in negative, atavistic terms. It is presented as dysfunctionally insular and traditional, riven by internal dissent and unable to organise itself even in the face of racist mobilisations.' For a more objective overview, including popular reactions to the novel, see Ruth Maxey, '"Representative" of British Asian Fiction? The Critical Reception of Monica Ali's *Brick Lane*'.
35   Walker, *'Brick Lane'*.
36   Hussain, *Writing Diaspora*, p. 17, p. 92.
37   Sandhu, *'Brick Lane'*.
38   Ali, *Alentejo Blue*, p. 44. Hereafter *Alentejo*. Subsequent references cited parenthetically.

Further reading

Jane Hiddleston, 'Shapes and Shadows: (Un)veiling the Immigrant in Monica Ali's *Brick Lane*', *Journal of Commonwealth Literature*, 40:1 (2005), pp. 57–72.

Ruth Maxey '"Representative" of British Asian Fiction? The Critical Reception of Monica Ali's *Brick Lane*', in Neil Murphy and Wai-Chew Sim (eds), *British Asian Fiction: Framing the Contemporary* (New York: Cambria, 2008), pp. 217–36.

James Procter, 'New Ethnicities, the Novel, and the Burdens of Representation', in James F. English (ed.), *A Concise Companion to Contemporary British Fiction*, ed. (Massachusetts: Blackwell, 2006), pp. 101–20.

Sara Upstone, '"Same Old, Same Old" Zadie Smith's *White Teeth* and Monica Ali's *Brick Lane*', *Journal of Postcolonial Writing*, 43:3 (2007), 336–49.

9

Suhayl Saadi

We have become bulimic with TV comedy dramas about Asian res-
taurants, dancers chained forever to their bangles, arranged/multiple
marriages and everywhere, as though in some smokey dwam of
metaphysical trans-substantiation, the odor of curry – it seems that
as soon as the prospect of a brown face appears on the page or the
screen, the repertoire, the vision, of commissioning bodies suddenly
become terrifyingly limited ... Even when the writing is urban realist, about 'gangstas' or whatever, usually the writers maintain a
sense of linguistic decorum, which in a sort of pre-Kelman, Billy
Bunter hallucination internally perpetuates the class-based, subject-
object viewpoint.[1]

On Saturday 30 June 2007, a car filled with explosives was
driven into the glass frontage of Glasgow International Airport.
While the bomb attack was a 'failure', resulting in only five
members of the public receiving minor injuries, this 'terrorist
attack' shifted the geographical focus of concerns with Asian
identity. The two occupants of the car, Bilal Abdulla and Kafeel
Ahmed, were accused of being connected to a small terrorist cell of Islamic extremists, and of involvement in another
failed bombing campaign in London a day earlier. That the two
were identified as producing their explosives out of a house
in a small village community, Houston, just outside Glasgow,
having bought their equipment from various stores around
Scotland, and that Abdulla – who was British-born – was a
doctor working at the Royal Alexandra Hospital in Paisley,
made this an explicitly 'Scottish' event.[2] Abdulla explained the
motivation for his attack as the Iraq War. In doing so, he identified a Scottish airport as a legitimate target of protest against the
'British' establishment. His actions at once identified Scotland
as British and its Muslim population as subject to the same disillusionment as its English counterparts. The Glasgow bomb
only increased the hostility towards Muslims in Scotland that
has been evident since the events of 9/11. In the wake of the

World Trade Center attacks, Scottish Muslims experienced the same backlash as their British counterparts: mosques were fire-bombed, women wearing hijab were harassed, Muslim men with beards or wearing traditional dress faced abuse in the streets, and the rate of racist attacks rose strongly.[3]

Yet, in a broader sense, the experience of being Muslim in Scotland is not directly comparable to being a Muslim in England.[4] In comparison with discussions around British or English identity, there is a relative lack of commentary on racism in Scotland. This has been attributed to the 'common perception ... that racism has not been as serious a problem in Scotland as it has been in England'.[5] While this assumption has been called into question by much criticism from as early as the 1980s,[6] nevertheless the perception persists that racism in Scottish cities is less of a problem than in English ones, particularly in relation to the Asian population.[7] Indeed, that the situation might be different in *some specific ways*, despite the existence of racism, is something borne out by survey: while 25 per cent of surveyed respondents in England in 1996, for example, thought immigrants were not good for the economy, only 16 per cent of Scots felt the same way; similarly while 17 per cent of English respondents did not think immigrants opened the country up to new cultures, only 12 per cent of Scots agreed.[8]

Various reasons are used to explain this difference, from the rather positive reading of Scots as 'an essentially welcoming, tolerant people',[9] to the more negative sense in which prejudice in Scotland is directed not towards ethnic minorities, but rather towards an alternative 'other': the English.[10] The small number of ethnic minorities in Scotland (2 per cent in 2001),[11] and their concentration in its four major cities, is very different to the British situation.[12] Yet at the same time, to be Asian in Scotland is to have a particular significance lacking in the British context: the Pakistani community is the dominant ethnic minority group in Scotland, making up 33.8 per cent of this population in 1999.[13] This Pakistani presence exists within a context where, in addition, the largest ethnic minority religious affiliation is Muslim.[14] This makes Asians, and Asian Muslims more specifically, therefore, 'the most prominent of the New Scots'.[15]

In Scotland, being Scottish takes preference over being British.[16] Yet such preference is not repeated when one examines the English relationship to Britishness.[17] In such terms, the debates surrounding the designation 'British Asian' take on a new complexity. What does it mean to be British Asian, if not only the Asian, but also the British part of this description is frequently problematised? In the Scottish context ethnic identity becomes subject to a new set of relations which extend existing conflicts. A 'British Asian' in Scotland may be equally unhappy with being described as British, as being described as Asian. Any feelings of alienation must be contextualised within an identity that is potentially doubly 'othered': as both ethnically marginalised, and nationally unrecognised, within dominant constructions of Britishness.

Suhayl Saadi's fiction embodies a 'Scottishness' representative of how assumptions of a universal British Asian identity are not just problematic, but radically problematic. His texts are set in Britain, yet they clearly identify not with this broader category of the nation-state, but rather with Britain's constituent nations: the majority are set in Scotland, with characters who define themselves not as British, but Scottish; likewise, Saadi's English characters do not seem to relate to a broader British identity: Joe in *The Spanish House* (2008), for example, 'had never regarded himself as anything other than English'.[18] That Saadi is not just Scottish, but also Muslim, means his fiction represents a fusion of cultural elements which even singularly would interrogate the category of British Asian. Adding Scottish identity to the already problematic relationship between Islam and Britishness, Saadi's fiction exemplifies the diversity within British Asian cultures, and the need to define these in relation to specifics of time and place.

Saadi himself is testament to the problematic nature of using British Asian as a descriptive term. His work has not been subject to the same critical attention as Asian writers based in England. This is despite his prolific output, which includes not only several novellas (*The Spanish House* (2008), *The White Cliffs* (2004), 'The Saelig Tales' (2006), *The Aerodrome* (2005)), a collection of short stories (*The Burning Mirror* (2000)), and two novels (*Psychoraag* (2004) and *The Snake* (1997), the latter published under the pseudonym Melanie Desmoulins), but also a number of additional short stories published online,[19] several stage and radio plays (*The Dark Island* (2004), *The White Cliffs* (2005), *Saame Sita* (2003), *Garden of the Fourteenth Moon* (2006)), edited collections of fiction (*Shorts: the Macallan Scotland on a Sunday Short Story Collection* (2003), including the jointly edited *A Fictional Guide to Scotland* (2003) and *Freedom Spring: Ten Years On* (2005)), journalism, song lyrics, and an opera libretto, *Queens of Govan* (2007), which is based on a story from *The Burning Mirror*, and was produced as part of the Scottish Opera's 2008 'Five: 15' project, which also included works by Ian Rankin and Alexander McCall Smith.

The lack of critical attention is also in contrast to the recognition Saadi has received, with *The Burning Mirror* shortlisted for the 2001 Saltire First Book Prize and one of its stories, 'Ninety-Nine Kiss-O-Grams', runner up in the Macallan short story competition,[20] and *Psychoraag* winning a PEN Oakland/ Josephine Miles Literary Award, shortlisted for the James Tait Black Memorial Prize, and nominated for the International IMPAC Dublin Literary Award and the Patras Bokhari Prize in Pakistan. This lack of critical attention is, for Saadi, evidence of the metropolitan focus of literary elites. Declaring that 'Scotland is not a literary backwater' he argues that there is a focus in both publishing and English print media on the fiction of Southern England, to the detriment of both Scottish and Northern writers.[21] This 'politics of fiction' is for Saadi driven by the middle-class, Oxbridge-educated metropolitan elites that dominate these industries and – inadvertently supporting government discourses – reproduce a narrow range of values in the fiction they endorse, what Saadi lyrically refers to as the 'Hyper-Hip Multicoloured Metropolitan London-Oxbridge "Liberal" Literary Mafia'.[22] Although Asian writers may be supported by such elites, they must meet the remits of 'safe multiculturalism': as the epigraph to this chapter suggests, being either exotic, or unthreatening. In positing this reality, Saadi himself raises the issue of how notions of British Asian identity may in fact act to level out differences and prevent diversity, rather than in fact encouraging a more representative British literature. As a Pakistani, concerned with working-class identity, Saadi has said: 'I am not fashionably ethnic. I am just ethnic.'[23]

That the notion of 'Asian cool' is in fact an intensely limited one is taken up in Saadi's novel, *Psychoraag*. The story of one night in the life of Zaf, a Scottish-Muslim DJ in Glasgow, Asian identity is described in the following terms:

> Until recently, Latino had been hip and Paki hadn't ... Indian had always been hip but only if you were a guru, a communist, or a sitar player. All that had changed in the last few years and now it wis cool – that was the word – cool to be connected, in some way, to the land which lay somewhere to the east of the Middle East. For some odd reason, however, Pakistan was seen completely differently. In fact, most of the time, it wasn't seen at all ... Pakistanis had remained completely inaudible. They had no music, no voice, no breath. In

many ways, they were seen as incorporatin everythin that wis bad,
dysfunctional and regressive about South Asia. Whereas that good
old fat, post-imperial clever clogs, Mata Barat, nee India, nee nee
the Jewel-in-the-... mysteriously (and, quite possibly, cosmically)
had acquired all that wis admirable, even enviable, about oriental
culture. Sexy – in a kind of golden shower, pure, ashramic kind of
way. And, as such, it remained perpetually cool ... Folk thought of
young, hip guys 'n' gals as Indian. Whereas the crabby auld-timers
with the specs, the sticks, the jumpers and the assertive teeth were
assumed to be inherently Pakistani (or else Bangladeshi but that wis
another story).[24]

Saadi's 'Scottishness'

The redundancy of 'British Asian' as a descriptive term in the
Scottish context has been explored in a number of sociological studies. In the 2001 census, the ethnic category of 'Asian,
British Asian' was modified to 'Asian, Asian Scottish or Asian
British' to reflect this fact.[25] In selecting dual identities that
include national affiliation, young Scottish Muslims seem
to be responding differently to their British Muslim counterparts, who – some studies suggest – are increasingly rejecting
Britishness as incompatible with Islamic belief.[26] If one cannot,
according to Gilroy, be black and British then one can, it seems,
be Asian and Scottish.

It is this possibility – to be both Asian and Scottish – which
Saadi foregrounds. All of his Asian protagonists are Scottish by
birth, representative of a reality in which 75.6 per cent of the
Scottish Pakistani population were born in Scotland.[27] As such,
they have access to the primary indicator of national belonging in Scotland.[28] As recent studies argue that birth facilitates
one's Scottish identity in a way largely, although not entirely,
independent of race, so Saadi's characters do not appear to
suffer from lacking Scottish ancestry.[29] Instead, their experience proves that 'not to be born in Scotland, and especially
to be born in England, is a greater barrier to inclusion than
to be non-white'.[30] Declaring that 'In our hearts, we were all
Glaswegian' (360) Zaf embodies such a reality. Indeed, the division of *Psychoraag* between Zaf's confident Glasgow persona and
the story of his parents reflects this access to Scottish identity
through one's birth. Zaf's parents' generation have been 'desic-
cated slowly by the unremmittin need to transmute themselves,
day after day, from something they had once been to what the
"new life" demanded of them' (42). Without this 'newness',

Zaf's generation are relieved from the pressures of assimilation-ist politics: they exist in a different age to that of the 'casual hate' (195) of their parents' experience which called into question the notion of Glasgow as 'The Friendly City' (196).

That Saadi's characters are Muslim makes such a possibility more significant. In a post–9/11 context, Saadi's characters question the assumption propagated in the media that to be a young British Muslim is to be set apart from 'mainstream' culture. This is presented in one of the most powerful stories in *The Burning Mirror*, 'The Queens of Govan', which recounts the experience of a young Muslim girl, Rubina. While the mullah tells Ruby and her father that 'the dogs of the West had taken control' the reality calls into question the media representation of Muslims as being coerced into such perspectives:

> He [the mullah] had wanted them to join the Young Muslims an tae go about wi clean-cut attitudes an big chips on their shooders. Beards an hijaabs. But her bhai watched TV, instead, an she ... she had got a job in the kebab house.[31]

Of course, it is the nature of stereotypes that they dynamically transform even as one is writing: so as *Psychoraag*, too, calls into question the image of the devoutly religious Muslim man or woman, and in particular the passive or weak Muslim male, so at the same time it becomes part of newly emerging stereotypes. Saadi's texts support new constructions of British Asian males as socially threatening, encompassing the Muslim terrorist, but also a broader 'problem'.[32] What Claire Alexander defines as the 'new folk devil', the 'Asian Gang' is evident in the violence which explodes in *Psychoraag*'s later pages.[33] The 'street culture' of this youth movement is embodied when the violence of the street invades the radio studio and, subsequently, Zaf moves his own aggressive personality out on to the Glasgow streets.[34] This is reaffirmed in the story 'Bandanna' where Sal – the central pro-tagonist, too, of 'Ninety-nine Kiss-o-grams' – is part of an Asian street gang. Saadi in part critiques this individual: Sal's laying down of his bandanna to pray at the end of the story speaks not of hybridity, but of hypocrisy. Yet his generation's violence is a rejection of the deference of their parents' generation, who would ask for nothing in 'another man's country'.[35] Gang violence may be negative: but its existence – like the protest in *Brick Lane* – points to a confident assertion of belonging and citizenship rights from the next generation, who see themselves not as migrants, but as 'true Gangstas'.[36] The claim made to space here is of the same character as that represented by Srivastava and Ali. As a Kashmiri born in the wake of Partition, in a space of borders, Sal speaks of Bhabha's hybridity that is always present.[37] Yet, at the same time, he maps a new Asian presence:

> Nothing was static. Life was movement, juddering, twitching, filmistar movement. Peasant to refugee, refugee to kisaan, emigrant to immigrant, Paki tae dkokandaar, shopkeeper tae gang-member' (113)

Somewhere in these last two transformations, Scottishness emerges: 'to' becomes 'tae'.

This confidence does not mean that acculturation is unproblematic, and several of Saadi's characters do desire assimilation: Sal in 'Ninety-nine Kiss-o-grams' desires a 'long-legged, thin-waisted goree tae wave like a white flag at the world' (7); Zaf dreams of being 'like a white man' (45), his description of his self-hatred (134–5) borrowing heavily from the philosophy of Frantz Fanon; Ruby in 'The Queens of Govan' wears make-up and works out to try and appear 'as straight an white as possible' (26); in 'The Dancers' Zarqa hates the mirror for reminding her of her mixed-race parentage.[38] It is not easy, however, to see these characters as 'caught between cultures'. Zarqa's statement that 'she'd nivir been certain whether the green she'd waved at Celtic matches had been the hara of Punjab or the Republican banner of west Belfast' (125) speaks to the mutability of cultural reference points, a reference to Scotland's own historical ethnic tensions that Saadi frequently employs. The ending of the story with Zarqa 'spinning round and round in the darkness' (130) also speaks to this ambivalence: the darkness suggests loss but, equally, posits dance culture as one in which physical difference ceases to be evident. Equally, while Ruby in 'The Queens of Govan' at times feels like she is 'nowhere', she is also 'kinda in-between' (28) and 'used tae the double-life' (29). She sees arranged marriage as little worse that the 'drunken romances' (28) of Glasgow street culture. In her employer, Qaisara, moreover, she encounters a strong, independent Muslim woman who offers an alternative way forward to her parents, a successful dualism represented in powerful visual terms by 'a sunflower-yellow shalvar-kamise wi the sleeves rolled up' (28). In comparison to Ruby's parents, Qaisara represents the possibility of existing successfully as a Muslim woman within Scottish culture. These young women are Scottish-Muslims in transition, coming to terms with their dual identities; coming to terms with *becoming* Scottish.

Becoming Scottish

It is ironic that Saadi is, in fact, English. Born Sohail Ahmed in Beverley, Yorkshire, in 1961, to Afghan-Pakistani parents, he moved to Paisley, Scotland as a child in 1965, and is now based with his family in Glasgow, where he went to university and studied medicine (he still works as a General Practitioner).

Saadi's relocation to Scotland appears to mean he presents a cultural identity that does not 'work' within popular notions of British Asian identity. One might reflect more positively on this exclusion, however, if one considers how Saadi has been identified, *despite his place of birth*, as Scottish. Although Saadi's writing has been largely ignored in English literary circles, he has received considerable recognition within Scotland: the Scottish Book Trust lists *Psychoraag* as one of the Best Scottish books of all time,[39] while *The Snake* has been described as 'the very first novel ever written by a black Scot'.[40] Moreover, Saadi himself has in interview proclaimed his belief in a 'distinct Scots Asian identity' that he himself feels part of.[41]

The acceptance of Saadi as Scottish seems to suggest that Scots, with their own history of colonial subjugation, may be more willing to identify with the 'other', and may therefore also be more willing to accept broader definitions of national identity. The continuance of colonial tensions between England and Scotland do not seem to have abated since devolution in 1999, and the strength of the independence movement in Scotland attests to the hostility towards the incorporation of what are perceived as hegemonic English practices and attitudes, with Scotland seen by some as a `stateless nation'.[42] There is the assumption in such claims that Britishness fails to sufficiently incorporate Scottish identities; indeed that it is simply convenient shorthand for Englishness.[43] In literary terms, this is expressed by readings of white Scottish literature itself as postcolonial, as it responds to the hegemonic role of Englishness in constructions of what it means to be British, and foregrounds Scottish nationalism as an anti-imperialist assertion of indigenous rights. There is a strong association between Scottish nationalism and what has been described as a 'literary renaissance among urban Scottish writers'.[44]

Saadi's acceptance as Scottish, then, points to the realisation of a postcolonial Scottish nationalism that is a direct challenge to exclusive imperialist ideologies. Although not born in Scotland, his valorisation by Scottish literary critics, his unproblematic identification by these critics as Scottish, and his own assertion of belonging, points to what Ross Bond defines as the possibility for *becoming* Scottish: the awareness that, although birth is the most significant factor for social acceptance, nevertheless individuals not born in Scotland do come to see themselves as Scottish, both because and in spite of the social attitudes of the wider community.[45]

That *becoming Scottish* is related to length of residence is of particular significance for this book: not being born in a place, but being raised there, makes one's experience tangibly different from that of the 'arrivants'.[46] Undoubtedly, this is a factor in Saadi's acceptance. In the same way that writers such as Ravinder Randhawa and Meera Syal identified with the feminist community and participated in the Asian Women Writers' Collective to construct a British Asian feminist presence, so Saadi has worked within the Scottish community to forge a similar identification with national concerns, founding the Pollockshields Writers' Group in Glasgow for ethnic minority authors. Yet at the centre of this identification of Saadi as Scottish is his use of language. A large number of Saadi's stories, and also his novel *Psychoraag*, are written in Scots dialect. Some of these, equally, focus on white Scots, rather than issues of ethnicity. Stories such as 'Imbolc', 'Beltane', and 'Samhain', written entirely in heavy dialect and alluding to Celtic mythology, resonate with a tradition that owes more to Robert Louis Stevenson than Salman Rushdie.[47] In doing this, Saadi utilises the same strategy as others who identify accent as the most effective alternative to birth as an assertion of Scottish identity, a means of displaying the 'Scottish behaviour' which can make residence an acceptable marker of Scottishness.[48] Secondary to birth, accent has been identified as making 'a significant contribution to having one's claim to be a Scot accepted', as accent may act 'as some sort of proxy for being brought up in a country other than that in which the person was born', allowing claims for birth to be made.[49] In particular, Saadi's usage not just of a generic Scots, but of a specifically 'Weegie patter' marks him out for critics as a 'genuine' Scots orator, rather than a mimic.[50]

In stories such as 'Ninety-nine Kiss-o-grams', Saadi fuses Scots dialect with Urdu, so that it offers a uniquely Scottish-Asian presence. Look at the glossary to *The Burning Mirror* and one encounters a fusion of Urdu and Scottish Gaelic terms, interwoven in the same list. *Psychoraag*, however, is the most developed use of this form. So the novel opens:

Salaam alaikum sat sri akaal, Namaste ji, good evenin oan this hoat, hoat summer's night! Fae the peaks ae Kirkintilloch tae the dips ae Cambuslang, fae the invisible mines as Easterhoose tae the mudflats ae Clydebank, welcome, ivirywan, welcome, Glasgae, welcome, Scoatland, tae *The Junnune Show.* Sax oors, that's right, sax oors, ae great music, rock an filmi an weird, weye-oot-there happenins an ma rollin voice. Whit a combination, eh? It's wan ye cannae resist. Wance ye tune in, the dial sticks. Aye. Ah'm in control ae yer radio sets – aw the music plays through me. Ye're oan ma wavelength an that's a pretty weird place tae be! Radio Chaandi broadcasting oan ninety-nine-point-nine meters FM. Moonlight, moonlight, moonlight! *Arey,* Mister Moonlight, stay oot ae ma windae – this is ma show! Right? (1)

Here confidence in Scots identity in particular is foregrounded: the glossary for this text *does not* include Scots terms, only Urdu ones, suggesting an increasingly defiant linguistic positioning.

In 'Ninety-nine Kiss-o-grams', Saadi makes a claim for how birth and dialect, *together,* facilitate Scottishness. The central character of Sal explicitly rejects national identification with Pakistan: 'This was his country, the land ae his forefaithers and yet, the stink ae it sickened him tae his gut ... Nae, he thought, and kicked the soil again, this isnae ma country. No ony mair. Mibbee, it nivir was.' (2) Instead, 'he longed for the cool spaces of Scola, the feel ae the rain on his back' (5). Losing his father's deeds at the end of the story, Sal has 'at last, become invisible' (8) in his 'homeland'. Yet this is represented as freedom, rather than loss: 'at last' indicates a change anticipated and longed for; the story's final image, of a bird taking off into flight, is a symbol of liberation. The migrant's dream of return is overturned: Sal dreams of returning to Scotland; his is a diaspora in reverse. That such claim is expressed in dialect cements only the extent to which to see Sal as Pakistani is to obscure the reality of his identity. Sal will substitute the ninety-nine virgins of Islamic lore for ninety-nine kiss-o-grams: he will fuse in his belief system both Scottish practice and his Islamic culture. Dialect offers in this context an additional way into the cultural centre, a means to counter prejudice constructed through other markers of identity.

Saadi here reinforces readings of Scottish nationalism as civic rather than ethnic, as a challenge to the basis of the 1981 Immigration Act in ancestry.[51] While such nationalism may be conceptualised as 'weak', his texts prove its value.[52] That Scottish nationalism is broad enough to encompass ethnic identities is, of course, open to debate, given the conventional understanding of nationalism as a movement deeply rooted in an imagined cultural consensus.[53] Recent projects of the devolved Scottish administration, however – such as the 'New Scots' strategy and the *One Scotland, Many Cultures* project, focused on 'an inclusive Scottishness determined by factors such as birthplace and residency rather than more exclusive determinants like ethnicity and parentage' – point towards a desire, at least, for such a reality.[54] The establishment by the SNP of the campaign group 'Asians for Independence' associated nationalism with an inclusive sense of Scottishness. Statements of participants include: 'I don't see any racism here … It's not like in England'.[55] That in surveys Scots themselves express a preference for a nation based on such principles is a further reinforcement.[56]

When Zaf imagines his radio audience, he captures this New Scottishness, an identity defined only by location:

> It wasn't just Zaf who wis on multiple wavelengths, the whole bloody population of Glasgow wis tunin in on totally different levels – each person wis listenin to a different Zaf, a separate show … Sometimes Zaf would try to picture his audience … Tired ex-ganstas … hot blades … young women … minicab drivers … doctors and nurses … lovers with thin walls … members of wacky religious sects … madrasah junkies … off-duty, multiculturally-inclined strippers … on-duty, curry-lovin polis; hookers … junkies … mothers whose babies woudn't go down; city biviis with kisaan-heid hubbies … mitai-makes … multi-balti-millionaires … tramps … migrants from north, south, east an west; those who'd never fitted in; clerks with scores to settle; parkin wardens wearin false moustaches; aficionados of cross-over; the Kings of the Night; kebab-shop runners; and internet-crazed insomniacs. (19)

Capturing the documented reality of minority arts engagement in Scotland where, in contrast to the migrant generation, Scotland's young ethnic minorities fuse 'ethnic' and mainstream arts as 'an expression of their dual identity' *Psychoraag* offers a dense interweaving of musical intertexts speaking to a complex fusion of cultural influences.[57] Artists such as Rafi, Susheela Raman, Talat Mahmood, Gauhar Jan, Kavita Krishnamurthy, Sonu Nigam, K. L. Saigal, and Chaba Fadela feature in *Psychoraag* to represent Urdu, Hindi, and/or Bollywood musical traditions, while bands such as The Beatles, The Stranglers, The Stone Roses, The Kinks and Primal Scream represent Western influences. In between these, artists including Asian Dub Foundation, Cornershop, Nitin Sawhney and Kula Shaker speak to the intermingling of such traditions in contemporary Britain. This is supplemented by Celtic references, such as the citation of Robert Burns' poetry, and references to the bands The Colour of Memory, Country Joe and the Fish, and The Wind-Machines. The latter tradition is claimed by Zaf for Asian culture at the end of the novel as the final assertion of a confident Scottish-Asian identity: 'the voice, the breath, did not belong just to Babs or to Scotland or to the *Gàidhealtachd* but also to Zaf, to the people of Asia' (406). Although Netto sees such artistic practice as evidence of the 'caught between two cultures' model, Saadi does not suggest this; music marks generational difference, but the practice is an unproblematic fusion, rather than an opposition. The harmonies of music, and the shared rhythms of different cultures, speak to the possibility of positive cultural synthesis.[58] This here, then, is what Karen Qureshi and Shaun Moores speak of as the 'identity remix' of British Asian music. [59] Yet whereas for Moores and Qureshi 'remix' is associated with the fusion of new and old Asian musical forms in the British-born generation, so for Saadi the Scottish music tradition, too, becomes part of this, evidence of the unidirectional, 'dialogic mutation' of British music which sees a two-way dialogue between different musical traditions as a creative act of *translation*.[60] The radio station serves as a microcosm of the perfect pluralist town, city or nation; posited by Saadi as a utopian space it symbolises the possibility for cultural fusion that respects individual traditions at the same time that it resists dissociative behaviour or separatism, because music 'knows nae boundaries' (30). The struggle to make this art – and its message – visible is, again, however, a factor of real-world relevance: the precarious position of the radio station – Glasgow Asian Community Radio – mirrors the recognised difficulty for ethnic artists who must contend with the fact that Scotland is still struggling to establish its own national culture, without taking account of ethnic concerns.[61] Undoubtedly, given Saadi's outspoken views, this experience is also metaphoric of the writer's similar struggle: to be recognised as Scottish, firstly, but then also for this Scottish literature to gain the recognition it deserves in a market dominated by London literary culture.

Indeed, Saadi points to how 'authentic' Scottish culture is a matter of recuperation for everyone, even those whose ancestry is Scottish, stolen by the ravages of capitalism and industrial decline. Everyone is *becoming* Scottish. Saadi's white Scots are actively involved in recuperating Scottish identity from the legacy of this deprivation: so in the story 'Beltane' Scott and

Deirdre 'twirled an whooped the celidh by the loch and felt really totally Scots and guid and whole, no like the fuckin druggies in the shoap wi thur sick plastic an deid eyes'.[62] Like Irvine Welsh and James Kelman, Saadi critiques 1980s Thatcherite rhetoric, identified with a rise in race hate in Britain. Akin to Paul Gilroy's suggestion that in this period race became the contemporary manifestation of class difference – that 'racial structuration ... is imposed by capital' – Saadi identifies the continued neglect of ethnic voices to be 'primarily about the class system'.[63] His fiction exposes the legacy of Thatcherite policy in Scotland, revealing it as the most obvious barrier to a racially inclusive Scottish identity, and reinforcing the ways Scottish nationalism and anti-Thatcherite politics are firmly welded together in the Scottish imagination.[64] In 'The Queens of Govan', the violence of Govan, with its racial and religious intolerance, and its protection rackets, is 'the rage ae the dead ships an the closed factory gates' (32). Outside the radio station in *Psychoraag* is the world of Pollockshields and Kinnin Park: walking up Maryhill Road, the 'To Let' and 'For Sale' signs tell Zaf that 'Mary wis long gone and her hill wis up for sale' (407). Zaf is clear of the origins of this circumstance: 'he'd been weaned at Thatcher's breast and, boy, had the milk been sour!' (49). The flipside of this depressing reality is the possibility for such Scottish identity to be re-made in its recuperation to include, but not be limited by, its ancestral features.

Post-ethnic nationalism?

In this description, one may be tempted to see Saadi as a mimic of Kureishi's own practices. As for Kureishi, Saadi's concern with race is placed within the context of a broader concern for the breakdown of dialectical oppositions: in *The White Cliffs*, for example, the 'dark' cliffs which threaten the central characters are white, not black, reversing the conventional racist coding of such terms. The epigraph to *The Burning Mirror* from the life of Rabi 'a al-'Adawiyya equally announces such concern: 'to quench the fires of Hell and burn Heaven, so that both these barriers to understanding shall vanish', an epigraph which is literally explored in the haunting and disturbing 'Darkness', where a personified death announces itself as that which can 'outrun the Devil ... outfly God'.[65] A focus on post-ethnic tales which examine identity from perspectives broader than race is, as established in Chapter 2, Kureishi's forte. Saadi's own preference for such narratives, equally, is explored through promiscuous, drug-taking, outspoken young protagonists who, as much as those presented by Kureishi, pander to a postmodern liberalism which denies the legitimacy of more 'traditional' cultural practices. Yet, unlike Kureishi, there does seem to be more sensitivity in Saadi's work to these practices. For example, while Kureishi's liberal Western perspective is betrayed by his reliance on the popular music of the Beatles and Prince as intertexts in works such as *The Buddha of Suburbia* and *The Black Album,* Saadi's much more diverse musical intertexts speak to a more genuine cross-cultural transformation.

At the same time, while both Kureishi's and Saadi's protagonists fail to conform to traditional images of Muslim identity, yet the way they approach this characterisation is crucially very different. Unlike Kureishi, Saadi is clear that there is a religion that exists outside fundamentalism: the latter is in *Psychoraag* described as 'an artificial version of Islam' (381). Saadi's work engages deeply with the complexities of religious belief in both organised and pagan forms, from Protestant and Catholic divisions, to the transformation of churches into the 'new religion' of dance music, to 'faery fowk' and Sussex mythology. This interest is most developed in 'The Seventh Chamber', the final of a trilogy of stories in *The Burning Mirror* on this theme.[66] Here, the character of Terri, whose spiritual journey the stories have mapped, is presented finally as a nun. Terri faces temptation and doubt, yet the story concludes ultimately with an affirmation of her spiritual choice. In *Psychoraag*, equally, Zaf is prompted to 'Thank the Lord', though he is less certain of who this 'Lord' is (207); he may not have been to a *masjid* for a long time, but the novel points to his need for such experience: 'talking to God was a symphonic affair and Zaf hadn't even grabbed the melody' (278). There is therefore the sense that while Saadi may complicate what it means to an Asian Muslim in Britain, nevertheless, his work does not reject, or render unacceptable, those individuals who might chose to align themselves with traditional practices. Rather, his work is profoundly sympathetic to the problems of living a spiritual life in a secular environment; art is a compliment to – rather than a substitute for – the ethical, sacred, spiritual, and otherworldly.

Yet perhaps most significantly, but not unconnectedly, Saadi is not Kureishi because his nationalism speaks to the importance of geographical affiliation, even as it denies race as a basis for this. The confidence exhibited by Saadi's protagonists is explicitly a Scottish confidence. It is in the specifics of Glasgow's concrete jungle, for example, that Zaf's heterogeneous music emerges:

> These peripheral estates consisted of great borin blocks of fast-food housing where nuthin ever happened. The inevitable video shops, the corporate pubs, the off-licences filled with cheap toxic wine. Yet, from these post-war afterthoughts with their ration-sized rooms, there had arisen this amazing band of Riviera joy, of Californian harmonies and Rajasthani rock. (193)

This is a literal embodiment of the hybrid, rather than exclusionary multiculturalism, which Yasmin Alibhai Brown's concept of 'a new vision which brings together all the tribes of Britain' points towards.[67] But it exists, ironically, not in a New British context, but rather in the more limited geography of New Scottish identity. In privileging Scottish biculturalism, Saadi reflects the choices of young Asian Scots to reject Britishness.[68] His texts point to the fact that whist the notion of British Asianness, so lauded as the new emerging youth identity for ethnic Britons, is largely absent, this is not because young ethnic Scots of South Asian descent are rejecting biculturalism, but because they are rejecting Britishness as the location for this. That biculturalism is in fact more likely in a Scottish context speaks to the social relevance of Saadi's representation.[69] The conflict between nationalism and the Muslim *umma* is mediated by the fact that this is a nationalism which recognises the value of religious commitment: it is possible to be both Muslim *and* Scottish, and there is no suggestion from Saadi that Englishness, and by extension Britishness, could be easily substituted in these terms. For whereas Saadi feels able to proclaim 'I've certainly not felt excluded within Scottish literary circles' yet in contrast he feels 'very excluded ... from the mainstream England-based literary world'.[70]

Conclusion

In making such a connection, Saadi, like other authors in this book, illustrates how the allegiances forged by British-born Asians may not subscribe to the patterns predicted by postmodern theory, or celebrated in postcolonial literature. Although Saadi rejects Britishness, he does this not in favour of a broader, more fluid positioning, but instead in favour of a narrow national affiliation. Britishness is rejected not because it is too real, but rather because it is too imaginary; Scottishness is the 'real' that can be identified with, and must therefore be focused upon. As other writers identify with London as a space within, and often in contrast to, a broader Britishness, so Scotland functions similarly for Saadi. The impact of Asian identity on Scotland does not make Scotland redundant. Instead, it remakes Scotland in a dynamic process of two-way hybridisation from which Scottish nationality emerges not weaker, but stronger. To be bicultural here is not to be alienated, but to be an embodiment of modern culture, with a multi-faceted, multifarious, identity that is represented as one to be celebrated. If we consider the most recent British Asian texts as post-ethnic then what Saadi's fiction indicates, in extension of this, is the extent to which such texts must also be considered '*Post-British*'.[71] Although Saadi's Scottish identity may be the most obvious example of such possibility, he should not be taken as its only proponent. Rather, he stands only as the most obvious example of the questionable reality of the term British Asian, and the rather surprising alternative allegiances which British-born Asians may instead be forging.

Discussion

- How does Saadi's musical reference serve as a metaphor for British Asian identity?
- To what extent are the stories in *The Burning Mirror* post-ethnic?
- 'There were rules you couldn't break because the rules constituted the fabric of your being.' (*Psychoraag* 365). What position on national and ethnic identity is offered by Saadi's fiction?

Notes

1 Saadi, 'Psychoraag: The Gods of the Door'.
2 McLaughlin, 'Glasgow Bombing Prosecutors Claim Two Doctors at Centre of UK Terror Campaign'.
3 See Hopkins, 'Young Muslim Men in Scotland'.
4 See Ameli and Merali, *British Muslims' Expectations of the Government*, p. 34.
5 Saeed *et al.*, 'New Ethnic and National Questions', p. 821.
6 Saeed *et al.*, 'New Ethnic and National Questions'. See also Bowes *et al.*, 'Racism and Harassment of Asians in Glasgow', pp. 76–7; Miles and Muirhead, 'Racism in Scotland'; Miles and Dunlop, 'Racism in Britain'; Cant and Kelly, 'Why is There a Need for Racial Equality

Activity in Scotland?'.
7   Miles and Muirhead, 'Racism', p. 127; Cant and Kelly, 'Why is There a Need for Racial Equality Activity', p. 9.
8   Jowell *et al.*, *British Social Attitudes*, p. 147.
9   Bond, 'Belonging and Becoming', p. 614.
10 Netto, 'Multiculturalism in the Devolved Context', p.51. McCrone and Bechhofer, 'National Identity and Social Inclusion', p. 1249.
11 Bond, 'Belonging and Becoming', p. 614.
12 Netto, 'Multiculturalism', p. 52.
13 Saeed, Blain and Forbes, 'New Ethnic and National Questions', p. 827.
14 Hopkins, 'Young Muslim Men', p. 258.
15 Kelly, 'Asians in Scotland: the Formation of an Elite?', p. 296.
16 Brown *et al.*, *Politics and Society in Scotland*, second edition; Rosie and Bond, 'Routes into Scottishness?'.
17 McCrone, 'Who Are We? ', p. 17. See also Curtice and Heath, 'Is the English Lion About to Roar?', p. 158; Curtice and Seyd, 'Is Devolution Strengthening or Weakening the UK?', p. 237; Heath *et al.*, 'Who Do We Think We Are?', p. 11.
18 Saadi, *The Spanish House*, p. 3.
19 See www.suhaylsaadi.com and also www.storyglossia.com
20 Saadi, 'Ninety-Nine Kiss-O-Grams', *The Burning Mirror*, pp. 1–8. Subsequent references are cited parenthetically.
21 Saadi, 'Psychoraag: The Gods of the Door'.
22 *Ibid.*
23 *Ibid.*
24 Saadi, *Psychoraag*, pp. 73–4. Subsequent references cited parenthetically.
25 See Aspinall, 'Who is Asian?', p. 92.
26 See Archer, 'Muslim Brothers, Black Lads, Traditional Asians', pp. 87–8.
27 Saeed *et al.*, 'New Ethnic and National Questions', p. 827
28 McCrone notes that 48 per cent respondents think birth very relevant in definitions of Scottishness, compared to 36 per cent ancestry, and 30 per cent residence, *Understanding Scotland*, p. 173. In England, figures are more evenly split, with 29 per cent of respondents thinking birth 'very important', 25 per cent ancestry, and 23 per cent residence (see Curtice and Heath, 'Is the English Lion about to Roar?', p. 169).
29 '[W]hen asked about a non-white person possessing all the relevant markers, that is, someone who lives in Scotland, was born there and speaks with a Scottish accent, nine out of ten people would accept such a non-white person's claim to be Scottish'; this rises from 7 out of 10 when birth is not certain (McCrone and Bechhofer, 'National Identity', pp. 1254–55). While in Scotland the most nationalist are the less exclusive, in England this tendency is reversed: see Curtice and Heath, 'Is the English Lion About to Roar?', p. 169.
30 McCrone and Bechhofer, 'National Identity', p. 1261.
31 Saadi, 'The Queens of Govan', *Burning Mirror*, pp. 21–36, p. 23. Subsequent references cited parenthetically.
32 See Hopkins, 'Youthful'. For further discussion see Alexander,

'Embodying Violence'.
33 Alexander, *The Asian Gang*, p. xiii.
34 Hopkins, 'Youthful', p. 338.
35 Saadi, 'Bandanna', *Burning Mirror*, pp. 109–20, p. 112. Subsequent references cited parenthetically.
36 *Ibid.*, p. 119.
37 This background echoes Saadi's parents' experience, who met in a Lahore refugee camp in 1947.
38 Saadi, 'The Dancers', *Burning Mirror*, pp. 121–30, p. 124. Subsequent references cited parenthetically. A 'Ruby' also appears in *Psychoraag*. However, it is not clear if this is the same young woman.
39 Marney, 'Psychoraag – Suhayl Saadi (2004): 100 Best Scottish Books of All Time'.
40 'Famous and Successful People from Paisley'.
41 Sardar, *Balti Britain*, p. 72, p. 77.
42 McCrone, *Understanding*, p. 47.
43 McCrone, 'Who Are We?', p. 16.
44 Cant and Kelly, "Why is There a Need for Racial Equality Activity', p. 11.
45 Bond, 'Belonging and Becoming' p. 621.
46 *Ibid.*
47 Saadi, 'Imbolc', *Burning Mirror*, pp. 61–7; 'Beltane', *Burning Mirror*, pp. 67–80; 'Samhain, *Burning Mirror*, pp. 81–6.
48 Kiely *et al.*, 'The Markers and Rules of Scottish National Identity', p. 41.
49 McCrone and Bechhofer, 'National Identity', p. 1257.
50 Calder, 'Saadi's All the Rag'.
51 McCrone, *Understanding*, p. 155.
52 *Ibid.*, p. 15.
53 See, for example, Anderson, *Imagined Communities*; Bhabha, 'Narrating the Nation'. Nairn reads Scottish nationalism in such terms: *The Break-Up of Britain*, p. 153.
54 Rosie and Bond, 'Routes into Scottishness', p. 142.
55 Matthew Brown, 'Fear of a Fortress Scotland'.
56 Hussain and Miller, 'Islamophobia and Anglophobia', p. 165.
57 Netto, 'Multiculturalism', p. 52; p. 54.
58 Saadi takes up this theme in broader terms in his novella *The Spanish House*, which he associates with 'the polyvalent and sometimes contradictory relationships between song-forms like flamenco, reggae or rock and politics'.
59 Qureshi and Moores, 'Identity Remix'. See also Back, *New Ethnicities and Urban Culture*, pp. 219–29.
60 Sharma, 'Noisy Asians or "Asian Noise"', p. 40.
61 Netto, 'Multiculturalism', p. 58.
62 Saadi, 'Beltane', p. 77.
63 Gilroy, *There Ain't No Black in the Union Jack*, p. 10. Saadi, 'Psychoraag: The Gods of the Door'.
64 See McCrone, 'Who Are We?', pp. 30–1.
65 Saadi, 'Darkness', *Burning Mirror*, pp. 189–98, p. 196.

66 Saadi, 'The Seventh Chamber', *Burning Mirror*, pp. 155–64.
67 Alibhai-Brown, 'Stuff Your "British Test"'.
68 In Saeed *et al.*, 'New Ethnic and National Questions', 22 per cent identified with the term Scottish, only 9 per cent saw themselves as British, p. 831.
69 Grouping identity into Hutnik's categories, 88 per cent of the respondents identified themselves as acculturative, in that they see themselves 'as both Pakistani and Scottish' (Saeed *et al.*, 'New Ethnic and National Questions', p. 837). This contrasts with studies in Britain, such as Modood's *Ethnic Minorities in Britain*, which identified acculturation in 69 per cent of respondents.
70 Sardar, *Balti Britain*, p. 77.
71 Saeed *et al.*, 'New Ethnic and National Questions', p. 824.

Further reading

David McCrone, *Understanding Scotland: The Sociology of a Nation, second edition* (London: Routledge, 1996)
Suhayl Saadi, 'Psychoraag: The Gods of the Door', *Spike Magazine*, January 2006, www.spikemagazine.com/0206-suhayl-saadi-censorship-in-the-uk-php>.

Conclusion

Is a conclusion the same as an ending? In some ways, this book marks just a beginning. The authors it focuses on are all still writing, seven of them are under the age of fifty. Their presence has realised Salman Rushdie's 'newness': a reinvigoration of British fiction from a perspective that can be compared to neither the postcolonial writing of their parents' generation nor an earlier British literature written from a predominantly white, predominantly Christian, perspective. Such 'newness', as we have seen, takes many divergent forms. It cannot be reduced to a singular definition of the 'British Asian text'. Rather it offers complex interventions into issues not just of race or ethnicity, but also broader questions of gender, religion, community, and – ultimately, as with all fiction – what it means to live. It cannot be associated simplistically either with a rejection of cultural traditions or with diasporic desires for recuperation; it cannot be defined either entirely as realist or experimental; it cannot be encapsulated either in notions of strident protest or equally confident passivity. Yet an intervention it marks nevertheless, as these differing features are combined dynamically to examine the tensions and pretensions of twenty-first-century Britain.

This beginning is marked, moreover, by the emergence of a number of new voices – all in their thirties, and all born in Britain, who have benefited from the interest in Asian culture, and the success of the writers in this study. Nisha Minhas's sequence of novels *Chapattis or Chips?* (2002), *Saris and Sins* (2003), *Passion and Poppadoms* (2004), *Bindis and Brides* (2005), *The Marriage Market* (2006) and *Tall Dark and Handsome* (2007) illuminates that the British Asian take on 'chick-lit' established by Atima Srivastava is alive and well. Zahid Hussain's *The Curry Mile* (2006) transfers Monica Ali's concern with inter-generational conflict in a starkly realist context to urban Manchester. In the realm of children's literature, Bali Rai and B. K. Mahal are offering young British Asians the opportunity to engage with issues surrounding their own identities. Most critically notable amongst these writers, Niven Govinden, Gautam Malkani and Nirpal Singh Dhaliwal all in 2006 published novels which reinforce the existence of a strident British-born generation, confident in its identity, and refusing to be 'othered' by archaic ancestral notions of Britishness. In *Tourism* Dhaliwal's successful British Asian protagonist Bhupinder immerses himself in the sexual, alcoholic and drug-related excesses of contemporary London: his alienation is a matter of his childhood, not his adult life in the 'miscegenist heaven' that is West London, a place he describes as 'home' having 'known nowhere else'.[1] The novel has more in common with the lads' fiction of Tony Parsons and Nick Hornby than the work of Rushdie or V. S. Naipaul. Govinden's teenage protagonists in *Graffiti My Soul* are equally confident, rejecting racist slogans as the language of 'the 1980s'.[2] Malkani's *Londonstani* is dominated by hypermasculine bravado, centred on characters who feel no need to reclaim Britain because they already own at least some part of it: there is, here, 'no kind of confused roots issue'.[3]

Yet, at the same time, the conclusion marked here is a kind of ending. Comparing these authors to those focused upon in this book suggests a subtle shift in representation. In some senses, these writers are not the contemporaries of Kureishi, but his own inheritors: Govinden's *Black Album* is not that written by Prince, but by the hip-hop artist Jay-Z.[4] Whereas liminality may not define the majority of writers in this book, it continues to haunt them. In contrast, Dhaliwal, Malkani, and Govinden no longer even speculate on their location as either traumatic or a reason for alienation. The title itself of Dhaliwal's novel marks this: tourism speaks to the pleasure of easy movement against the strictures and pressures of migration or exile. Malkani's central characters, likewise, play ironically with notions of racial stereotype. The novel's opening chapter, in a section entitled 'Paki', stands as introduction to the book's ethos; it recounts the beating of a white boy for using this very term of racist abuse, only to end with the revelation that 'nobody round here ever, ever used that word'.[5] These authors know their geographies; the legibility that Srivastava assumes can now, it seems, be taken for granted. Whereas Kureishi's character of Karim sees the suburbs as a space of narrow vision against London's multicultural power, Malkani's suburbs – in his case not Bromley, but Hounslow – are now thoroughly 'urban': immured in a black

British street culture that means the old spatial demarcations no longer apply. Govinden's Veerapen, equally, embroiled in the influences of urban street culture, proclaims: 'Surrey – Hackney. There's no difference'.[6]

This confidence is evidenced in further movement towards the post-ethnic reality that Kureishi's later fiction embodies, and which writers such as Monica Ali, Suhayl Saadi and Hari Kunzru have taken up. *Londonstani* is the most extreme example of this, due to its startling ending. The novel's protagonist, Jas, is involved in an 'Asian Gang' and readers naturally assume that Jas himself is Asian. The end of the novel reveals, however, that he is white: Jas is Jason. Malkani represents therefore an environment not only in which ethnicity has ceased to be the primary marker of collective identity but, even more powerfully, has become something that can no longer be judged by behaviour. That we cannot detect that Jas is white points to the intermixing of cultural practices amongst an urban youth generation to the extent that ideas of authenticity have faded entirely from view. He is the most extreme embodiment of David Hollinger's vision of a world in which ethnicity is not abandoned, [7] but is chosen rather than ascribed, a post-9/11 experiment in what may lie beyond a world where 'race remains the self-evident force of nature in society'.[8]

This constant performativity is reinforced by its existence within a broader culture of similar actions: young men, for example, whose 'ghetto' identities are fabrications which belie their middle-class backgrounds. In some reviews, critics challenged *Londonstani* on the familiar grounds of its authenticity, Malkani subject to the same pressure of the burden of representation as earlier Asian authors. This drive neglects the fact that the whole novel is about the erosion of this 'authentic' culture: the fictional business run by the manipulative Sanjay, 'middle class kids, who live in five-bedroom houses and they want to be rude-boys and they're pretending to be something they ain't'.[9] Govinden writes fictions that are less cleverly, but more explicitly, post-ethnic: citing Kureishi as a significant influence on his work he has followed the earlier author in creating fictions that are not centred on Asian protagonists, yet offer a broader focus on identity politics. His first novel, *We are the New Romantics* (2004), is vague about racial identity: one narrator, Amy, is blonde, another, DJ, is 'dark', but the complexities of identity are debated not principally through the relevance of these descriptions, but through the novel's engagement with homosexuality; indeed, it is more common to find discussion of Govinden's novels in terms of sexuality. The narrator of *Graffiti My Soul*, Veerapen, does have an Asian background, but both his own identity and his affiliations are a perfect example of post-ethnicity in practice: half-Tamil, half-Jew, none of Veerapen's friends are Asian, and their own backgrounds are unimportant: the novel's love interest has the exotic name of Moon Suzuki, but her sister is called Gwyn.

That writers such as Govinden and Malkani are comfortable to begin their careers with such fictions might, ultimately, suggest that the notion of British Asian literature has passed into redundancy even before it has gained any notable currency. It takes a level of optimism to suggest this might in fact be the case, for it would mean that race and ethnicity has ceased to function as a marker of difference in British society. This is most evident in Govinden's case, where he seems to be being read outside of an ethnic framework. More pessimistically, it may point towards the utopian nature of these fictions, their function not as reflections of the reality of race relations, but as radical calls for reform of contemporary relations. Such a possibility, while politically exciting, is depressing in the sense that it suggests less has changed than such fictions might suggest. In the wake of the rise in Islamophobia after the 9/11 attacks on the World Trade Center and the July 2005 London Tube and bus bombings this pessimistic conclusion unfortunately seems more feasible.

Whether utopian or not, one particular feature of note in these new fictions is the way, indeed, they call the enthusiasm surrounding this post-ethnic reality into question. Claims for a society that no longer functions according to recognition of race or ethnicity have been celebrated in a number of quarters as the solution to social tensions and the route to a more equal, inclusive, national community. Paul Gilroy, for example, posits the utopian possibility of a 'planetary humanism': a post-racial and post-ethnic society where 'the old, modern idea of "race" can have no ethically defensible place', and where an alternative politics of 'sameness' leads to the eventual recognition not only of diversity, but universal rights.[10] Hollinger, equally, argues that racial and cultural politics need to be disentangled, so that the idea of identity is replaced by that of 'affiliation by revocable consent'.[11] These critics are right that such hopes offer the welcome possibility of societies in which the prejudices, oppressions and violence of racialised communities have been consigned to history. Yet Malkani, in particular, problematises this assumption by presenting a largely dystopic post-ethnic reality. Loss of even an illusion of ethnic authenticity is presented ambivalently: the exhilaration we might feel on being made aware by Malkani's ending that ethnicity is no longer easily identifiable is undercut by the vacant, empty lives of his central protagonists. This is evident in Malkani's Asians, young men who 'don't have an East meets West contradiction because they don't know enough about the East'.[12] For these men, achieving post-ethnicity means not being conscious about one's cultural background.

Moreover, hyper-masculinity replaces ethnic identification with equally narrow gendered identity stereotypes. So while, for Gilroy, planetary humanism means transcendence not just of race but also gender, for Malkani's young men shifting away from racial identification is simply in the name of alternative prejudices.[13] Consumed by the need to be 'real men' Hardjit and his friends – in positions of ethnic dominance – aggressively form themselves not in reaction to white racism, which might have a certain tragic justification, but rather simply to ensure their control of the Hounslow streets. That such loss is equally evident in the character of Jas further complicates this representation. While there is something powerful in the fact that the mimicry is reversed – Jas's desire to be 'Asian' might be a powerful example of the empire writing back – yet his lament 'my surname too fuckin long an too fuckin shameful to fit on my own fuckin gravestone' renders the reality anything but celebratory.[14] In the same way as Rushdie points to the failure of Gibreel's assumption of colonial methods of territorialisation, so Malkani suggests that making the former colonisers subject to the same disabling desires as those they once colonised only perpetuates the negative consequences of such actions: Jas's former friend Daniel, as he is being beaten at the opening of the novel, confronts him with 'What's happened to you over the last year? ... You've become like one of those gangsta types you used to hate'.[15] Here Malkani plays into debates surrounding the loss of male white identities, something *Tourism* also focuses on with its awareness of women like Ghislaine: 'a careerist and a mother, she took care of her figure and was married to a feminised invertebrate who was easy to push around'.[16]

Such cultural loss is presented in terms of Asian culture by both Govinden and Dhaliwal: Bhupinder comes to realise the denial of his Asian culture through his relationship with Sarupa, who 'had a better idea of who I was and what I was about than Sophie would ever get'.[17] In *Graffiti My Soul* Veerapen's awareness of his own post-ethnic affiliations, his inheritance of Kureishi's liberal culture, is not something he celebrates, but ultimately laments:

> But I'm dead inside, man, blunted by TV, and girls, and the promise of what I can do when I slip on my running shoes, and the sniff of freshly burning weed at five paces. I got no energy left to be all radical, no time left for brotherhood – maybe for a kid who's grown up the way I did, but not for some be-pleasing-you-sir who's just stepped off the boat. They mean nothing to me. It might sound rough, but that's how it is.[18]

Post-ethnicity has not eroded the exclusionary politics of urban life. Equally, ethnicity itself continues to exist in the prevalence of particular norms. That these norms emerge from ethnic minority cultures – not only Asian but also Afro-Caribbean and African-American youth identities – is no more inclusive than the previous dominance of white culture. That they are hybrid, equally, does not prevent them from being hegemonic in the refusal to make space for alternative social formations; in *Londonstani* the Asians who listen to R.E.M. are branded 'coconuts' even when binary racial oppositions have ceased to function.[19]

In *Tourism*, this recognition takes the form of a shift away from racism, towards cultural prejudice. In Bhupinder's world, post-ethnic language is not a form of protest, but 'the Caribbean slang that is the lingua franca of London's multi-ethnic underclass'.[20] Bhupinder himself is a purveyor of this cultural prejudice, as he locates himself as insider against a new wave of immigrants – 'these people' – from Australia, South Africa, and Eastern Europe, people who 'make niggers look smart'.[21] Religion serves a similar function. While the comments made by Bhupinder's (black) friend Michael are not to be taken seriously – they are not a 'proper conversation' – nevertheless their essence is relevant, even if the expression is designed to be provocative:

> These dummies are making life easy for black people. Same as Muslims are good for black people. 9/11 was a break for niggers. White people are cutting us some slack, now we're not top of their shit-list. Right now, they need all the friends they can get ... Niggers might rob you and rape your girlfriend, but they won't land a fucking plane on you. Another stunt like that, and we'll be in the clear.[22]

Malkani, equally, recognises this reality: Jas can be one of the gang, but Samira, who is a Muslim, is 'outta bounds'.[23] Again *Londonstani*'s violent opening can be returned to as evidence of this: that Jas is white does not stop Daniel being beaten for being a 'gora', something which is transformed by Jas's presence in the group to be less a matter of the opposition between two discrete ethnicities, and more a marker of the interrogation of an alternative masculinity – not being a 'gangsta' – which Daniel embodies. Daniel's alternative may be less 'post-ethnic', but it is the 'post-ethnic' fusion of cultures which impresses itself violently on others in a manner that is anything but liberal. So while for Gilroy the shift away from racial difference promises a world in which 'sameness can be acknowledged and made significant', *Londonstani* only proves this to be impossible: race may fade, but difference does not.[24] Instead, it rather affirms the reality of racism as something much broader than skin colour: the 'ultimate racism of thought, beliefs and ideas' which persists in the novel even when race seemingly disappears.[25]

That performance here is not conscious may be a mark of normality, but it is a movement to a society with less agency, performativity with more in common with Judith Butler's Foucaulian pronouncement of performance than anything more radical. In *Tourism*, young black men are described as adopting 'a sordid boorish persona that bears no relation to their actual lives': indoctrinated into hyper-masculinity by music culture, there is little choice in the resulting performances.[26] The boys in *Londonstani* are not making politically engaged statements: their reaction to Mr Ashwood's outlining of right-wing global politics is that 'dis politics shit, it all bout poncey, grey-haired bald people talkin posh'.[27] Post-ethnic reality has led not to social equality, but to other forms of difference and – equally – to the transformation of liberal ideology into totalitarian presence. What has been lost is not simply racism, but also the cultural reference points which counter alienation and prevent the movement into other, equally violent, forms of compensatory identities. There is also, in such movement, no accommodation of Britishness; post-ethnicity does not mean the realisation of the Labour government's dream of 'community cohesion':

> Can you imagine a desi in London getting excited bout the Union Jack? That shit's just for, like, football hooligans, the royal family an all those dicks who go round singin 'Rule Britannia'.[28]

This is not to suggest that either Malkani or Govinden advocate a return to the idea of a racial or ethnic essence. The dangers of this project are equally clear in Dhaliwal's writing, where the book's anti-white discourse may suggest irreverent confidence, but is also at times in poor taste and even perhaps offensive.[29] It does suggest, however, that multiculturalism – in the sense of discrete identities existing alongside each other – may have been prematurely disallowed. Even if we move to a post-ethnic reality, this does not solve the problem that comes from the human desire to define oneself structurally in terms of binary oppositions. If the problem is 'the other' then post-ethnicity may merely displace, rather than decline, this reality.

Such complexity is evidence of the increasingly convoluted fictions which British Asian authors are constructing to embrace an experience that is less about being an outsider, or even an insider who feels like an outsider, and more about how such terms have themselves become increasingly destabilised. Writing not from the margins, but with a history that allows them to see where these boundaries lie, British Asian writers are at the centre of offering twenty-first-century voices that have the potential to forge both a renaissance in the British novel, and a remaking of the very national identifications upon which such definitions rely.

Notes

1   Dhaliwal, *Tourism*, p. 45, p. 52, p. 240.
2   Govinden, *Graffiti*, p. 153.
3   Interview with author, 25 April 2007.
4   Govinden, *Graffiti*, p. 9.
5   Malkani, *Londonstani*, p. 13.
6   Govinden, *Graffiti*, p. 124.
7   Hollinger, *Postethnic America*, p. 220.
8   Gilroy, *After Empire*, p. 11.
9   Interview with author, 25 April 2007.
10 Gilroy, *Between Camps*, p. 2, p. 6, p. 101.
11 Hollinger, *Postethnic America*, p. 188.
12 Interview with author, 25 April 2007.
13 Gilroy, *Between Camps*, p. 16.
14 Malkani, *Londonstani*, p. 294.
15 *Ibid.*
16 Dhaliwal, *Tourism*, p. 143.
17 *Ibid.*, pp. 195–6.
18 Govinden, *Graffiti*, p. 163.
19 Malkani, *Londonstani*, p. 22.
20 Dhaliwal, *Tourism*, p. 64.

21 *Ibid.*, p. 24, p. 67.
22 *Ibid.*, p. 68.
23 Malkani, *Londonstani*, p. 49.
24 Gilroy, *After Empire*, p. 3.
25 Sardar, *Balti Britain*, p. 288.
26 Dhaliwal, *Tourism*, p. 64.
27 Malkani, *Londonstani*, p. 130.
28 *Ibid.*, p. 216.
29 It is unclear how ironic Dhaliwal is being here. Certainly Bhupinder can be read as an anti-hero, and one should not assume that his problematic racial attitudes are endorsed by the author.

Bibliography

Abbas, Tahir, 'British South Asian Muslims: Before and After September 11', in Abbas (ed.), *Muslims in Britain*, pp. 3–17.

Abbas, Tahir (ed.), *Muslims in Britain: Communities Under Pressure* (London: Zed, 2005).

Aboulela, Leila, *The Translator* (Edinburgh: Polygon, 1999).

—— *Minaret* (London: Bloomsbury, 2005).

Adams, Tim, 'Many Unhappy Returns for a Teenage Terrorist', *Observer* (2 Sept. 2007).

Afzal-Khan, Fawzia, *Cultural Imperialism and the Indo-English Novel: Genre and Ideology in R. K. Narayan, Anita Desai, Kamala Markandaya, and Salman Rushdie* (Pennsylvania: Pennsylvania State University Press, 1993).

Ahmad, Aijaz, *In Theory: Classes, Nations, Literatures* (London: Verso, 1992).

Ahmad, Rukhsana and Rahila Gupta (eds), *Flaming Spirit: Stories from the Asian Women Writers' Collective* (London: Virago, 1994).

Ahmed, Leila, 'The Discourse of the Veil', in Gaurau Desai and Supriya Nair (eds), *Postcolonialisms: An Anthology of Cultural Theory and Criticism* (Oxford: Berg, 2005), pp. 315–38.

Ainsley, Rosa (ed.), *New Frontiers of Space, Bodies and Gender* (London: Routledge, 1998).

Aldama, Frederick Luis, 'Hari Kunzru In Conversation', *Wasafiri*, 45 (2005), 11–14.

Alexander, Claire, *The Asian Gang: Ethnicity, Identity, Masculinity* (Oxford: Berg, 2000).

—— 'Beyond Black: Rethinking the Colour/Culture Divide', *Ethnic and Racial Studies*, 25:4 (2002), 552–71.

—— 'Imagining the Asian Gang: Ethnicity, Masculinity and Youth After "the Riots"', *Critical Social Policy*, 24:4 (2004), 526–49.

—— 'Embodying Violence: "Riots", Dis/order and the Private Lives of "the Asian Gang"', in Claire Alexander and Caroline Knowles (eds), *Making Race Matter* (London: Palgrave, 2005), pp. 199–217.

Ali, Monica, *Brick Lane* (London: Doubleday, 2003).

—— *Alentejo Blue* (London: Black Swan, 2004).

Alibhai-Brown, Yasmin, *Who Do We Think We Are?: Imagining the New Britain* (London: Allen Lane, 2000).

—— 'Stuff Your "British Test"', *The Independent* (16 Dec. 2001), www.independent.co.uk/opinion/commentators/yasmin-alibhai-brown/

yasmin--alibhai-brown-stuff-your-british-test–620294.html.

Allen, Chris, 'From Race to Religion: The New Face of Discrimination', in Abbas (ed.), *Muslims in Britain*, pp. 49–65.

Allen, Richard, 'A Post-Colonial World: *Look Back in Anger* and *The Enigma of Arrival*', in Richard Allen and Harish Trivedi (eds), *Literature and Nation: Britain and India 1800–1900* (London: Routledge, 2000), pp. 138–53.

Ameli, Saied R. and Arzu Merali, *British Muslims' Expectations of the Government: Dual Citizenship: British, Islamic, or Both? Obligation, Recognition, Respect and Belonging* (Wembley: Islamic Human Rights Commission, 2004).

Amin, Ash, 'Unruly strangers? The 2001 Urban Riots in Britain', *International Journal of Urban and Regional Research*, 27 (2003), 460–3.

Anderson, Benedict, *Imagined Communities: Reflections on the Origin and Spread of Nationalism*, revised edition (London: Verso, 1991).

Anonymous, 'Homeless is Where the Art Is' (1994), rpt in Reder (ed.), *Conversations*, pp. 162–6.

Ansari, Humayun, *The Infidel Within: Muslims in Britain since 1800* (London: Hurst and Company, 2004).

Anwar, Muhammad, 'Young Asians Between Two Cultures', *New Society* (16 Dec. 1976), pp. 563–5.

Arana, Victoria and Lauri Ramey, 'Introduction', in Victoria Arana and Lauri Ramey (eds), *Black British Writing* (New York: Palgrave, 2004), pp. 1–8.

Archer, Louise, 'Muslim Brothers, Black Lads, Traditional Asians': British Muslim Young Men's Constructions of Race, Religion and Masculinity', *Feminism Psychology*,11 (2001), 79–104.

Ashcroft, Bill, Gareth Griffiths and Helen Tiffin, *The Empire Writes Back: Theory and Practice in Post-colonial Literatures* (London: Routledge, 1989).

Asian Women Writers' Workshop, *Right of Way: Prose and Poetry* (London: The Women's Press, 1988)

Aslam, Nadeem, *Season of the Rainbirds* (London: Andre Deutsch, 1993).

—— *Maps for Lost Lovers* (London: Faber, 2004).

—— *The Wasted Vigil* (London: Faber, 2008).

—— 'God and Me', *Granta 93: God's Own Countries*, Spring 2006, www. granta.com/extracts/2646.

Aspinall, Peter J., 'Who is Asian? A Category That Remains Contested in Population and Health Research', *Journal Public Health Medicine*, 25 (2003), 91–7.

Back, Les, *New Ethnicities and Urban Culture: Racisms and Multiculture in Young Lives* (London: University College London Press, 1996).

Ballard, Roger, 'Introduction: The Emergence of Desh Pardesh', in Roger Ballard (ed.), *Desh Pardesh: The South Asian Presence in Britain* (London: Hurst, 1994), pp. 1–34.

Baucom, Ian, *Out of Place* (Princeton, NJ: Princeton University Press, 1999).

Beckett, Andy, 'Don't Call Me Comrade', *Guardian* (25 Aug. 2007).

Bedell, Geraldine, 'Full of East End Promise', *Observer* (15 June 2003), http://observer.guardian.co.uk/bookgroup/story/0,13699,991603,00. html.

Beezmohun, Sharmilla, 'Where are all the British Asian Writers?', *Journal of Gender Studies*, 7:2 (1998), 227.

Begum, Halima and John Eade, 'All Quiet on the Eastern Front? Bangladeshi Reactions in Tower Hamlets', in Abbas (ed.), *Muslims in Britain*, pp. 179–93.

Bentley, Eric, 'On the Other Side of Despair' (1964), rpt in D.J. Palmer (ed.), *Comedy* (Basingstoke: Macmillan, 1984), pp. 135–50.

Bentley, Nick, *Contemporary British Fiction* (Edinburgh: Edinburgh University Press, 2008).

Bergson, Henri, 'Laughter' (1900), in Sypher (ed.), *Comedy*, pp. 61–190.

Bhabha, Homi, *The Location of Culture* (London: Routledge, 1994).

—— 'Narrating the Nation', in Homi Bhabha (ed.), *Nation and Narration* (London: Routledge, 1990), pp. 1–7.

—— 'The Vernacular Cosmopolitan', in Ferdinand Dennis and Naseen Khan (eds), *Voices of the Crossing: the Impact of Britain on Writers from Asia, the Caribbean and Africa* (London: Serpent's Tail, 2000), pp. 133–42.

Bhattacharya, Soumya, 'Goodbye, young lovers', *Observer* (July 18, 2004), http://books.guardian.co.uk/reviews/generalfiction/ 0,6121, 1263491 ,00.html.

Birt, Yahya, 'Notes on Islamophobia', *Musings on the Britannic Crescent* (31 Dec. 2006), www.yahyabirt.com/?p=48.

Blackmore, Susan, *Consciousness: A Very Short Introduction* (Oxford: Oxford University Press, 2005).

Bloom, Clive, *Bestsellers: Popular Fiction Since 1900* (Basingstoke: Palgrave Macmillan, 2002).

Boehmer, Elleke, *Colonial and Postcolonial Literature: Migrant Metaphors* (Oxford: Oxford University Press, 2005).

Bond, Ross, 'Belonging and Becoming: National Identity and Exclusion', *Sociology*, 40:4 (2006), 609–626.

Bowes, Alison M., Jacqui McCluskey and Duncan F. Sim, 'Racism and Harassment of Asians in Glasgow', *Ethnic and Racial Studies*, 13:1 (1990), 71–90.

Boyce Davies, Carol, *Black Women, Writing and Identity: Migrations of the Subject* (New York: Routledge, 1994).

Brah, Avtar, *Cartographies of Diaspora: Contesting Identities* (London: Routledge, 1996),

Brennan, Timothy, *Salman Rushdie and the Third World* (New York: St Martin's Press, 1989).

Bromley, Roger, *Narratives for a New Belonging: Diasporic Cultural Fictions* (Edinburgh: Edinburgh University Press, 2000).

Brown, Alice, David McCrone and Lindsay Patterson, *Politics and Society in Scotland*, second edition (Basingstoke: Macmillan, 1998).

Brown, Malcolm D., 'Orientalism and Resistance to Orientalism: Muslim identities in Contemporary Western Europe', in Sasha Roseneil and Julie Seymour (eds), *Practicing identities: Power and Resistance* (Basingstoke: Palgrave Macmillan, 1999), pp. 180–98.

Brown, Matthew, 'Fear of a Fortress Scotland', *The Big Issue in Scotland*, 154 (22–28 June 1998), 11.

Brulotte, Gaëtan, 'Laughing at Power', in John Parkin, John Phillips and Peter Collier (eds), *Laughter and Power* (Oxford: Peter Lang,

2006), pp. 11–18.

Bryce, Jane and Kari Doko, 'Textual Deviancy and Cultural Syncretism: Romantic Fiction as a Subversive Stain in Africana Women's Writing', in Janice Lee Liddell and Yakini Belinda Kemp (eds), *Arms Akimbo: Africana Women in Contemporary Literature* (Gainesville, FL: University Press of Florida, 1999), pp. 219–29.

Burdsey, Daniel, '"One of the lads"? Dual Ethnicity and Assimilated Ethnicities in the Careers of British Asian Professional Footballers', *Ethnic and Racial Studies*, 27:5 (2004), 757–79.

Butler, Judith, *Gender Trouble* (1990) (London: Routledge, 2006).

—— *Undoing Gender* (New York: Routledge, 2004).

Calder, Angus, 'Saadi's All the Rag', 25 April 2004, http://sarmed.netfirms. com/suhayl/NEW/books/psycho/calder_review.htm.

Cant, Bob and Elinor Kelly, 'Why is There a Need for Racial Equality Activity in Scotland?', *Scottish Affairs*, 12 (1995), 9–26.

Carby, Hazel V., 'Schooling in Babylon', in Paul Gilroy and Pratibha Parmar (eds), *The Empire Strikes Back: Race and Racism in 1970s Britain* (Birmingham: Centre for Contemporary Cultural Studies, 1982), pp. 183–211.

Cavalier, Philip, 'Urban Capital: Henry James, William Dean Howells, and Beyond', Conference Paper Presented at *The Idea of the City: Early Modern, Modern, and Post-Modern Locations and Communities*, Northampton University, 8 June 2007.

Chatterjee, Debani (ed.), *The Redbeck Anthology of British South Asian Poetry* (Bradford: Redbeck, 2000).

Childs, Peter and Patrick Williams, *AN Introduction to Post-Colonial Theory* (Hemel Hempstead: Harvester, 1996).

Chrisman, Laura, *Postcolonial Contraventions: Cultural Readings of Race, Imperialism, and Transnationalism* (Manchester: Manchester University Press, 2003).

Clement Ball, John, *Imagining London: Postcolonial Fiction and the Transnational Metropolis* (Toronto: University of Toronto Press, 2004).

—— 'The Semi-Detached Metropolis: Hanif Kureishi's London, *Ariel*, 27:4 (1996), 7–27.

Cobham, Rhondha and Merle Collins (eds), *Watchers and Seekers: Creative Writing by Black Women in Britain* (London: The Women's Press, 1987).

Cohen, Robin, *Global Diasporas: An Introduction* (London: University College London Press, 1997).

Cook, Jon, 'Relocating Britishness and the Break-up of Britain', in Stephen Caunce, Ewa Mazierska, Susan Sydney-Smith and John K. Walton (eds), *Relocating Britishness* (Manchester: Manchester University Press, 2004), pp. 17–37.

Cooke, Rachel, 'I'm the Bloke who got the Big Advance', *Observer* (16 May 2004), http://observer.guardian.co.uk/review/story/0,6903,1217521 ,00.html.

Corner, Martin, 'Beyond Revisions: Rushdie, Newness and the End of Authenticity', in John Mcleod and David Rogers (eds), *The Revisions of Englishness* (Manchester: Manchester University Press, 2005), pp. 154–67.

Cudjoe, Selwyn R., *V. S. Naipaul: A Materialist Reading* (Amherst, MA: University of Massachusetts Press, 1988).

Curtice, John and Anthony Heath, 'Is the English Lion About to Roar? National Identity After Devolution', *British Social Attitudes: the 17th Report* (London: Sage, 2000), pp. 155–75.

Curtice, John and Ben Seyd, 'Is Devolution Strengthening or Weakening the UK?', *British Social Attitudes: The 18ᵗʰ Report* (London: Sage, 2001), pp. 227–44.

Davis, Erik, *Techgnosis: Myth, Magic and Mysticism in the Age of Information* (London: Serpent's Tail, 1999).

Dawson, Ashley, *Mongrel Nation: Diasporic Culture and the Making of Postcolonial Britain* (Ann Arbor, MI: University of Michigan Press, 2007).

Degabriele, Maria, 'Prince of Darkness Meets Prince of Porn: Sexual and Political Identities in Hanif Kureishi's *The Black Album*', *Intersections*, 2 (1999), www.sshe.murdoch.edu.au/intersections/issue2/Kureishi. html.

Delrez, Marc, 'Political Aesthetics: Cross-Cultural Desire and the Capitulation of Form in the Work of Kazuo Ishiguro and Salman Rushdie', *BELL: Belgian Essays on Language and Literature* (1994), 7–16.

Dennett, Daniel, *Consciousness Explained* (1991) (London: Penguin, 1993).

Desmoulins, Melanie, *The Snake* (London: Velvet, 1997).

Dessau, Bruce, 'The Buddha of Bromley', *Time Out* (3 March 1999), p. 11.

Dhaliwal, Nirpal Singh, *Tourism* (London: Vintage, 2006).

Dhingra, Leena, 'Breaking Out of the Labels', in Rhondha Cobham and Merle Collins (eds), *Watchers and Seekers: Creative Writing by Black Women in Britain* (London: The Women's Press, 1987), pp. 103–7.

Dhondy, Farrukh, 'The Gutter Inspector's Report?', in Amitava Kumar (ed.), *The Humour and the Pity: On V. S. Naipaul* (New Delhi: Buffalo, 2002), pp. 47–56.

Dodd, Philip, 'Requiem for a Rave', *Sight and Sound*, 1 (1991), pp. 9–13.

—— 'Challenges for New Labour', in Griffiths and Leonard (eds), *Reclaiming Britishness*, pp. 2–6.

Döring, Tobias, 'Subversion Among the Vegetables: Food and the Guises of Culture in Ravinder Randhawa's Fiction', in Neumeier (ed.), *Engendering Realism*, pp. 249–64.

D'Souza, Aruna and Tom McDonagh, 'Introduction', in Aruna D'Souza and Tom McDonagh (eds), *The Invisible Flâneuse? Women, Men and Public Space in Nineteenth Century Paris* (Manchester: Manchester University Press, 2006), pp. 1–17.

Dunker, Patricia, *Sisters and Strangers: An Introduction to Contemporary Feminist Fiction* (Oxford: Blackwell, 1992).

Dürrenmatt, Friedrich, 'Comedy and the Modern World' (1958), rpt in Palmer (ed.), *Comedy*, pp. 131–4.

Eagleton, Mary, 'Genre and Gender', in Clare Hanson (ed.), *Re-Reading the Short Story* (Basingstoke: Macmillan, 1989), pp. 56–68, rpt in David Duff (ed.), *Modern Genre Theory* (Harlow: Pearson, 2000), pp. 250–62.

The Economist, 'A Travesty of Honour', *The Economist*, 372:8382 (3 July 2004).

Esposito, John, *The Islamic Threat: Myth or Reality?* (Oxford: Oxford University

Press, 1992).

Falconer, Delia, 'Brick Lane', *Sydney Morning Herald* (2 August 2003), www. smh.com.au/articles/2003/08/01/1059480538023.html.

Fisher, M. H., S. Lahiri and S. S. Thandi, *A South-Asian History of Britain: Four Centuries of Peoples from the Indian Sub-continent* (Oxford: Greenwood, 2007).

French, Patrick, *The World Is What It Is* (New York: Alfred A. Knopf, 2008).

Frye, Northrop, 'The Argument of Comedy' (1949), rpt in Palmer (ed.), *Comedy*, pp. 74–84.

Gandhi, Leela, '"Ellowen, Deeowen": Salman Rushdie and The Migrant's Desire', in Ann Blake, Leela Gandhi and Sue Thomas (eds), *England Through Colonial Eyes in Twentieth-Century Fiction* (Basingstoke: Palgrave, 2001), pp. 157–70.

Geaves, Ron, 'Negotiating British Citizenship and Muslim Identity, in Abbas (ed.), *Muslims in Britain*, pp. 66–77.

Ghosh-Schellhorn, Martina, 'Transitional Identities: The Novels of the Black British Writer Ravinder Randhawa', in Neumeier (ed.), *Engendering Realism*, pp. 237–47.

Gikandi, Simon, *Maps of Englishness: Writing Identity in the Culture of Colonialism* (New York: Columbia University Press, 1996).

Gilroy, Paul, *There Ain't No Black in the Union Jack* (1987) (London: Routledge, 1992).

—— *Between Camps* (London: Allen Lane, 2000).

—— *After Empire: Melancholia in Convivial Culture* (Abingdon: Routledge, 2004).

Gorra, Michael, *After Empire: Scott, Naipaul, Rushdie* (Chicago: University of Chicago Press, 1997).

—— 'East Enders', *The New York Times* (7 Sept. 2003), *The New York Times Online*, http://query.nytimes.com/gst/fullpage.html?res=9C01E6DB1E39F934 #A3575AC0A9659C8B63.

Govinden, Niven, *We are the New Romantics* (London: Bloomsbury, 2004).

—— *Graffiti My Soul* (Edinburgh: Canongate: 2006).

Greenberg, Robert M., 'Anger and the Alchemy of Literary Method in V. S. Naipaul's Political Fiction: The Case of *The Mimic Men*', *Twentieth Century Literature*, 46 (2000), 214–37.

Greenslade, William, 'Fitness and the Fin de Siècle', in John Stokes (ed.), *Fin de Siècle/Fin du Globe* (Hampshire: Macmillan, 1992), pp. 37–51.

Grewal, Shabnam, Jackie Kay, Liliane Landor, Gail Lewis, Pratiba Parmar, 'Preface', in Grewal *et al.*, *Charting the Journey*, pp. 1–6.

—— (eds) *Charting the Journey: Writings by Black and Third World Women* (London: Sheba Feminist Publishers, 1988).

Griffiths, Phoebe and Mark Leonard (eds), *Reclaiming Britishness: Living Together After September 11 and the Rise of the Right* (London: The Foreign Policy Centre, 2002).

Gurnah, Abdulrazak, 'Displacement and Transformation in *The Enigma of Arrival* and *The Satanic Verses*', in Lee (ed.), *Other Britain, Other British*, pp. 5–20.

Gurr, Andrew, *Writers in Exile* (Brighton: Harvester, 1981).

Haffenden, John, 'Salman Rushdie' (1985), rpt in Reder (ed.), *Conversations*, pp. 30–56.

Halliday, Fred, 'West Encountering Islam: Islamophobia Reconsidered', in Ali Mohammadi (ed.), *Islam Encountering Globalization* (London: Routledge Curzon, 2002), pp. 14–35.

Hand, Felicity, 'Shaking Off Sharam: The Double Burden of British Asian Women', in Fernando Galván and Mercedes Bengoechea (eds), *On Writing (and) Race in Contemporary Britain* (Alcalá, Spain: University of Alcalá, 1999), pp. 133–8.

—— 'How British are the Asians?', *Wasafiri*, 10 (1995), 9–13.

Haraway, Donna J., *The Haraway Reader* (New York: Routledge, 2004).

—— 'The Biopolitics of Postmodern Bodies: Constitutions of Self in Immune System Discourse', in Donna J. Haraway, *Simians, Cyborgs, and Women: The Reinvention of Nature* (London: Free Association, 1991), pp. 203–30.

—— 'A Cyborg Manifesto: Science, Technology, and Socialist-Feminism in the Late Twentieth Century', in Donna J. Haraway, *Simians, Cyborgs, and Women: TheReinvention of Nature* (London: Free Association, 1991), pp. 149–82.

—— 'PRAGMATICS: Technoscience in Hypertext', in Donna Haraway, *Modest Witness@Second_Millenium FemaleMan©_Meets_OncoMouse™* (New York: Routledge, 1997), pp. 125–30.

—— 'Introduction: A Kinship of Feminist Figurations', in Haraway, *The Haraway Reader*, pp. 1–6.

—— 'There are Always More Things Going On Than You Thought! Methodologies as Thinking Technologies', Kvinder, *Køn og Forskning*, 4 (2000), 52–60, rpt in Haraway, *The Haraway Reader*, pp. 321–42.

—— 'The Promises of Monsters: A Regenerative Politics for Inappropriate/s Others', in Lawrence Grossberg, Cary Nelson and Paula Treichler (eds), *Cultural Studies* (New York: Routledge, 2002), pp. 294–337, rpt in Haraway, *The Haraway Reader*, pp. 63–124.

Harrison, James, *Salman Rushdie* (New York: Twayne, 1992).

Hayward, Helen, *The Enigma of V. S. Naipaul: Sources and Contexts* (Basingstoke: Palgrave Macmillan, 2002).

Heath, Anthony, Jean Martin and Gabriella Elegenius, 'Who Do We Think We Are? The Decline of Traditional Social Identities', *British Social Attitudes: the 23rd Report* (London: Sage, 2007), pp. 1–34.

Hennard Duthell de la Rochère, Martine, *Origin and Originality in Rushdie's Fiction* (Bern, Switzerland: Peter Lang, 1999).

Hollinger, David, *Postethnic America, Tenth Anniversay Edition: Revised and Updated* (New York: Basic Books, 2005).

Holmes, Frederick M., 'The Postcolonial Subject Divided Between East and West: Kureishi's *The Black Album* as an Intertext of Rushdie's *The Satanic Verses*', *Papers on Language and Literature*, 37 (2001), 296–313.

Hopkins, Peter E., 'Young Muslim Men in Scotland: Inclusions and Exclusions', *Children's Geographies*, 2:2 (2004), 257–72.

—— 'Youthful Muslim Masculinities: Gender and Generational Relations', *Transactions of the Institute of British Geographers*, 31:3 (2006), 337–52.

Huggan, Graham, *The Postcolonial Exotic: Marketing the Margins* (London: Routledge, 2001).

Huntington, Samuel P., *The Clash of Civilizations and the Remaking of World Order* (New York: Simon and Schuster, 1996).

Huq, Rupa, 'Asian Kool? Bhangra and Beyond', in Sanjay Sharma, John Hutnyk and Aswani Sharma (eds), *Dis-Orienting Rhythms: The Politics of the New Asian Dance Music* (London: Zed, 1996), pp. 61–80.

Hussain, Asifa and William Miller, 'Islamophobia and Anglophobia in Post-Devolution Scotland', in Catherine Bromley, John Curtice, David McCrone and Alison Park (eds), *Has Devolution Delivered? The New Scotland Four Years On* (Edinburgh: Edinburgh University Press, 2006), pp. 159–86.

Hussain, Yasmin, *Writing Diaspora: South Asian Women, Culture and Ethnicity* (Aldershot: Ashgate, 2005).

Hussain, Zahid, *The Curry Mile* (London: Suitcase Books, 2006).

Hussein, Aamer, 'Changing Seasons: Post-colonial or "Other" Writing in Britain Today', *Wasafiri*, 20 (1994), 16–18.

Hutnik, Nimmi, *Ethnic Minority Identity: A Social Psychological Perspective* (Oxford: Clarendon Press, 1991).

Ilona, Anthony, 'Hanif Kureishi's *The Buddha of Suburbia*: "A New Way of Being British"', in Richard J. Lane, Rod Mengham and Philip Tew (eds), *Contemporary British Fiction* (Cambridge: Polity, 2003), pp. 87–105.

Innes, C.L., *A History of Black and Asian Writing in Britain 1700–2000* (Cambridge: Cambridge University Press, 2002).

—— 'Wintering: Making a Home in Britain', in Lee (ed.), *Other Britain*, pp. 21–34.

—— 'Review of *A Wicked Old Woman*', *Wasafiri*, 8 (1988), 32–3.

Institute for the Study of Islam and Christianity, *Islam in Britain: The British Muslim Community in February 2005* (Pewsey: Isaac Publishing, 2005).

Israel, Nico, 'Tropicalizing London: British Fiction and the Discipline of Postcolonialism', in James F. English (ed.), *A Concise Companion to Contemporary British Fiction* (Malden, MA: Blackwell, 2006), pp. 83–100.

Jackson, Stevi, 'Women and Heterosexual Love: Complicity, Resistance and Change', in Lynne Pearce and Jackie Stacey (eds), *Romance Revisited* (New York: New York University Press, 1995), pp. 49–62.

Jaggi, Maya, 'A Buddy from Suburbia', Guardian (1 March 1995), www.guardian.co.uk/books/1995/mar/01/fiction.reviews.

Jowell, Roger, John Curtice and Alison Park *et al.* (eds), *British Social Attitudes: The 13th Report* (Aldershot: Dartmouth, 1996).

Julien, Isaac and Kobena Mercer, 'De Margin and de Centre', *Screen*, 29:4 (1988), 2–10.

Kaleta, Kenneth C., *Hanif Kureishi: Postcolonial Storyteller* (Austin, TX: University of Texas Press, 1998).

Kapur, Akash, 'A Million Neuroses', in Amitava Kumar (ed.), *The Humour and the Pity: On V. S. Naipaul* (New Delhi: Buffalo, 2002), pp. 67–80.

—— 'Little Murders', *New York Times* (22 May 2005), *New York Times Online*, http://query.nytimes.com/gst/fullpage.html?res=9A0CE7D91030F9 31A15756C0A9639C8B63.

Katz, Cindi, 'Banal Terrorism: Spatial Fetishism and Everyday Insecurity', in Derek Gregory and Allan Pred (eds), *Violent Geographies: Fear, Terror and Political Violence* (New York: Routledge, 2007) pp. 349–61.

Kay, Jackie and Pratibha Parmar, 'Interview with Audre Lorde', *Spare Rib*, 188 (1988), 37–41.

Kelly, Elinor, 'Asians in Scotland: The Formation of an Elite?', in Gerry Hassan and Chris Warhurst (eds), *Anatomy of the New Scotland: Power, Influence and Change* (Edinburgh: Mainstream, 2002), pp. 295–305.

Kermode, Frank, *The Sense of an Ending: Studies in the Theory of Fiction* (Oxford: Oxford University Press, 1967).

Kiely, Richard, Frank Bechhofer, Robert Stewart and David McCrone, 'The Markers and Rules of Scottish National Identity', *The Sociological Review*, 49:1 (2001), 33–55.

King, Bruce, *V. S. Naipaul*, second edition (Basingstoke: Palgrave Macmillan, 2003).

—— *The Oxford English Literary History. Volume 13: 1948–2000: The Internationalization of English Literature* (Oxford: Oxford University Press, 2004).

—— 'The New Internationalism', in James Acheson (ed.), *The British and Irish Novel Since 1960* (London: Macmillan, 1991), pp. 193–210.

Kirby, Kathleen M., 'Re: Mapping Subjectivity: Cartographic Vision and the Limits of Politics', in Nancy Duncan (ed.), *BodySpace* (London: Routledge, 1996), pp. 45–55.

Koehler, Robert, 'Neo-Fantasies and Ancient Myths: Adam Curtis on *The Power of* Nightmares', *Cinemascope*, 23, www.cinema-scope.com/cs23/int_ koehler_curtis.htm.

Koning, Christina, '*Anita and Me* by Meera Syal', *Times Online*, http://entertainment.timesonline.co.uk/tol/arts_and_entertainment/books/book_reviews/article1488848.ece.

Korosec-Serfaty, Perla, 'Experience and Use of the Dwelling', in Irwin Altman and Carol M. Werner (eds), *Home Environments* (New York: Plenum, 1985), pp. 65–86.

Krishnan, S., '*Midnight's Children*: An Un-Indian Book About All Things Indian', *Aside*, 6:3 (1982), pp. 51, 53.

Krishnaswamy, Revathi, 'Mythologies of Migrancy: Postcolonialism, Postmodernism and the Politics of (Dis)location, *ARIEL*, 26:1 (1995), 125–46.

Kundnani, Arun, 'The Death of Multiculturalism', *Race & Class*, 43:4 (2002), 67–72.

Kundu, Rama, 'Naipaul: "An Indian who is not an Indian"', in Mohit K. Ray (ed.), *V. S. Naipaul: Critical Essays, Volume 1* (New Delhi, Atlantic, 2003), pp. 119–48.

Kunzru, Hari, *The Impressionist* (London: Hamish Hamilton, 2002).

—— *Transmission* (London: Hamish Hamilton, 2004).

—— *My Revolutions* (London: Hamish Hamilton, 2007).

—— 'Futurism: Daniel Dennett' (1995), www.harikunzru.com/hari/futurism.htm.

—— 'You are Cyborg' (1997), *Wired*, http://wired.com/wired/archive/5.02/ffharaway_pr.html.

—— 'Deus Ex Machina' (1998), *Noise* (London: Penguin, 2005), pp. 14–28.

—— 'Sunya' (1999), www.harikunzru.com/hari/sunya.htm.

—— 'Art, Writing: White Teeth' (2000), www.harikunzru.com/hari/whiteteeth. htm.
—— 'Art, Writing: Salman Rushdie' (2003), www.harikunzru.com/hari/ rushdie.htm.
—— 'Society: Making Friends with the Mail' (2003), www.harikunzru. com/hari/jlr/htm.
Kureishi, Hanif, *Playscripts 102: Outskirts, The King and Me, Tomorrow Today* (London: John Calder, 1983).
—— *My Beautiful Laundrette* (1986) (London: Faber, 1996).
—— *The Buddha of Suburbia* (London: Faber, 1990).
—— *The Black Album* (London: Faber, 1995).
—— *Love in a Blue Time* (London: Faber, 1997).
—— *Intimacy* (London: Faber, 1998).
—— *Hanif Kureishi: Plays* (London: Faber, 1999).
—— *Midnight All Day* (London: Faber, 1999).
—— *Sleep with Me* (London: Faber, 1999).
—— *Gabriel's Gift* (London: Faber, 2001).
—— *Collected Screenplays 1* (London: Faber, 2002).
—— *The Body and Seven Stories* (London: Faber, 2002).
—— *My Ear at his Heart*: *Reading my Father* (London: Faber, 2004).
—— *When Night Begins* (London: Faber, 2004).
—— *Something to Tell You* (London: Faber, 2008).
—— 'Dirty Washing', *Time Out*, 795 (1985), 25–6.
—— 'Bradford' (1986), rpt. in *The Word and the Bomb* (London: Faber, 2005), pp. 75–80.
—— 'The Rainbow Sign', in *My Beautiful Laundrette and The Rainbow Sign* (London: Faber, 1986).
—— 'Film Diary: Sammy and Rosie Get Laid', *Granta*, 22 (1987), 61–76.
—— 'Esther', *Atlantic Monthly*, 263.5 (1989), 56–62.
—— 'Eight Arms to Hold You' (1991), *My Beautiful Laundrette and Other Writings* (London: Faber, 1996), pp. 103–120.
—— 'Wild Women, Wild Men', *Granta*, 39 (1992), 171–9.
—— 'Umbrella', *Granta*, 65 (1999), pp. 227–37.
Kureishi, Yasmin, 'Review of *A Wicked Old Woman*', *Spare Rib*, 183 (October 1987), 29.
—— 'Review of *Charting the Journey*', *Spare Rib*, 191 (June 1988), 33.
—— 'Intimacies: A Sister's Tale', *Guardian* (7 May 1998), p. 21.
Lamming, George, *The Emigrants* (London: Joseph, 1954).
Lammy, David, Rediscovering Internationalism', in Griffiths and Leonard (eds), *Reclaiming Britishness*, pp. 36–43.
Langer, Susanne, 'The Comic Rhythm' (1953), rpt in Palmer (ed.), *Comedy*, pp. 124–30.
Lawson Welsh, Sarah, 'Critical Myopia and Black British Literature: Reassessing the Literary Contribution of the Post-Windrush Generation(s)', *Kunapipi*, 21:1 (1998), 132–42.
Lee, Robert, A., 'Changing the Script: Sex, Lies and Videotapes in Hanif Kureishi, David Dabydeen and Mike Phillips', in Lee (ed.), *Other Britain, Other British*, pp. 69–89.
Lee, Robert A. (ed.), *Other Britain, Other British: Contemporary Multicultural*

Fiction (London: Pluto, 1995).

Leonard, Mark, *Britain™* (London: Demos, 1997).

Lewis, Philip, *Islamic Britain: Religion, Politics and Identity among British Muslims* (London: I. B. Tauris, 1994).

—— *Young, British and Muslim* (London: Continuum, 2007).

Lima, Marina Helen, 'Interview with Kadija Sesay', *Obsidian*, 5:2 (2004), 21–34.

Linklater, Alexander, 'Death of the Ego: Hanif Kureishi Has at Last Found his Mature Voice', *Guardian* (16 Nov. 2002), p. 27.

Lynch, Kevin, *The Image of the City* (Cambridge, MA: MIT Press, 1960).

Lyon, Stephen, 'In the Shadow of September 11: Multiculturalism and Identity', in Abbas (ed.), *Muslims in Britain*, pp. 77–91.

MacCabe, Colin, 'Interview: Hanif Kureishi on London', *Critical Quarterly*, 41:3 (1999), 37–56.

McClintock, Anne, *Imperial Leather: Race, Gender, and Sexuality in the Colonial Conquest* (New York: Routledge, 1995).

McCrone, David, *Understanding Scotland: The Sociology of a Nation*, second edition (London: Routledge, 1996)

—— 'Who Are We? Understanding Scottish Identity', in Catherine Di Domenico *et al.* (eds), *Boundaries and Identities: Nation, Politics and Culture in Scotland* (Dundee: University of Abertay Press, 2001), pp. 11–35.

McCrone, David and Frank Bechhofer, 'National Identity and Social Inclusion', *Ethnic and Racial Studies*, 31:7 (2008), 1245–66.

McDonagh, 'Introduction', in Aruna D'Souza and Tom McDonough (eds), *The Invisible Flâneuse? Women, Men and Public Space in Nineteenth Century Paris* (Manchester: Manchester University Press, 2006), pp. 1–17.

McDowell, Linda, 'Spatializing Feminism: Geographic Perspectives', in Nancy Duncan (ed.), *BodySpace* (London: Routledge, 1996), pp. 28–41.

McEwan, Ian, *Atonement* (London: Vintage, 2001).

—— *Saturday* (London: Jonathan Cape, 2005).

McLaughlin, Martyn, 'Glasgow Bombing Prosecutors Claim Two Doctors at Centre of UK Terror Campaign', *The Scotsman* (10 October 2008), http://news.scotsman.com/latestnews/-Glasgow-bombing-prosecutors-claim.4578889.jp.

McLeod, John, *Beginning Postcolonialism* (Manchester: Manchester University Press, 2000).

—— *Postcolonial London: Rewriting the Metropolis* (London: Routledge, 2004).

Mahanta, Aparna, 'Allegories of the Indian Experience: The Novels of Salman Rushdie', *Economic and Political Weekly*, 19:6 (1984), 244–7.

Malkani, Gautam, *Londonstani* (London: Fourth Estate, 2006).

Mani, Bakirathi, 'Undressing the Diaspora', in Parvati Raghuram and Nirmal Puwar (eds), *South Asian Women in the Diaspora* (Oxford: Berg, 2003), pp. 117–35.

Marney, Laura, 'Psychoraag – Suhayl Saadi (2004): 100 Best Scottish Books of All Time', *List Magazine* (1 January 2005), www.list.co.uk/article/2802-psychoraag-suhayl-saadi–2004/.

Mars-Jones, Adam, 'East Meets West', *Observer*, Sunday 31 March 2002, http://www.guardian.co.uk/books/2002/mar/31/fiction.features1.

Mattin, David, 'My Revolutions', *The Independent*, 2 Sept. 2007, www. independent.co.uk/arts-entertainment/books/reviews/my-revolu-tions-by-hari-kunzru–463612.html.

Maxey, Ruth, '"Representative" of British Asian Fiction? The Critical Reception of Monica Ali's *Brick Lane*', in Murphy and Sim (eds), *British Asian Fiction*, pp. 217–36.

Meadows, Susannah, 'Son of a Sort of Goddess', *New York Times*, 12 May 2002, http:// query.nytimes.com/gst/fullpage.html?res= 9A06E6DF1331F931A25756C0A9649C8B63.

Mendelsohn, Daniel, 'Karma Chameleon', *New York Magazine*, 1 Apr. 2002, http://nymag.com/nymetro/arts/books/reviews/5843/.

Meredith, George, 'An Essay on Comedy' (1877), in Wylie Sypher (ed.), *Comedy* (Baltimore, MD: John Hopkins, 1956), pp. 3–57.

Michel, Martina, 'Und(der)-Cover: Ravinder Randhawa's *A Wicked Old Woman*', in Irmgard Maassen and Anna Maria Stuby (eds) *(Sub)Versions of Realism: Recent Women's Fiction in Britain* (Heidelberg, Germany: Universitätsverlag C Winter, 1997), pp. 143–57.

Miles, Robert and Anne Dunlop, 'Racism in Britain: the Scottish Dimension', in Peter Jackson (ed.), *Race and Racism* (London: Allen and Unwin, 1987), pp. 119–41.

Miles, Robert and Leslie Muirhead, 'Racism in Scotland', in David McCrone (ed.), *The Scottish Government Yearbook 1986* (Edinburgh: Unit for the Study of Government in Scotland, 1986), pp. 108–36.

Minhas, Nisha, *Chapatti or Chips?* (London: Pocket, 2002).

—— *Saris and Sins* (London: Pocket, 2003).

—— *Passion and Poppadoms* (London: Pocket, 2004).

—— *Bindis and Brides* (London: Pocket, 2005).

—— *The Marriage Market* (London: Pocket, 2006).

—— *Tall Dark and Handsome* (London: Pocket, 2007).

Mishra, Vijay, *Literature of the Indian Diaspora: Theorizing the Diasporic Imaginary* (London: Routledge, 2007).

——'Postcolonial Differend: Diasporic Narratives of Salman Rushdie', *ARIEL*, 26:3 (1995), 7–44.

—— 'The Familiar Temporariness: Naipaul, Diaspora and the Literary Imagination: A Personal Narrative', in Rajesh Rai and Peter Reeves (eds), *The South Asian Diaspora: Transnational Networks and Changing Identities* (London: Routledge, 2008), pp. 193–208.

—— 'Rushdie-Wushdie: Salman Rushdie's Hobson-Jobson', Kingston University Literary Series, Kingston University, England, 28 October 2008.

Mitchell, Katharyne, 'Different Diasporas and the Hype of Hybridity', *Environment and Planning D*, 15 (1997), 533–53.

Modood, Tariq, *Multicultural Politics: Racism, Ethnicity and Muslims in Britain* (Edinburgh: Edinburgh University Press, 2005).

—— 'Political Blackness and British Asians', *Sociology* 28.4 (1994), 859–76.

—— *Ethnic Minorities in Britain: Diversity and Disadvantage* (London: Policy Studies Institute, 1997).

Modood, Tariq, Sharon Beishon and Satnam Birdee, *Changing Ethnic Identities* (London: Policy Studies Institute, 1994).

Molteno, Marion, 'In Her Mother's House', *A Language in Common* (London: The Women's Press, 1987), pp. 19–41.

Monteith, Sharon, 'On the Streets and in the Tower Blocks: Ravinder Randhawa's *A Wicked Old Woman* (1987) and Livi Michael's *Under a Thin Moon* (1992)', *Critical Survey*, 8:1 (1996), 26–36.

Moore-Gilbert, Bart, *Hanif Kureishi* (Manchester: Manchester University Press, 2001).

Morey, Peter, 'Salman Rushdie and the English Tradition', in Abdulrazak Gurnah (ed.), *The Cambridge Companion to Salman Rushdie* (Cambridge: Cambridge University Press, 2008), pp. 29–43.

Mudge, Alden, 'Identity Crisis: The Many Faces of an Amazing Traveler', *Bookpage* (March 2002), www.bookpage.com/0204bp/hari_kunzru.html.

Mukerjee, Bharati, 'Prophet and Loss: Salman Rushdie's Migration of Souls', *Village Voice Literary Supplement*, 72 (March 1989), 9–12.

Murphy, Neil and Wai-Chew Sim (eds), *British Asian Fiction: Framing the Contemporary* (New York: Cambria, 2008).

Mustafa, Fawzia, *V. S. Naipaul* (Cambridge: Cambridge University Press, 1995).

—— *Mr Stone and the Knight's Companion* (London: Andre Deutsch, 1963).

Naipaul, V. S., *The Mimic Men* (1967) (London: Picador, 2002).

—— *Guerrillas* (London: André Deutsch, 1975).

—— *The Enigma of Arrival* (1987) (London: Vintage, 1988).

—— *A Way in the World* (London: Vintage, 1995).

—— *Letters Between a Father and Son* (London: Little, Brown and Company, 1999).

—— *Half a Life* (London: Picador, 2001).

—— *Magic Seeds* (London: Picador, 2004).

—— 'London' (1958), *The Overcrowded Barracoon and Other Articles* (London: Andre Deutsch, 1972), pp. 9–16.

—— 'Jasmine' (1964), *The Overcrowded Barracoon and Other Articles* (London: Andre Deutsch, 1972), pp. 23–29.

—— 'The Perfect Tenants', *A Flag on the Island* (1967) (Harmondsworth: Penguin, 1969), pp. 85–100.

—— 'Tell Me Who to Kill', *In a Free State* (1971) (Harmondsworth: Penguin, 1973), pp. 59–102.

—— 'Reading and Writing', *Reading and Writing: A Personal Account* (New York: New York Review Books, 2000), pp. 1–38.

Nairn, Tom, *The Break-Up of Britain*, New Edition (London: Verso, 1981)

Nash, Geoffrey, 'Re-siting Religion and Creating Feminised Space in the Fiction of Ahdaf Soueif and Leila Aboulela', *Wasafiri*, 35 (2002), 28–31.

Nasta, Susheila, *Home Truths: Fictions of the South Asian Diaspora in Britain* (Basingstoke: Palgrave, 2002).

—— 'Introduction', in Susheila Nasta (ed.), *Motherlands: Black Women's Writing from Africa, the Caribbean and South Asia* (London: The Women's Press, 1991), pp. xiii–xxx.

—— 'Homes Without Walls: New Voices in South Asian writing in Britain', in Ralph J. Crane and Radhika Mohanram (eds), *Shifting Continents/*

Colliding Cultures: Diaspora Writing of the Indian Subcontinent (Amsterdam: Rodopi, 2000), pp. 83–101.

—— Nava, Mira, *Visceral Cosmopolitanism: Gender, Culture and the Normalisation of Difference* (Oxford: Berg, 2007).

Neti, Leila, 'Siting Speech: The Politics of Imagining the Other in Meera Syal's *Anita and Me*', in Murphy and Sim (eds), *British Asian Fiction*, pp. 97–118.

Netto, Gina, 'Multiculturalism in the Devolved Context: Minority Ethnic Negotiation of Identity through Engagement in the Arts in Scotland', *Sociology*, 42:1 (2008), 47–64.

Neumeier, Beate (ed.), *Engendering Realism and Postmodernism: Contemporary Women Writers in Britain* (Amsterdam: Rodopi, 2001).

Niven, Alaistair, 'V. S. Naipaul Talks to Alastair Niven', *Wasafiri*, 21 (1995), 5–6.

Nixon, Rob, *London Calling: V. S. Naipaul, Postcolonial Mandarin* (New York: Oxford University Press, 1992).

Nkweto Simmonds, Felly, 'Love in Black and White', in Pearce and Stacey (eds), *Romance Revisited*, pp. 210–24.

O'Connor, Michael, 'Writing Against Terror – Nadeem Aslam', *Three Monkeys Online* (July 2005), www.threemonkeysonline.com/article_nadeem_aslam_interview.htm.

O'Neill, Patrick, *The Comedy of Entropy: Humour/Narrative/Reading* (Toronto: University of Toronto Press, 1990).

Olson, Elder, 'The Comic Object' (1968), rpt in Palmer (ed.), *Comedy*, pp. 151–6.

Oswell, David, 'Suburban Tales: Television, Masculinity and Textual Geographies', in David Bell and Azzedine Haddour (eds), *City Visions* (Harlow: Pearson, 2000), pp. 73–90. Pally, Marcia, 'Kureishi like a Fox', *Film Comment*, 22:5 (Oct. 1986), 50–5.

Palmer, D. J., 'Introduction', in Palmer (ed.), *Comedy*, pp. 8–22.

Palmer, D. J. (ed.), *Comedy: Developments in Criticism* (Hampshire: Macmillan, 1984).

Parameswaran, Radhika, 'Reading Fictions of Romance: Gender, Sexuality, and Nationalism in Postcolonial India'. *Journal of Communication*, 52:4 (2002), 832–51.

Parekh, Bhikhu, *The Future of Multi-Ethnic Britain* (London: Runnymede Trust, 2000).

Parry, Benita, *Postcolonial Studies: a Materialist Critique* (London: Routledge, 2004).

Paul, Kathleen, *Whitewashing Britain: Race and Citizenship in the Postwar Era* (Ithaca, NY: Cornell University Press, 1997).

Pearce, Lynne and Jackie Stacey, 'The Heart of the Matter: Feminists Revisit Romance', in Pearce and Stacey (eds), *Romance Revisited* (London: Lawrence and Wishart, 1995), pp. 11–48.

Persson, Ingmar, 'Self-Doubt: Why We are Not Identical to Things of Any Kind', in Galen Strawson (ed.), *The Self?* (Oxford: Blackwell, 2005), pp. 26–44.

Phillips, Caryl, 'V. S. Naipaul', in Phillips, *A New World Order: Selected Essays* (London: Secker and Warburg, 2001), pp. 187–219.

Phillips, Melanie, *Londonistan: How Britain is Creating a Terror State Within* (London: Gibson House, 2006).

Phillips, Mike and Trevor Phillips, *Windrush: The Irresistible Rise of Multiracial Britain* (London: HarperCollins, 1998).

Poole, Elizabeth, *Reporting Islam* (London: I.B. Tauris, 2002).

Procter, James, *Dwelling Places* (Manchester: Manchester University Press, 2003).

—— 'New Ethnicities, the Novel, and the Burdens of Representation', in James F. English (ed.), *A Concise Companion to Contemporary British Fiction* (Cambridge, MA: Blackwell, 2006), pp. 101–20.

Punter, David, *Postcolonial Imaginings: Fictions of a New World Order* (Edinburgh: Edinburgh University Press, 2000).

Puri, Kailash, 'Circle Line', in Debjani Chatterjee (ed.), *The Redbeck Anthology of British South Asian Poetry* (Bradford: Redbeck, 2000), p. 125.

Qureshi, Karen and Shaun Moores, 'Identity Remix: Tradition and Translation in the Lives of Young Pakistani Scots', *European Journal of Cultural Studies*, 2:3 (Sept. 1999), 311–30.

Radway, Janet, *Reading the Romance: Women Patriarchy and Popular Literature* (Chapel Hill, NC: North Carolina University Press, 1984).

Raghuram, Parvati and Nirmal Puwar (eds), *South Asian Women in the Diaspora* (Oxford: Berg, 2003).

Rahim, Habibeh, 'The Mirage of Faith and Justice: Some Sociopolitical and Cultural Themes in Post-colonial Urdu Short Stories', in John C. Hawley (ed.), *The Postcolonial Crescent: Islam's Impact on Contemporary Literature* (New York: Peter Lang, 1998), pp. 229–48.

Ramsey-Kurtz, Helga, 'Humouring the Terrorists or the Terrorised? Militant Muslims in Salman Rushdie, Zadie Smith, and Hanif Kureishi', in Reichl and Stein (eds), *Cheeky Fictions*, pp. 73–86.

Ranasinha, Ruvani, *Hanif Kureishi* (Tavistock: Northcote House, 2002).

—— *South Asian Writers in Twentieth-Century Britain: Culture in Translation* (Oxford: Oxford University Press, 2007).

Randhawa, Ravinder, *A Wicked Old Woman* (London: The Women's Press, 1987).

—— *Hari-jan* (London: Bijlee, 1992).

—— *The Coral Strand* (London: House of Stratus, 2001).

—— 'India' (1985), in Rosemary Stones (ed.), *More to Life than Mr Right: Stories for Young Feminists* (London: Fontana Lions, 1987), pp. 11–29.

—— 'Sunni', in Christina Dunhill (ed.), *A Girl's Best Friend* (London: Women's Press, 1987), pp. 126–36.

—— 'Mickey Mouse', *Critical Quarterly*, 33:4 (1991), 66–74.

—— 'Games', in Asian Women Writers' Workshop, *Right of Way: Prose and Poetry*, pp. 120–30.

—— 'Time Traveler', in Neumeier (ed.), *Engendering Realism*, pp. 379–90.

—— 'The Heera', in Asian Women Writers' Workshop, *Right of Way: Prose and Poetry*, pp. 70–83.

—— 'Pedal Push', in Asian Women Writers' Workshop, *Right of Way: Prose and Poetry*, pp. 7–13.

—— 'War of the Worlds', in Asian Women Writers' Workshop, *Right of Way: Prose and Poetry*, pp. 155–62.

Reder, Michael R. (ed.), *Conversations with Salman Rushdie* (Jackson, MS: University Press of Mississippi, 2000).

Rees, Jasper, 'Nadeem Aslam', *Telegraph* (22 June 2004), www.telegraph. co.uk/arts/main.jhtml;jsessionid=LS4WXI35EGNZ3QFIQMGCFFW AVCBQUIV0?xml=/arts/2004/06/20/boaslam.xml.

Reese, Jennifer, *'Life Isn't All Ha Ha Hee Hee* by Meera Syal', *The New York Times* (25 June 2000), in New York Times' Staff, *The New York Times Book Reviews* (New York: Taylor and Francis, 2000), p. 1192.

Regis, Pamela, *A Natural History of the Romance Novel* (Philadelphia, PA: University of Pennsylvania Press, 2003).

Reichl, Susanne and Mark Stein, 'Introduction', in Susanne Reichl and Mark Stein (eds), *Cheeky Fictions: Laughter and the Postcolonial* (Amsterdam: Rodopi, 2005), pp. 1–26.

Rich, Adrienne, 'Compulsory Heterosexuality and Lesbian Existence', *Signs: Journal of Women in Culture and Society*, 33:3 (1980), pp. 675–96, rpt in Vincent B. Leitch *et al.* (eds), *The Norton Anthology of Theory and Criticism* (New York: Norton, 2001), pp. 1762–80.

Robbins, Ruth, *Subjectivity* (Basingstoke: Palgrave Macmillan, 2005).

Robinson, Alan, 'Faking It: Simulation and Self-Fashioning in Hari Kunzru's *Transmission*', in Murphy and Sim (eds), *British Asian Fiction*, pp. 77–96.

Robson, David, 'The deadly honour', *The Telegraph* (13 July 2004),www. telegraph.co.uk/arts/main.jhtml?xml=/arts/2004/07/11/boasl11. xml&sSheet=/arts/2004/07/11/bomain.html.

Rosie, Michael and Ross Bond, 'Routes into Scottishness?', in Catherine Bromley, John Curtice, David McCrone, Alison Park and Anthony John Parker (eds), *Has Devolution Delivered?* (Edinburgh: Edinburgh University Press, 2006), pp. 141–58.

Ross, Jean W., *'Contemporary Authors* Interview: Salman Rushdie' (1984), rpt in Reder (ed.), *Conversations*, pp. 1–7.

Ross, Michael L., *Race Riots: Comedy and Ethnicity in Modern British Fiction* (Montreal: McGill-Queens University Press, 2006).

Runnymede Trust, *Islamophobia: A Challenge for Us All* (London: Runnymede Trust, 1997).

Rushdie, Salman, *Midnight's Children* (1981) (London: Picador, 1982).

—— *Shame* (London: Picador, 1983).

—— *The Satanic Verses* (1988) (London: Vintage, 1998).

—— *Imaginary Homelands* (London: Granta, 1991).

—— *East, West* (London: Jonathan Cape, 1994).

—— *The Ground Beneath Her Feet* (London: Vintage, 1999).

—— 'Imaginary Homelands' (1982), in *Imaginary Homelands*, pp. 9–21.

—— 'The New Empire in Britain' (1984), in *Imaginary Homelands*, pp. 129–38

—— 'Hobson Jobson' (1985), in *Imaginary Homelands*, pp. 81–4.

—— 'Choice Between Light and Dark', *Observer* (22 Jan. 1989), p. 11.

—— 'In Good Faith' (1990), in *Imaginary Homelands*, pp. 393–414.

—— 'The Courtier' (1994), in *East, West*, pp. 175–211.

Russell, Ralph, *The Pursuit of Urdu Literature: A Select History* (London: Zed, 1992).

Saadi, Suhayl, *The Burning Mirror* (Edinburgh: Polygon, 2000).
—— *Psychoraag* (Edinburgh: Black and White, 2004).
—— *The White Cliffs* (Dingwall: Sandstone, 2004).
—— *The Aerodrome, Scotia Review* (2006), www.scotiareview.org/files/downloads/SSaadi.pdf.
—— 'The Saelig Tales', in Jennie Renton (ed.), *Textualities 1: Magic Afoot* (2006).
—— 'Psychoraag: The Gods of the Door', *Spike Magazine* (January 2006), www.spikemagazine.com/0206-suhayl-saadi-censorship-in-the-uk-php.
—— *The Spanish House, The Bottle Imp*, 3 (2008), www.arts.gla.ac.uk/ScotLit/ASLS/SWE/TBI/TBIIssue3/TheSpanishHouse.pdf
Saadi, Suhayl (ed.), *Shorts: The Macallan Scotland on Sunday Short Story Collection* (Edinburgh: Polygon, 2003).
Saadi, Suhayl, Meaghan Delahunt and Elizabeth Reader (eds), *A Fictional Guide to Scotland* (Glasgow: OpenInk, 2003).
Saadi, Suhayl and Catherine McInerney (eds), *Freedom Spring: Ten Years On* (New Lanark: Waverley, 2005).
Sachdeva Mann, Harveen, '"Being Borne across: Translation and Salman Rushdie's *The Satanic Verses*', *Criticism*, 37:2 (1995), 281–308.
Saeed, Amir, Neil Blain and Douglas Forbes, 'New Ethnic and National Questions in Scotland:Post-British Identities Among Glasgow Pakistani Teenagers', *Ethnic and Racial Studies*, 22:5 (1999), 821–44.
Safi, Omar (ed.), Progressive *Muslims: On Justice, Gender and Pluralism* (Oxford: Oneworld, 2003).
Said, Edward, *Covering Islam: How the Media and the Experts Determine How We See the Rest of the World* (London: Routledge and Kegan Paul, 1981).
Salgado, Gamini, 'V. S. Naipaul and the Politics of Fiction', in Boris Ford (ed.), *The Present: Volume 8, The New Pelican Guide to English Literature* (Harmondsworth: Penguin, 1983), pp. 314–27.
Sandhu, Sukhdev, *London Calling: How Black and Asian Writers Imagined a City* (London: Harper Collins, 2003).
—— 'Pop Goes the Centre', in Laura Chrisman and Benita Parry, *Postcolonial Theory and Criticism* (Cambridge: Brewer, 1999), pp. 133–54.
—— '*Brick Lane* by Monica Ali', *London Review of Books* (9 Oct. 2003), www.lrb.co.uk/v25/n19/sand01_.html.
Sanga, Jaina C., *Salman Rushdie's Postcolonial Metaphors: Migration, Translation, Hybridity, Blasphemy, and Globalization* (Westport, CT: Greenwood, 2001).
San Juan Jnr, E., *Beyond Postcolonial Theory* (New York: St. Martin's Press, 1999).
Sardar, Ziauddin, *Orientalism* (Buckingham: Open University Press, 1999).
—— *Balti Britain: A Journey Through the British Asian Experience* (London: Granta, 2008).
—— 'alt.civilisations.faq: Cyberspace as the Darker Side of the West', in Ziauddin Sardar and Jerome R. Ravetz (eds), *Cyberfutures: Culture and Politics on the Information Superhighway* (London: Pluto, 1996), pp. 14–41.
—— 'The Excluded Minority: British Muslim Identity After September 11', in Griffiths and Leonard (eds), *Reclaiming Britishness*, pp. 51–5.

Sartre, Jean-Paul, *Intimacy and Other Stories*, trans. Lloyd Alexander (London: Peter Nevill, 1949).

Sawhney, Sabina and Simona Sawhney, 'Reading Rushdie after September 11, 2001', *Twentieth Century Literature*, 47:4 (2001), 431–43.

Sawhney, Simona, 'Satanic Choices: Poetry and Prophecy in Rushdie's Novel', *Twentieth Century Literature*, 45:3 (1999), 253–77.

Sayyid, S., *A Fundamental Fear: Eurocentrism and the Emergence of Islamism*, second edition (London: Zed, 2003).

Schechtman, Marya, 'Self-Expression and Self-Control', in Galen Strawson (ed.), *The Self?* (Malden, MA: Blackwell, 2005), pp. 45–62.

Schlote, Christine, '"I'm British But ..." Explorations of Identity by Three Postcolonial British Women Artists', *EnterText*, 2:1 (2001/2002), 95–123.

—— 'Confrontational Sites: Cultural Conflicts, Social Inequality and Sexual Politics in the Work of Rukhsana Ahmad', in Emma Parker (ed.), *Essays and Studies 2004: Contemporary British Women Writers* (Cambridge: D. S. Brewer, 2004), pp. 85–103.

—— '"The Sketch's the thing wherein we'll catch the conscience of the audience": Strategies and Pitfalls of Ethnic TV comedies in Britain, the United States, and Germany', in Reichl and Stein (eds), *Cheeky Fictions*, pp. 177–90.

Schoene, Berthold, 'Herald of Hybridity: The Emancipation of Difference in Hanif Kureishi's The Buddha of Suburbia', *International Journal of Cultural Studies*, 1:1 (1998), 109–28.

Schoene-Harwood, Berthold, 'Beyond (T)race: Bildung and Proprioperception in Meera Syal's *Anita and Me*', *Journal of Commonwealth Literature*, 34 (1999), 159–68.

Selvon, Samuel, *The Lonely Londoners* (Harlow: Longman, 1956).

Sen, Asha, 'Re-Writing History: Hanif Kureishi and the Politics of Black Britain', *Passages: Journal of Transnational and Transcultural Studies*, 2:1 (2000), 61–80.

Sesay, Kadija, 'Transformations Within the Black British Novel', in Victoria Arana and Lauri Ramey (eds), *Black British Writing* (New York: Palgrave, 2004), pp. 99–108.

Sharify-Funk, Meena, 'From Dichotomies to Dialogues: Trend in Contemporary Islamic Hermeneutics', in Abdul Aziz Said, Mohammed Abu-Nimer and Meena Sharify-Funk (eds), *Contemporary Islam: Dynamic, Not Static* (London: Routledge, 2006), pp. 64–80.

Sharma, Sanjay, 'Noisy Asians or "Asian Noise"', in Sanjay Sharma, John Hutnyk and Aswani Sharma (eds), *Dis-Orienting Rhythms: The Politics of the New Asian Dance Music* (London: Zed, 1996), pp. 32–57.

Shohat, Ella, 'Notes on the "Post-Colonial"', in Fawzia Afzal-Khan and Kalpana Seshadri-Crooks (eds), *The Pre-Occupation of Postcolonial Studies* (Durham, NC: Duke University Press, 2000), pp. 126–39.

Simmons, Gwendolyn Zoharah, 'Are we up to the challenge? The Need for a Radical Re-ordering of the Islamic Discourse on Women', in Omar Safi (ed.), *Progressive Muslims: On Justice, Gender and Pluralism* (Oxford: Oneworld, 2003), pp. 235–48.

Singh, Manjit Inder, *V. S. Naipaul*, second edition (Jaipur: Rawat, 2002).

Skinner, John, 'Black British Interventions', in Brian Schaffer (ed.), *A Companion to the British and Irish Novel 1945–2000* (Oxford: Blackwell, 2005), pp. 128–43.

Smale, David (ed.), *Salman Rushdie: Midnight's Children/The Satanic Verses: A Reader's Guide to Essential Criticism* (Basingstoke: Palgrave Macmillan, 2001).

Smith, Zadie, *White Teeth* (London: Penguin, 2000).

—— *The Autograph Man* (London: Hamish Hamilton, 2002).

Socorro Suárez Lafuente, María, 'Changing Places … Changing the Rate of Exchange', in Fernando Galván and Mercedes Bengoechea (eds), *On Writing (and) Race in Contemporary Britain* (Alcalá, Spain: University of Alcalá, 1999), pp. 123–32.

Soguk, Nevzat, 'Reflections on the 'Orientalised Orientals'', *Alternatives*, 18 (1993), 361–84.

Sooke, Alastair, 'Signs of the Times', *New Statesman* (6 Sept. 2007), www.newstatesman.com/books/2007/09/hari-kunzru-revolutions-mike.

Sookhdeo, Patrick, *Islam in Britain: The British Muslim Community in February 2005* (Pewsey: Isaac Publishing, 2005).

Spivak, Gayatri Chakravorty, 'Can The Subaltern Speak?', in Cary Nelson and Lawrence Grossberg (eds), *Marxism and the Interpretation of Culture* (Chicago: University of Illinois Press, 1987), pp. 271–313.

—— 'Reading The Satanic Verses', *Outside in the Teaching Machine* (New York: Routledge, 1993), pp. 217–41.

Srivastava, Atima, *Transmission* (London: Serpent's Tail, 1992).

—— *Looking for Maya* (London: Quartet, 1999).

—— 'Dragons in E8', *Barcelona Review* 25, July–Aug. 2001, http://www.barcelonareview.com/25/e_as.htm.

Strawson, Galen (ed.), *The Self?* (Malden, MA: Blackwell, 2005).

Stein, Mark, *Black British Literature: Novels of Transformation* (Columbus, OH: Ohio State University Press, 2004).

Stetz, Margaret D, British *Women's Comic Fiction, 1890–1990: Not Drowning, But Laughing* (Aldershot: Ashgate, 2001).

Stotesbury, John A., 'Genre and Islam in Recent Anglophone Romantic Fiction', in Susana Onega and Christian Gutleben (eds), *Refracting the Canon in Contemporary British Literature and Film* (Amsterdam: Rodopi, 2004), pp. 69–82.

Suleri, Sara, *The Rhetoric of English India* (Chicago: The University of Chicago Press, 1992).

Swinden, Patrick, *The English Novel of History and Society, 1940–80* (London: Macmillan, 1984).

Syal, Meera, *My Sister Wife*, in Kadija George (ed.), *Six Plays by Black and Asian Women Writers* (London: Aurora Metro, 1993), pp. 111–58.

—— *Life Isn't All Ha Ha Hee Hee* (1999) (London: Black Swan, 2000).

—— *Anita and Me* (1996) (London: Flamingo, 2002).

—— 'The Traveller', in Asian Women Writers' Workshop, *Right of Way: Prose and Poetry*, pp. 96–105.

Sypher, Wylie, 'The Meanings of Comedy', in Wylie Sypher (ed.), *Comedy* (Baltimore, MD: Johns Hopkins University Press, 1980), pp. 193–255.

Taylor, Charles, *Sources of the Self: The Making of the Modern Identity* (Cambridge: Cambridge University Press, 1989).

Tester, Keith, 'Introduction', in Keith Tester (ed.), *The Flâneur* (London: Routledge, 1994), pp. 1–21.

Teverson, Andrew, *Salman Rushdie* (Manchester: Manchester University Press, 2007).

Theroux, Paul, *V. S. Naipaul: An Introduction to His Work* (London: Andre Deutsch, 1972).

Thieme, John, *The Web of Tradition: Uses of Allusion in V. S. Naipaul's Fiction* (Hertford: Hansib, 1987).

Thomas, Susie, *Hanif Kureishi: A Reader's Guide to Essential Criticism* (Basingstoke: Palgrave Macmillan, 2005).

Thurtle, Phillip, and Robert Mitchell, 'Introduction: Data Made Flesh: The Material Poiesis of Informatics', in Robert Mitchell and Philip Thurtle (ed.), *Data Made Flesh: Embodying Information* (New York: Routledge, 2004), pp. 1–26.

Ticktin, Miriam, 'Contemporary British Asian Women's Writing: Social Movement or Literary Tradition?', *Women: A Cultural Review*, 7:1 (1996), 66–77.

Tiffin, Helen, 'Rites of Resistance: Counter-Discourse and West Indian Biography', *Journal of West Indian Literature*, 3:1 (1989), 28–45.

Tripathi, Sali, 'The Last – and the Best – Salman Rushdie Interview in India!' (1983), rpt in Reder (ed.), *Conversations*, pp. 20–9.

Updike, John, *Terrorist* (New York: Alfred A. Knopf, 2006),

Upstone, Sara, *Spatial Politics in the Postcolonial Novel* (Aldershot: Ashgate, 2009).

—— 'Negotiations of London as Imperial Urban Space in the Contemporary Postcolonial Novel', in Christoph Lindner (ed.), *Urban Space and Cityscapes: Perspectives from Modern and Contemporary Culture* (London: Routledge, 2006), pp. 88–100.

—— '"Same Old, Same Old" Zadie Smith's *White Teeth* and Monica Ali's *Brick Lane*', *Journal of Postcolonial Writing*, 43:3 (2007), 336–49.

—— 'A Question of Black or White: Returning to Hanif Kureishi's The Black Album', *Postcolonial Text*, 4:1 (2008), http://postcolonial.org/index.php/pct/article/viewArticle/679.

Walcott, Derek, 'A Far Cry from Africa' (1956), rpt in Stephen Greenblatt et al. (eds), *The Norton Anthology of English, Volume Two*, eighth edition (New York: Norton, 2006), pp. 2587–8.

—— 'The Garden Path, *New Republic* (13 April 1987), 26–31.

Walder, Dennis, *Post-colonial Literatures in English: History, Language, Theory* (Oxford: Blackwell, 1998).

Walker, Nicola, 'Brick Lane', *The Age* (23 Aug. 2003), www.theage.com.au/articles/2003/08/20/1061368348340.html.

Walsh, William, *V. S. Naipaul* (Edinburgh: Oliver and Boyd, 1973).

Walters, Natasha, 'Citrus Scent of Inexorable Desire', *Guardian*, 14 June 2003, Guardian Online,http://books.guardian.co.uk/booker-prize2003/story/0,13819,1019773,00.html.

Webb, W.L., 'Salman Rushdie: Satanic Verses' (1988), rpt in Reder (ed.), *Conversations*, pp. 87–100.

Weber, Prina, *Imagined Diasporas among Manchester Muslims* (Oxford: James Currey, 2002).

Weedon, Chris, 'Redefining Otherness, Negotiating Difference: Contemporary British Asian Women's Writing', in Neumeier (ed.), *Engendering Realism,* pp. 223–35.

Weidner, Stefan, 'A Cosmos of Traditionalist Muslim Migrants', trans Tim Nevill, *Art and Thought* (2006), www.arabia.pl/english/content/view/ 80/16/.

Weiss, Timothy F., *On the Margins: The Art of Exile in V. S. Naipaul* (Amherst, MA: University of Massachusetts Press, 1992).

—— 'V. S. Naipaul's "Fin de Siècle": "The Enigma of Arrival" and "A Way in the World"', *ARIEL* 27:3 (1996), 107–24.

Wheatcroft, Geoffrey, 'A Terrifying Honesty', in Amitava Kumar (ed.), *The Humour and the Pity: Essays on V. S. Naipaul* (New Delhi: Buffalo, 2002), pp. 97–107.

Whelehan, Imelda, *The Feminist Bestseller* (Basingstoke: Palgrave Macmillan, 2005).

Wilcox, James, 'Hairy Neddy and the Mad Mitchells', *The New York Times* (10 August 1997), *The New York Times on the Web*, www.times.com/ books/97/08/10/reviews/970810.10wilcoxt.html.

Wilson, Elizabeth, 'The Invisible Flâneur', *New Left Review,* 191 (1992), 90–110.

Wolff, Janet, 'The Invisible *Flâneuse*: Women and the Literature of Modernity', *Theory, Culture & Society,* 2:3 (1985), 37–46.

—— 'The Artist and the *Flâneur*: Rodin, Rilke and Gwen John in Paris', in Keith Tester (ed.), *The Flâneur* (London: Routledge, 1994), pp. 111–37.

—— 'Gender and the Haunting of Cities (or, the retirement of the *flâneur*)', in Aruna D'Souza and Tom McDonough (eds), *The Invisible Flâneuse? Women, Men and Public Space in Nineteenth Century Paris* (Manchester University Press: Manchester, 2006), pp. 18–31.

Wood, Michael, 'Enigmas and Homelands', in Zachary Leader (ed.), *On Modern British Fiction* (Oxford: Oxford University Press, 2002), pp. 77–92.

Young, Robert, *Colonial Desire: Hybridity in Theory, Culture and Race* (London: Routledge, 1995).

Yousaf, Nahem, 'Hanif Kureishi and the Brown Man's Burden', *Critical Survey,* 8:1 (1996), pp. 14–25.

Online sources

'Famous and Successful People from Paisley', *Paisley Community Website,* http://paisley.org.uk/famous_people/suhayl_saadi.php.

'Hari Kunzru, Penguin Authors', *Penguin UK,* www.penguin.co.uk/nf/ Author/AuthorPage/0,,1000054681,00.html?sys=QUE.

'Interview with Hari Kunzru', www.book-club.co.nz/features/harikunzru. htm.

'Nadeem Aslam on *Maps for Lost Lovers*', www.faber.co.uk/article_detail. html?aid=23652.

Transcript: *The Power of Nightmares'*, www.daanspeak.com/TranscriptPower
OfNightmares1.html.

Films

Adulthood, dir. Noel Clarke (Independent, 2008).
Beautiful Thing, dir. Hettie Macdonald (Channel Four Films, 1996).
Bend it Like Beckham, dir. Gurinder Chadha (Redbus Film, 2002).
Bhaji on the Beach, dir. Gurinder Chadha (Channel Four Films, 1993).
Brick Lane, dir. Sarah Gavron (Optimum Releasing, 2007).
Bride and Prejudice, dir. Gurinder Chadha (Pathé Pictures, 2004).
East is East, dir. Damien O'Donnell (Channel Four Films, 1999).
Kidulthood, dir. Menhaj Huda (Revolver Entertainment, 2006).
London Kills Me, dir. Hanif Kureishi (Rank Film, 1991).
The Mother, dir. Roger Michell (Momentum Pictures, 2003).
My Beautiful Laundrette, dir. Stephen Frears (Mainline Pictures, 1985).
My Son the Fanatic, dir. Udayan Prasad (Feature Film, 1997).
Sammy and Rosie Get Laid, dir. Stephen Frears (Palace Pictures, 1987).
Venus, dir. Roger Michell (Buena Vista Pictures, 2006).

Index

Note: literary works can be found under authors' names.
Note: 'n.' after a page reference indicates the number of a note on that page.

Index